Target: Heydrich

by

Miroslav Ivanov

Translated from the French by Patrick O'Brian

Macmillan Publishing Co., Inc.

NEW YORK

Macmillan Publishing Co., Inc.
866 Third Avenue, New York, N. Y. 10022

Target: Heydrich was originally published
under the title *L'Attentat Contre Heydrich*
by Éditions Robert Laffont, Paris.
Library of Congress Catalog Card Number: 72-11277

First Printing 1974

Printed in the United States of America

75-4542 MCL

CONTENTS

(*Illustrations following page 148*)

AUTHOR'S PROLOGUE

A radiant sun in the blue sky, shining down into the gardens and gilding the blossom on the trees; now and then a cloud drifting across, sending a deep shadow over the streets. People going to and fro, just as they had done yesterday or the day before—women carrying their shopping baskets or pushing baby carriages. Sometimes a car going by or the raucous din of a motorcycle. A May morning.

Not one of the people hurrying along the pavement or going into the shops had the least suspicion that anything was about to happen. And some way off, below the level of the road, the Vltava flowed gently along its curve; a little group of men working under the bridge; a van delivering polish—boot polish and floor wax.

In a few moments everything was going to change—everything, including the fate of a great many people. For a few moments more Reinhard Heydrich, SS Obergruppenführer and general of police, sat there next to his chauffeur, staring out over the hood of the car that had just brought him from his country house, watching the road stream by. On his knees he held a briefcase, and automatically his fingers stroked the leather. No one must know what was inside it. Top Secret.

A few miles to go and he would be in Prague: a special plane was waiting at the airfield to take him to Hitler. The plane would in fact do nothing of the kind, but this was something that Heydrich did not know.

There he sat, his thin lips set in a hard line. A woman in black crossed the road. He glanced at her. Not that her face interested him, but he liked the colour. He liked everything black.

The car was travelling towards the corner. A few hundred yards, no more. A young man moved away from the wall and flashed a mirror, just as a child might do for fun. Heydrich scowled. But this mirror foretold his fate, though he did not know it yet.

The van delivered its floor wax and polish; a slim, beautiful girl was sunbathing in a nearby garden; two bicycles stood not far from the hedge. It was half past ten on the morning of 27 May 1942.

Still nothing happened. The black car moved closer and closer to this bend in the road that passed through the district of Prague called Liben. The seconds-hand moved on. Some way off there was the sound of a streetcar. An old woman passed slowly by.

The crash of an explosion.

In a Europe enslaved by the black uniforms there were still courageous men.

1

The hideout in the rocks

(Antonin Sedlacek)

ABOUT 1938 some factory owners in the nearby town came here to rent a hunting lodge. And they wanted a gamekeeper. I had a job on the state roads at that time, and the roadmender said to me, "You might put in for it, Lojza." My grandfather and my father had been gamekeepers, so I went along.

It was a good job—feeding the game, going the rounds; not so pleasant in winter, but it brought in a little money. When you have a lot of children—and I have seven—you certainly need that.

It was before New Year's Eve in 1941—I don't remember just how many days before and I was in bed but unable to sleep—lying there thinking and staring into the darkness, when all at once I heard a rumbling noise, which was either a great way off or very high up. Then the noise came closer and passed over our house; and the dogs in the village started barking. Quietly I put on my slippers and threw my coat over my shoulders to go out and see what it was. But as I opened the door my wife said, "Where are you going, Father? It's still dark." "Stay in bed," I told her, "I'm going to look at the rabbits." She turned over and went back to sleep.

I took the ladder without making a noise and leant it against the wall to get up on to the roof. Lord, what a night! Everything sparkled. Deep snow covered the fields, and above it shone the stars and moon. The rumbling was growing distant. I dare say the plane was moving off. A few seconds later something seemed to

13

fall from the stars, swinging like a parachute. A few moments later it reached the ground, but a long way off from our place, somewhere behind the graveyard. I came slowly down the ladder, wondering what to do. I got back to the kitchen to finish dressing, but my wife sat up in bed and wanted to know what was wrong. What could I say? She would have been frightened. I was sure that it was parachutists, and if I'd told her I wanted to see them she would have given me no rest. So I kept my peace and went back to bed.

In those days of the Protectorate, it was best to keep your mouth shut. A man could put his life in danger without knowing it, and that's why I never told anyone what I'd seen that night.

About nine o'clock the next morning I was following the path through the fields behind our cottage, when suddenly I saw footprints in the snow—the tracks of two men.

I looked all round: there was nobody about, so I followed the trail backwards. It led behind the cemetery, to the very place where I had seen the parachute that night. And God help me, it led straight to where I put out forage for the game. Here the snow was all trampled and someone had piled it up in a heap. I gave it a kick, and there were ropes tangling round my boot. That smelled bad—it smelled of Gestapo trouble. I looked all round again, took off my rucksack and pretended to be taking out the forage. Leaning forward I gently brushed the snow aside—it was a parachute, of course. What was I to do?

Someone had only to stumble on it and report what he had seen. Then they would say, "Why, Lojza was there with his forage; he must have seen it and he's said nothing." But if I did report it, I would be a bad Czech, a rotten patriot. Right. So I shouldered my sack again and followed the footprints.

The tracks ran towards a gardener's hut not far from Nehvizdy, our village. There I found an empty biscuit tin with a foreign label. But they didn't stop there: they ran straight on into the fields. It made my blood run cold.

Just picture this white, untouched plain, and on it the tracks of two men. A few hundred yards along they had rested, for the snow was trampled; and then they had gone on, aiming for a little hill over a mile away, with a copse on the top of it. It was well chosen. All round our village there is only plain, except for that little rise with an old quarry near it and a pond among the rocks. I knew the place well; it was a wild, uninhabited spot, with a big cave in the rocks.

I reached the wood at last, and saw that the tracks slanted quickly away towards the quarry. I moved closer; I was already on the slope, when suddenly I saw them down below me.

They must have seen me too, but they pretended to be unaware. One of them was looking at a map and the other kept his hand in his hip-pocket. I thought, You've got a pistol, my friend: but aloud I said, "Good morning, boys," and I coughed.

They moved and called out good morning. Then they were silent, just looking at me. I lit a cigarette and said, "What are you doing here?"

They were rather small men, dressed perfectly ordinarily. "We want to start working this stone again," said one of them.

I had to smile. They could tell that to anyone else, but not to me. They saw I didn't believe them, and all at once I was afraid the one with his hand in his hip-pocket might do something silly. And so to be safe I said, "I've come to help you."

They put their heads together, actually touching, and after a moment the one who hadn't spoken yet called out, "All right. Come on down."

I went down the slope and in a minute I was in the ravine. "Look," I said, "I'm so-and-so: here are my papers so you can trust me. I saw you when you dropped during the night and this morning I found your parachutes. Why didn't you hide them better?"

For a few seconds they said nothing. Then one of them made up his mind and told me they had meant to hide them better later on—that was all they could manage in the dark not knowing where they were.

"And just where have we landed?" asked the smaller one.

"You're very near Prague," I said. They looked unbelieving. I showed them my keeper's card again and one of them read, "district of Brandys on the Elbe." They were upset, alarmed.

They told me that they were supposed to have been dropped somewhere else.

"Never mind," I said. "I'll help you."

They whispered together again for a moment and then told me solemnly that they had a transmitter with them and if I meant to betray them they would radio my name to their friends before I could even reach the police station. I smiled and brushed off the threat. "What do you need?" I asked.

"Are there any police in your village?"

"Indeed there are."

"Do they know anything?"

I promised to find out. Then I asked if they had anything to eat. No, nothing. And they needed some bandage. There is no druggist in the village, but as luck would have it a couple of months before I had broken my big toe and used bandage. There was still some left.

I went cautiously back to the village. I said nothing to my wife. I took some food and a bit of Christmas cake that we had left; I put some bandage in my pocket, and a little bottle of alcohol. I walked through the village in the direction of the police station, but everything was quiet there—one policeman busy doing something at home and the other sitting in the inn. I rested a while—then went back to the quarry.

It was certainly the best place they could have chosen. By the pond there was a deserted hut; a few birches were growing in the loose stones and nearby a small but thick wood; and above all there was this cave in the rocks. In summer boys often went there to play bandits but now, in winter, nobody came.

The cave had two mouths, and it was fairly deep and dark; by one mouth you came out behind the hut and by the other you reached the far side of the little valley. The men had brought pine branches from the nearby wood; they had made two beds and they had a little fire ready laid. When I came back that afternoon they were inside: I gave them the food and the bandage. One of them was limping—he had twisted his foot landing.

"Well, Uncle, what news?" they asked, when they saw me.

"Good. Nobody knows anything."

"And what about you? Aren't you frightened?"

What could I say? I didn't want to dash their spirits, so I said I wasn't; but it was not easy for me to say and they probably noticed it. So to ease my mind one of them said, "We shan't be staying here long."

"But where will you go? You'll get picked up."

But they laughed and told me they weren't afraid of anything. I told them that if anything dangerous turned up, I'd fire twice with my shotgun, and that would be to tell them they had to run.

"Is there another quarry like this in these parts?" asked the younger one, a chap with a face as round as a ball. I turned it over in my mind, and remembered that there was a tunnel off behind the road to the next village: there had been a little coal mine there once, long ago.

I went to the quarry again the next day, and after that I went at least once a day. Each time I went I took them something to eat. We talked a little; they wanted to know what was happening and whether Germans were moving around in the neighbourhood. They lent me an automatic in case anything happened when I was going to and fro. And once they wanted to give me cigarettes and chocolate, but I wouldn't take them. I said, "It's better not to, otherwise the children will say father brought them this marvellous chocolate. And then if someone asked me where I found it, what would I say? There's no chocolate in the shops." And it was the same with the cigarettes; there, with them in the cave, I smoked some, but I never took any away.

I was going to the Rocks—that's what we call the quarry here—one evening when the snow was coming down and the pond was frozen when suddenly I saw someone crouched against the cliff. I stopped: I didn't know what to do. But I had my gun on my shoulder and I said to myself, Come, you're a game-keeper and you have a right to be here. So I walked on. This man had hidden so as not to be seen; but I had to know who was wandering about in these parts and what he meant by it. So I shouted, "You there! What are you doing?"

He was frightened and he had to come out of the shadows. It was Baumann, the miller, from another village behind the forest.

"I've been skating," he said.

"And where are your skates?"

At first he made no answer, but looked at me warily. "And what do you mean by questioning me like this?" he said at last, in an angry voice.

"I'm a gamekeeper and there are poachers about. Haven't you seen the tracks of two men around here?"

He didn't know what to say, and while he was puzzling over it he turned his head towards the cave.

"Do you know anything about them?" I asked.

"Yes. You too?"

I nodded. Then we admitted that we were each bringing them food and information. They were cautious men and they had told neither the miller nor me that anyone else had come to see them. Once Baumann and I met right inside the cave. Later, when the whole thing collapsed, the Gestapo arrested and shot him. He kept his mouth shut and did not give me away; otherwise I shouldn't be here either.

One day I came back to the village from some place or other and I saw a German car standing in front of the last house. They had some kind of an upright post, and there were dozens of people all around. I didn't know what they were doing.

When I got home I snatched up my gun and rucksack and hurried off across the fields. The Germans let me pass: they were only measuring something—God knows whether they were looking for a transmitter or what. I took a roundabout way and I warned the men that things might take a nasty turn. That shook them and they asked me to take them to the tunnel. We waited until dark, gathered up everything in the cave and set out.

But it was a disappointment, smelling awful—very damp and mouldy.

They stayed one night and by then the Germans had gone and so they made up their minds to go back to the quarry unless I could tell them of some reliable acquaintance in the neighbourhood. I remembered a forest a few miles from our village, and that a man called Bartos lived there in the keeper's house. I sent them to him.

They say the parachutists left Bartos to go and stay with Stary at Sestajovice and that after that they managed to get to Prague. As for Stary, the Germans shot him too. I was very lucky. Almost everyone who helped the parachutists is dead; but somehow I came through.

2

The old doctor's account

(*Stanislav Hruby*)

THE DAY had begun in precisely the same way as usual, with washing and shaving, breakfast, the papers and then the consulting room. When I got there I found two old ladies sitting in the waiting room. Both were suffering from sciatica and I prescribed a liniment for each of them; then when I opened the door again I saw Piskacek and a young man of medium height I did not know. I beckoned and they came in. "Well, and what seems to be the matter?" I asked in a friendly way, looking at the young man.

Piskacek took two paces forward, looking cautiously round, and said in a confidential tone, "My friend has put a toe of his left foot out of joint."

"Take off your shoe," I said to the young man.

He took off his shoe and sock and showed me his foot. The big toe was all blue. I palpated it carefully, feeling the instep and the sole. The bones seemed unbroken. But still, as a precaution, I said, "This ought to be X-rayed."

The young fellow started and threw a questioning look at Piskacek, who turned to me, smiled, and asked, "Is it really necessary?"

At this I looked him straight in the eye, hard. He met my gaze, saying nothing.

"What is your name?" I asked his companion.

"Zdenek Vyskocil," he answered without hesitation.

"Where do you work?"

He did not reply and Piskacek broke in, "Listen, Doctor, couldn't he be helped with poultices?"

I shrugged and quickly wrote out a prescription. They both thanked me—Piskacek tried to slip some money into my pocket, but I refused—and they went out of the consulting room.

Some time later Piskacek came back again, but alone this time. "How is your patient?" I asked.

"He's better already," he said.

From his awkwardness it was plain to me that he was doubtful about telling me why he had come. "What's on your mind?" I asked, to encourage him.

"Doctor, it's hard to explain. That young man you saw, he's— he's come from abroad. We're taking care of him, and of another boy who came with him ... and we need your help for a while."

"My help?" I was so surprised that I got up and walked towards Piskacek.

"Yes: they have identity cards—from that point of view everything's in order. But we want work papers for them. And you could help us."

I said nothing, turning this unexpected request over in my mind. You staked your life at that little game; in cases like this the Nazis always had the same reaction. But what could I do? Was I to refuse what Piskacek asked for? I had never had anything to do with politics. I used to say that all a doctor needed was to know how to take tonsils out and look after contagious diseases, without meddling with public business as well. But now it was not a question of tonsils, nor of influenza. I am not fond of high-sounding words, so let us put it that that day I realized there were some realities more important than all that. I nodded.

Piskacek sighed with relief. "I was sure you wouldn't disappoint us."

I sent him, in my name, to some friends I had in the Health Insurance at Prague, and they were good enough to get him the necessary work papers.

After that Piskacek brought me the two young fellows and I gave them sickness-cards certifying that they were unfit for work. I wrote out the first in the name of Josef Strnad, with a diagnosis of duodenal ulcer. He was living with the Khodl family in Prague-Vysocany. The second I filled out in the name of Frantisek Prochazka, and I gave him an inflammation of the gall bladder. He too was living in the Vysocany district, at Piskacek's house in Na brehu Street.

In this way the young men could now walk about freely in Prague. They had work papers and they were officially sick. But there was still the problem of making their sickness last. I had to explain the whole business to my friend Dr. Lycka of Prague-Karlin, the medical inspector for the insurance. Every week he signed a cross-check certificate and filled in the extension of unfitness for work on their cards. And so that they should not have to come to my place I went there to treat Piskacek's mother-in-law for an attack of gout—all too convenient to be genuine.

Most of the day our two young charges wandered about Prague. We did not yet know what they were looking for nor what they meant to do.

Looking after parachutists had turned us into conspirators, and we met every Sunday in the S.K. Vysocany stadium. While the football match was going on we discussed how we could help them during the following days.

It was on one of these occasions that Piskacek told me how the two young fellows had come under his care. At the beginning of January 1942, a friend of his who lived in a village not far from Prague came to see him. This friend told him confidentially that he was sheltering two men whose presence in his house had not been declared to the police, and that these young fellows had to get to Prague. And that was the beginning of what subsequently turned into a daily burden of anxiety—shelter, food, identity papers. Many people helped out of sheer good will, without even knowing whether the men came from the East or the West and without having the least notion of what they had come to do here. It was only after the killing that I learnt that the two agents' real names were Jan Kubis and Josef Gabcik.

Almost all those who helped them paid for it with their lives. Piskacek's whole family was murdered, as well as Dr. Lycka's. It was the merest chance that I did not share their fate.

Now, when I walk in the evenings along the banks of the Vltava, I sometimes remember them all and I ponder about Kubis' and Gabcik's mission. Was what they did right? Necessary? Probably it was—I do not know.

3

First steps

(*Antonie Smrzova–Bejckova*)

SOMETIMES you do something dangerous without feeling any fear at all, for the simple reason that you do not acknowledge it— you refuse to think about it. I'm sure you must not think about danger. I like tidiness in everything, even in one's thoughts. I hate muddled notions. That's why I didn't take long to think it over when my sister Ema Khodlova told me one day in January 1942 that there were some parachutists in Prague and that they needed our help. They had certainly come to inflict damage on the Germans. Right. So they had to be helped. And that's what we did.

We were five brothers and sisters in the Smrz family: Ema, the eldest, then Vaclav, Jaroslav and me: Josef had been killed in the First World War. Ema had married Khodl, a good, decent man who worked as a fitter in the Kolben works. His work sometimes took him abroad, as far as Persia and Bulgaria. He was not often at home, apart from Sundays, and so there was room in their flat. How had we heard there were parachutists in Prague? I don't remember now. Maybe my brother Jaroslav, a saddler, who was the first of us to know it, told Piskacek about my sister Ema's flat, and that was how the parachutists turned up there one day. We did not know their real names.

Jaroslav, Ema and her husband, and I all lived in Vysocany, close together, and we often went to see each other. So we were all well acquainted with these two young fellows who lived at Ema's place. The Khodls had one son, a student of about twenty.

He very soon became friends with these two, walking about Prague with them and showing them everything they wanted to see. They even went to the Hradcany Castle together, and to the cinema and the winter stadium. The parachutists were glad to have a guide and my nephew Vasek was delighted to go with his new friends—he admired them for the loaded pistol they always had in their pocket and the way they never said a single word about their plans.

One day, Jaroslav went to see Vaclav and asked him whether he could unsew the cushions on his divan to hide a parachute.

"Why?" cried Vaclav, quite amazed.

"These men don't know what to do with their parachutes. Couldn't we hide them for good and all?"

"What about the villa at Svepravice?" suggested Vaclav.

The Khodls had a little place at Svepravice. In the attic there was a small room where Vasek slept. The house was empty in winter. So they put the parachutes in this little shut-up bedroom.

Ema was very fond of the two boys. She wouldn't have them worried or prestered and presently they took to calling her "Ma." The evenings were very pleasant; we all used to sit round the table and listen to what these young fellows told us or watch them play cards. Sometimes Ota—that was one of them—did conjuring tricks, and sometimes he talked about the war, quite easy and relaxed. They were both sure it would soon be over.

My sister loved hearing that. What they said made her forget, at least for a few moments, the continual danger her whole family was living in. The two young men promised her that if the Gestapo came, they would kill her and Vasek before killing themselves, so that none of them should fall into the hands of the Germans alive. By way of comfort, it was, well ... The nicest thing to hear was what they said about the coming end of the war. Maybe we should all live through it.

But whenever one of us asked them just what they were doing in Prague, they only smiled and avoided the question. Ota dealt with anyone who was inquisitive by saying, "We're counting the ducks on the Vltava."

They often vanished from the Khodls' place for days on end and nobody knew where they went or what they did. Once they asked my brother Vaclav to get them a bicycle, telling him they needed it urgently. Up until then they had always borrowed Ema's or Jaroslav's. None of us knew why they needed it or why they wanted another; but Vaclav did what they asked. At that time he was working at the Avia factory, and Avia had bought some new bicycles for their workers. He stole an Ogar—that was the brand—and brought it to them after having changed the manufacturer's number. He also changed the number on Jaroslav's bicycle. One of Vaclav's friends at the works helped him to file off the original numbers and stamp on others.

Once they had these bicycles, the young men went off more often. They used to come back to us all dirty and worn out. Sometimes, when they came back, they would have a bath and then sleep fourteen hours at a stretch.

All of us lived in a strange tension. It was not really fear, but it was certainly a state of nerves. How we prayed that this plan we knew nothing about should succeed! I knew very well that we were hanging between life and death. Life's better, of course, but death is not something you must avoid if it's useful. We trusted in this undertaking that the young men were preparing for— would they ever have been sent to Prague on a mission if it was not useful or necessary? And so we lived on from one day to the next.

From time to time the parachutists surprised us with new and very difficult demands. One day they wanted Vaclav to help them to find a place for a transmitter. He suggested the new Dablice graveyard, but there must have been something against it, because they never spoke of it again. Another time they asked my brother-in-law Khodl to get them a rope thirty or forty yards long. It had to be an inch thick. That day he was setting up some machinery at Hlinsko and there he found the rope they wanted, put it in a box and sent it home. It suited the young men. But as usual they never said what it was to be used for. For my part, it seemed to me that a rope like that, stretched across a road, could stop a car. Zdenek and Ota were delighted with it; they measured it, checked its thickness, and at last Zdenek, the smaller one, said, "It'll do the job."

I often thought about that. Later my sister came running to our place and before she could get her breath she said to me, "Do you know what's happened about that rope?"

I couldn't remember having read in the papers about any sabotage or anything like that. "No. I've no idea."

"They've sacked my husband. They found out that he took it. And could he even say why? He doesn't know himself how it is going to be used. He had to keep his mouth shut, and now here he is out of a job after nearly forty years at Kolbenka's. And people stare at us as though we were thieves."

I comforted Ema as best I could; I told her Zdenek and Ota certainly would never have wanted that rope without good reasons. When I think about it now ... Could any one of us then have imagined how unimportant that business was, in comparison with what was waiting for us? No one, thank God.

But my brother-in-law Khodl was desperately unhappy about it. He was eaten up with shame and wouldn't go out any more. We had to watch him to see he didn't do something rash. He used to say it was a stain on his honour as a worker and he'd rather kill himself than put up with being taken for a thief.

Another time, later on, Zdenek tackled Vaclav: "Uncle, could you get hold of a car for us?"

"A car?" said Vaclav, smiling. "So the bikes I found you aren't good enough any more?"

"No," said Zdenek gravely. "We are getting ready for a big manoeuvre near the crossing of the Melnik and Kralupy roads, by the Tumovka inn, and we'll need a car to get us back to Prague faster."

What could Vaclav do? He promised them that he'd do his best and he went to see the chief of the firemen at the Avia works.

"Josef, I want to get hold of a car."

"What for?"

"It's hard to say. Listen, there are two young men who've come from abroad. They're preparing something, we don't know what, but they say it'll be worth while. And they need a car that can take them to a crossroads not far from Prague and bring them back again."

Josef was a decent man; what Vaclav said was enough for him. "You shall have it, Vaclav."

Not long after this Vaclav's wife fell seriously ill and had to be taken to hospital, where she stayed until autumn 1942. That probably saved Vaclav's life. He had much less free time and had to leave the two young men to be looked after by Ema, Jaroslav and, a little, by me.

One day Zdenek came to tell me that someone would be bringing me a case. "Please will you keep it in your place for me, Madame Antonie?"

I promised him I would. A man came to the flat and left me this case. It had a fine piece of cloth in it. A tailor who knew my sister Ema went to their place, measured Zdenek and made him a very good suit. He looked fine in it. Zdenek gave me the old clothes he had been wearing up till then, to hide. After the war I handed them in to the Ministry of Defence and they gave me a certificate.

Then the young men moved. They said they had to change their quarters from time to time so as not to attract attention. But on Mother's Day, in May, they brought Ema a huge bunch of flowers. My sister was so delighted that she said over and over again, "Now I know you are good boys. Look, Vasek. They've remembered me and they've brought me flowers." She dabbed her eyes with her handkerchief and brought them a cake, in spite of all they could say.

"No, no, Ma. You mustn't give us anything. You were always too kind to us."

After that they vanished again.

After the killing, when the Gestapo burst into the Khodls' place, the Mother's Day bouquet was still there; and it too was confiscated.

Every day we thought about those boys and wondered what they could be doing. But the days went by, May was coming to an end, and nothing happened. We had no news. Josef, the fireman, worried in vain about the car. The rope still lay there at the Khodls'. As a precaution, we made up our minds to hide it, and Fanynka, Vasek's fiancée, helped me load it on to a little pushcart. We took it to Dolni Pocernice and threw it down the well. None of us knew anything at all. I didn't, at any rate; nor did Ema, I believe. The young men were cautious and no doubt they wanted to avoid compromising us. But in the end that didn't help much.

In actual fact, they were preparing to strike during the spring of 1942, and it seems that only my brother Jaroslav knew about their plan. Indeed, they say he helped directly in carrying out the attack.

4

Ꮪꜧe chemistry teacher's account: 1

(*Ladislav Vanek*)

CHEMISTRY calls for precision. Later, precision was equally necessary to me in my underground activities. But in this case another factor had to be taken into consideration: in chemistry you work with elements; in the resistance you work with human beings who may be killed. And nothing can replace a man's life.

One of the rules of living outside the law requires that the man who goes underground should leave his home and avoid all contact with those he loves. This life began for me in 1941. At that time I was teaching in the 4th Brno high school and I lived at Slavkov, going into Brno every day by train. My father-in-law, a retired schoolmaster, had an excellent library, but he was equally fond of gymnastics. My wife shared her father's tastes. She was arrested by the Gestapo in October 1941. I was warned, and I got out of the school as the Gestapo arrived to take me. I went to Prague, and there I began the life of a man who was no longer able to find peace. A man who has officially ceased living, but who nevertheless walks about the streets, knows what it is to be hungry and to long for an ordinary existence.

I lived with the Senolds at 12, Krale Jiriho. It was there that I took part in setting up the Sokol* resistance organization, the Jindra group.

I stayed with the Senolds about six weeks; then I lived for some time at Dejvice, and after that at Zahradni mesto, where I spent the Christmas of 1941. I lived with Madame Helena, the

*Sokol, the Czech national physical-culture organization.

wife of a friend who had fled abroad. After he had gone, we both decided that I should take his name and use his identity card, with my photograph on it, of course, and that in this way the chemistry teacher would vanish, to be replaced in Zahradni mesto by "Captain Ales."

I grew a little moustache; I wore my friend's clothes; and gradually I became another man. I abandoned chemical formulae and learnt the essential rules of clandestine warfare. I watched the German secret police as attentively as once I had watched my pupils. And that is how the year 1942 began for me.

Even as early as that the Jindra resistance movement was firmly organized. Pechacek, the former Sokol champion, was its leader in Bohemia, with local chiefs such as Piskacek in Vysocany under him. Stepan Drasal was the leader in Moravia. My task was the running of Jindra on the scale of the whole country. We made ready for action. We set up an intelligence network and installed transmitters. I was brought into the UVOD, the central internal resistance committee, which united various clandestine organizations, including the military group "Defence of the Nation" and the "Stay True" committee.

In those days I was personally acquainted with Captain Vaclav Moravek, one of the Balaban–Masin–Moravek trio. He was an interesting man, so brave that his courage became a legend. He organized a great deal of sabotage, procured false papers, maintained contact between the various resistance movements, and above all ran an excellent intelligence service. He had gone underground at the very beginning of the German occupation, that is to say as early as 1939. He had a transmitter, and he was in permanent contact with London. He planned terrorist activities on a wide scale, but it seemed to him that even in conjunction with Balaban and Masin, his own resources would never be sufficient to give it the breadth he wanted. That was why, as he acknowledged himself, he asked London to drop agents in Bohemia and Moravia—men who could accomplish "great things" there.

No doubt you wonder how Vaclav Moravek could have any influence with the Czech general staff in London. The fact is that

Moravek was in touch with Paul Thümmel, the Haupt-V-Mann in the Wehrmacht intelligence service for the Czech countries and the Balkans. Thümmel was a spy on the grand, international scale. Vaclav Moravek put very large sums of money at Thümmel's disposal, and Thümmel told him important secrets concerning the Third Reich's High Command. In June 1940, for example, Thümmel knew the details of the Nazis' plan for the invasion of England. Moravek sent this information, whose importance I do not have to emphasize, to London.

Vaclav Moravek used the *nom de guerre* of Leon. One day he asked me to get him some poison, but it had necessarily to be a poison that would only work some hours after it had been swallowed. I was astonished, and asked him to explain. "What do you mean to do with it, Leon?"

"If the Gestapo arrest me, I want to be able to laugh in their faces for two or three hours."

The Gestapo did in fact surround him several times, but he always managed to get away, clearing himself a road with his pistol. Once, at Prague-Nusle, he was caught as he was actually sending radio messages, for the Gestapo had invaded the building and they burst into the flat; but Moravek slipped down by the lightning-rod, escaping again. The metal cut off a finger, however, and after that Moravek wore a glove with one of the fingers stuffed. One day I noticed that this glove had seven uneven stitches in it, four big and three small, and I said to him, "What are those stitches for?"

He pursed his lips. "Four Gestapo killed and three wounded."

Yet he was perfectly well aware that he would end up by being taken. That was why he told me he meant to put me in touch with a man called René, so that I could carry on with his job when he could no longer do it himself. René was Paul Thümmel, but at that time we did not know his real identity.

Some time in January 1942—I forget the exact date—Pechacek told me that some parachutists were being looked after by our Jindra organization.

"How did you hear this?"

He repeated the information that Piskacek had brought from

Vysocany—the landing outside a village near Prague and the shelter in a cave that had been used for some time.

"Where do they come from?"

"From England, it seems."

"What do you know about them?" I asked urgently, because that was what mattered most to us.

"Almost nothing," admitted Pechacek sadly.

"Do our people trust them?"

"For the moment, yes."

"And what if they are agents provocateurs?"

"They came by plane: they were helped to hide their parachutes."

"How can you be sure that the men who were dropped are the same as those Piskacek is telling you about? And why shouldn't the Germans themselves be behind the dropping, so that these young fellows can win our confidence and infiltrate the network?"

Pechacek was silent. To tell the truth, I did not much care for what I had just heard. It did not seem to me likely that parachutists coming from London should behave as these two men were doing. They said nothing about themselves but they were very free in questioning anyone who came near them yet no one knew anything of crucial importance about them. Would it not be wiser to pull out of the whole thing?

I turned it over in my mind, looking into every possibility. The apparently impromptu way they had turned up here took me aback. But it also occurred to me, that if they did really come from London, they could have no idea what a shocking hold the Gestapo had on our unhappy country, and to what degree caution and silence had become essential. And I remembered how Moravek had asked London for help.

I hesitated for a long while before telling Pechacek that we should have to meet these mysterious characters face to face—see them with our own eyes and make them talk about themselves.

That is how we met. I was waiting for them, together with Pechacek, in the flat he had in the Smichov district of Prague. We were sitting there, not saying a word, either of us. In moments like this, a man sinks into his own thoughts. The sound of the

bell made us jump. Pechacek went to open the door and he came
back with Zelenka–Hajsky and a young man we did not know.
Only one of the parachutists had come.

I must say a few words about Zelenka–Hajsky. He was a
former headmaster who had escaped from the frontier zone in
September 1938, after Munich, when the region where he lived was
attached to the Reich. He worked faithfully for our movement
and had been assigned to help people who were living outside
the law. His group was called Rijen, and he himself had chosen
the name of Riha. Sometimes he also used that of Hajsky. It
was he who brought us these two unknown men.

The stranger was rather short and thickset. He had slightly
protruding cheekbones and thin lips. As he came in he glanced
round the room and seemed relieved to find me alone.

"I am Ota," he said.

"And I am Jindra," I replied.

We shook hands, each watching the other. Pechacek brought
tea and we drank it in silence—the conversation would not get
under way. I made up my mind to start.

"I'd just like to point out that this house is guarded and that
each of us has something in his pocket."

He smiled, and without a word took a pistol from his jacket.
Then he added, "I'm fond of these gadgets, too."

"Where do you come from?"

"I can't tell you."

"Why not?"

"Our mission is secret."

"But you've already told several people that you came from
England."

"What of it?"

"You mustn't be surprised at our lack of trust. There are a good
many agents provocateurs in this country."

Now he looked angry, ostentatiously shrugging his shoulders.

"Do you know any Czech officers in England?" I asked.

He gave satisfactory answers to this. Then I tried to trip him
up with other questions. Pechacek showed him the photo of his
son-in-law, who had gone abroad. Ota seemed to be relaxed;

but after all, if he was a Nazi agent provocateur, everything he told us might be a lesson he had learnt by heart.

All at once I noticed that he was using Moravian turns of speech.

"Do you come from Bohemia?"

"No. From Moravia."

"What a lucky coincidence. So do I!" Silence again. "Could you tell me what part?"

"Round about Trebic," he said, sulkily.

"I know those parts. Can you tell me what there is extraordinary about the railway station at Vladislav?"

Without hesitating, the young fellow answered, "There's a magnificent great bed of roses. I dare say one of the railwaymen is very keen on growing flowers."

I began to believe in him and to think that my fears were groundless. Pechacek and Zelenka–Hajsky followed the conversation closely and sometimes they put in a question themselves.

"You mustn't be angry if I say nothing about our mission," said the stranger earnestly. "All I can tell you is its code name—Anthropoid."

Anthropos, I said to myself, that's the Greek for man. And Anthropoid, what would that mean? The group with a name like that must have something in common with men—or maybe with something that was no longer a man? Moravek often said that it was necessary for a Nazi monster to be killed. Carrying on my train of thought I asked point-blank, "Haven't you come with the idea of killing Heydrich?"

The stranger jumped, giving me a startled look. "How did you know?"

The implicit acknowledgment brought us closer. Once again chance had turned the course of events. The young fellow could not understand how we came to know the object of his mission, and from then on he became much more open. And presently he added, "We need your help."

I nodded. Once we had reached this point, everything else followed easily and smoothly. We shared out the tasks. Zelenka–Hajsky took charge of the two parachutists—they would have to change quarters frequently.

"What kind of contact have you with London?" I asked.

"There are several of us here. My own companion has hurt his foot and that's why I came alone this evening. Other men were dropped the same night as us. They have a transmitter. We send our information to London through them and get back additional orders."

Zelenka was delighted at his obvious sincerity. "These are thoroughly decent lads. I've already warned them to be very careful. But we can trust them."

We drank another cup of tea. Outside it was dark—night falls early in January. We shook hands warmly as we parted. Everything was in order. But he had not told us his real name.

THE HISTORIAN STEPS IN : I

(*The author*)

We must go back a little in time.

On 21 September 1941, the Czech press agency CTK announced that the Protector of the Reich, Freiherr von Neurath, had found it necessary for reasons of health to beg Hitler to grant him a long period of leave. The article stated that in these circumstances the Führer was unable to refuse the Reichsprotektor's request and that he had entrusted the SS Obergruppenführer and General of Police Reinhard Heydrich with the functions of Reichsprotektor in Bohemia and Moravia during the illness of the minister von Neurath.

From that time on the SS flag flew over the castle of Prague. Heydrich took over the rule of the Protectorate and at once proclaimed a state of emergency. He signed the first list of death sentences: every patriotic Czech was threatened.

Leaders and members of the illegal Communist Party died before the firing squad: O. Synek, Fr. Taussig, Vi. Haken, J. Krejci, V. Kren, Vr. Santroch—their numbers continually increased. Partisans from the various movements were also put to death: Generals Vojta, Bily, Horacek, Dolezal and Sara, and other officers such as Balaban, Dvorack, Kasper. And scores of intellectuals, workers, craftsmen, apprentices, students. The grim Bekanntmachung posted on the walls of the city were crowded with names: Mandik, Vavra, Kabrt, Blazek, Pechlat, Cerny, Jelinek, Skvor, Vitek, Maly, Vesely—baker, jeweller, draftsman, clerk, compositor, postman, miner, electrician, officer, greaser, fisherman, office worker, glove maker, gunsmith—all Czechs.

And this brings us to the precise reason for Heydrich's arrival in Prague. Hitler needed a brutal, energetic Nazi in Bohemia and Moravia. Freiherr von Neurath was not of the right calibre; under his protectorate the situation was falling to pieces and the resistance movements were gaining strength. A striking piece of evidence proved this towards the end of the summer of 1941. The resistance movements appealed to the people to boycott Protectorate newspapers, and they responded in very great numbers. This success for the fighters on the home front was also a final warning for the Nazis, who now fully understood that Neurath was incapable of dealing with Czech patriotism.

On 17 September 1941, therefore, representatives of the Gestapo, the Sicherheitsdienst and SS commanders held a meeting in Prague and decided that Hitler must be given an exact account of the declining state of affairs in the Protectorate and advised that harsh coercive measures were essential.

The Führer replied unambiguously by sending Reinhard Heydrich, the faithful head of the central security bureau of the Reich (RSHA), to the Protectorate. This man was second in command to Reichsführer Heinrich Himmler, the supreme chief of all German police organizations, and in carrying out tasks assigned to him in the various occupied countries he had already clearly proved himself unmoved by humanitarian considerations. He was the perfect Nazi prototype—"the man with a heart of iron" as Hitler himself put it. On 2 August 1941, before his posting to Prague, Heydrich had sent Hitler and Himmler a report headed On the activity of the Communists in Germany and the occupied territories, before and after the beginning of the war with the Soviet Union. *Among other things, it stated that the strongest Communist movement in the occupied countries was very likely that of Bohemia and Moravia. This report must also have decided Hitler to pick Heydrich to "put things in order" in the Czech countries.*

On 27 September 1941 then, Reinhard Heydrich stepped out of his Mercedes and walked into Prague Castle as new Reichsprotektor. Five days later he summoned all Nazi authorities in the Protectorate to Cernin Palace and in a secret speech informed them of his policy: "The eastern territories are partly inhabited by Slavs, and in these territories it must be understood that all acts of goodwill are interpreted as weakness ... The Slav does not like being treated on an equal footing and he is not used to having his masters descend to his level . . . The inhabitants of these territories must become our servants.

"*The effect of the final solution must be as follows: this entire area will one day be definitively German, and the Czechs have nothing to expect here . . . The area is the heart of the Reich. We will try to Germanize these Czech vermin.*"

On 11 October 1941 Heydrich told Berlin he had the task in hand. Firing squads. Hangings. Beheadings.

A month later, on 12 November 1941, the Prague Gestapo produced a report on the activity of the illegal Communist movement. Two days later the Brno Gestapo did the same. Strikes broke out at Hradec Kralove, in Nachod, in the Prague shipbuilding yards in Prague-Liben, at the CKD Prague at Slany, in the Upice textile factories, at the waterworks in Prague-Jinonice, in the Ostrava mines, and elsewhere. In the region of Vsetin the first partisan bands were being formed.

Those resistance networks that had not been wiped out by the first "state of emergency" measures increased their activity. Among others was the group led by the officers Balaban, Masin, and Moravek. They had preserved their link with agent A54, otherwise Franta, René, Dr Holm or Eva—code names for Nazi officer Paul Thümmel, an agent of the Czech intelligence service in London, who regularly provided them with vital information.

After long negotiations, a Central National Revolutionary Committee (UNRV) was set up. It brought representatives of resistance movements of varying tendencies together on a basis of equality. The UNRV at once adopted a programme of active resistance. As early as August 1941 Moravek and his group—theirs was one of the most energetic movements—asked London to drop parachutists into Bohemia to help the resistance and to carry out diversionary action.

There is documentary evidence that some months prior to this request London was considering dropping teams into the Protectorate for special missions. An early note is to be found in the war diary of the Czech Minister of National Defence in London dated 30 April 1941: "*Received WO (War Office) authorization to send 4 officers and 5 non-commissioned officers for parachute training. Young officers and non-commissioned officers have been selected. The course will begin on 4 May this year and will last three weeks. The WO intends to train this nucleus of parachutists in a total number of pupils amounting to about 14 officers and 22 non-commissioned officers. The commanding officer of the brigade and Staff-Colonel Moravec have been informed."*

Another document, dated 19 May 1941, written on the paper of the Ministry of National Defence in London, numbered 1229 and stamped Very Urgent and Confidential, *points out that the date first set for the beginning of the course no longer applied.* It also says, "Staff-Colonel Moravec, the Head of the Intelligence Service, has arranged with the WO for other training for the prospective parachutists. The whole proposed force will be trained in two groups. The first, of 6 officers and 6 non-commissioned officers, will follow the course of the 25th of this month, lasting 3 weeks. The second group of 6 officers and 6 non-commissioned officers will follow the course of 6 June of this year, lasting 3 weeks. The military personnel selected will proceed to Manchester where they will be received by intelligence officers. The training of future military personnel will be arranged later."

We also find here the list supplied by the commanding officer of the 1st Czech Brigade, containing the names of carefully selected candidates. It is made up of several different choices in case "the minister should intend to carry out certain alterations." The selections attached to the letter show the candidates in the order that the commanding officer considered "the most useful."

On the first list is the name of one of the two men who would die heroically at Prague. He is last out of thirty-six candidates: Josef Gabcik. And after his name, in the handwriting of a London civil servant, there is the note "nose."

In the second set of possibilities is listed, inconspicuously in the second section, the name of First Lieutenant Alfred Bartos, who would later command parachute team Silver A.

On the last list, of candidates for eventual acceptance, we find the names of First Lieutenant Adolf Opalka, later leader of the parachutists during the church battle in Prague, and of Lieutenant Oldrich Pechal.

None of those who took part in the killing or the preparations for it yet appeared in these lists. But at that time—the spring of 1941—it was merely a question of parachute training, without taking into account any specific individual missions. The groups dropped in Czechoslovakia *were not formed until later. And in the interval other volunteers had gone through parachute courses.*

These courses took place in Scotland. *We know from the evidence of the survivors that they were tough and exhausting—hard physical training, day and night exercises, self-defence, theory, marksmanship, parachute jumps. Most of the volunteers were filled with a fierce, heartfelt desire to return to the struggle against those who were occupying their country, against Nazism.*

We have a report on the activity of the parachutists in the Protectorate, written by the German secret police in Prague and dated 2 June 1942. It was based on the interrogations of those parachutists who had turned traitor or had talked under torture after their arrest.

> *It has been established, through the interrogation of arrested parachuted agents, as well as those who gave themselves up to the state police and from persons who worked with certain agents now dead, that almost all the parachuted agents illegally joined the Czech Legion in Poland shortly after the setting up of the Protectorate. There they embarked at Gdynia for French ports. In other cases they reached the Czech Legion in France by way of the Balkans, Istanbul, Cairo and Marseilles. After the fall of France they were taken to England along with survivors of the British Expeditionary Force. The great majority of these agents opposed the setting up of the Protectorate and wished to give armed support to England and France in order to bring about the fall of Germany and the restoration of the Czechoslovak Republic. Only two cases are known of young Czechs who joined the Legion out of a love for adventure.*

Here a passing observation is called for. The two adventurers to whom the Gestapo referred turned traitor: their names were Curda and Gerik. And it was entirely due to them that in spring and summer of 1942 the Nazis succeeded in liquidating most of the parachutists then in Bohemia and Moravia.

The men were not always chosen for the courses with all the discrimination that could have been wished. Frantisek Pavelka, for example, the first parachutist sent by London and dropped near Caslav on 4 October 1941, proved a severe disappointment. The Gestapo stated, *"Pavelka was arrested in Prague on 25 October 1941 by local officers of the state police. According to his information he is the first parachuted agent to be sent by London. His mission was to deliver a transmitter and a code to the heads of the illegal radiotelegraphy group. Before he left, General Ingr, the self-styled Czechoslovak minister of national defence in London, personally said good-bye to him. All his material has been seized by the state police. The local inhabitants, six in number, by whom he was sheltered and whose names had been given to him in London, have been arrested by police headquarters in Prague."*

To return to the Gestapo's general report on the parachutists:

In the first place all the parachuted agents were given special training for a fortnight at the school in Manchester; this was carried out by English staff and it included the use of weapons, radiotelegraphy, and the Morse code as well as parachute training. This short course was followed by a period of six months spent with the agents' original units. After this they were detailed for a special six weeks course at the sabotage school at Cammus Darrah, near Mallaig, in Scotland: here too the instructors were all English, and taught hand-to-hand combat, the Morse code, map reading, the use of explosives, sabotage of railways and bridges, and the disruption of drinking-water supplies. At the end of the course, the agents returned once more to their units for six weeks.

After this they were brought together at a country house called Bellasis in Dorking, about twenty-five miles southeast of London, from where they were taken to various airfields as required. The radiotelegraphists underwent a special complementary course at the Czech transmitting station at Tune Neuk, a country house at Woldingham, near London.

The agents have usually been dropped in groups of three, each group commanded by a Czech officer. The espionage groups have been equipped with short-wave transmitters and spare parts for their sets. Several three man groups have been provided with a special short-wave instrument whose code name is Rebecca; it is designed to provide automatic radio guidance on a set wavelength for British aircraft within a range of 100–150 kilometres, showing them the direction of the target. The sabotage groups, also three man teams, have been given large quantities of various explosives.

In some cases individual agents have been dropped; their only mission is to supply cash, spare parts for radio equipment, poison capsules and fresh codes.

Up to the present only two groups of five men are known. In one case it is known that three of the men were assigned to spy and the other two to commit the assassination. An inquiry into the second group of five is still in progress.

Certain details in this German report, which was drawn up after the killing, are mistaken. Nevertheless, the weakness and treachery of a few men had given the Nazis information on the essential points. The report states that the group entrusted with the killing was composed of two men. How had this plan for their mission come into being?

In the autumn of 1941 a meeting was held in London, and during this meeting an attempt on Heydrich's life was decided upon. It was planned for 28 October 1941, the day upon which the nation celebrated the Czechoslovak Republic. That is to say six months before the event actually occurred.

This date, 28 October 1941, is confirmed by the evidence of Jindra, the chemistry teacher who became a Partisan. During a meeting in spring 1942 Gabcik said to him, "You are afraid that the killing may have terrible consequences and you say you are not prepared for it. What would you say if we had carried it out last October, when it was first planned?"

We possess the official record of a meeting on 3 October 1941 attended by Staff-Colonel Moravec, Lieutenant-Colonel Bartik, Major Palecek, Staff-Major Krcek, Sergeant Gabcik, and Sergeant Svoboda.

Staff-Colonel Frantisek Moravec addressed the two parachutists Gabcik and Svoboda in these terms: "The radio and the newspapers have told you about the insane, murderous slaughter that is going on at home, in our own houses. The Germans are killing the finest men we have. But even this is only a sign of the kind of war we are engaged in; and our duty is not to whine or complain but to fight. At home, our people have fought—now they are in a difficult position, one that limits their field of action. It is our turn to help them from outside. One of the objectives of this help from abroad will be entrusted to you. This October is the saddest October national holiday that our country has known since its independence—the holiday must be marked in a most outstanding fashion. It has been decided that it shall be done by a stroke that will go down in history in exactly the same way as the slaughter of our compatriots.

"*In Prague there are two persons who are representative of the killing. They are K. H. Frank and the newcomer Heydrich. In our opinion, and in the opinion of our leaders, we must try to make one of them pay for all the rest, so as to prove that we return blow for blow. That, essentially, is the mission with which you are to be entrusted. You will go back to our country in pairs, so that each can help the other. This will be necessary, since, for reasons that will be evident to you, you will have to carry out your task without the assistance of our compatriots who have stayed in the country. When I say without their assistance, I mean that help of this nature is out of the question until the task has been accomplished. Once it is done, they will provide assistance of every kind. You must decide for yourselves how the work is to be carried out and how much time you will devote to it. You will be dropped at a place that offers the best possible conditions for landing. You will be equipped with everything we can provide. As far as we know the position, you will receive the support of any of our fellow-countrymen you may turn to. But for your part, caution, prudence and forethought are essential. I do not have to tell you that your mission is of the utmost historical importance and that the danger is great. Its success depends on the conditions that your own shrewdness and ability bring into being. We will discuss this again when you come back from the additional exercise that has been arranged. As I have said, this is a mission of the utmost gravity. You must therefore think it over in a completely candid, fair-minded way. If you still have any doubts about what I have set out, you must say so.*" Both Gabcik and Svoboda formally agreed to undertake a mission of this kind. The anticipated date of departure is 10 October of this year.*

The killing was therefore entrusted to two men, Gabcik and Svoboda. But subsequently Svoboda was injured in an exercise, and this unexpected accident hampered the plan. The mission was therefore postponed.

Orders were then given to drop another group in the Protectorate. This group was made up of a commanding officer, First Lieutenant Alfred Bartos, pseudonym Emil Sedlak; Sergeant Josef Valcik, pseudonym Zdenek Tousek; and the non-commissioned radiotelegraphist Jiri Potucek, pseudonym Alois Tolar. This group's code name was Silver A, and that of the transmitter taken by the group Libuse.

Favourable weather conditions had to be waited for since the distance *was great—close to a thousand miles. The first attempt took place on 7 November 1941. That afternoon the Silver A parachutists reached the airfield, where their dispatcher, Captain Sustr, was waiting for them. The plane took off at 1814 hours. According to the flight log it reached the Belgian coast at 1921 hours, crossed the Thin at 2023 hours, and reached a point south of Prague at 2210 hours. At this juncture a snowstorm prevented the dropping; having tried to get round it in vain, the pilot decided to return to England. A second attempt on 30 November was no more successful: the plane turned back without having found the dropping-zone.*

During the following weeks, the Silver A team returned to training—two other parachutists, Gabcik and Kubis, took part in this course. They received orders setting 28 December 1941 as the date for a fresh attempt. The weather forecast was good. As well as Silver A, two other teams were to be dropped: Anthropoid, consisting of Sergeant Josef Gabcik, pseudonym Zdenek Vyskocil, locksmith, and Jan Kubis, pseudonym Ota Strnad, workman; and Silver B, consisting of Jan Zemek, pseudonym Vladimir Vrba, and Vladimir Skacha, pseudonym Jan Novak. There were seven men, therefore, in addition to the dispatcher, who were to take their places in the plane. Each of the parachutists signed an under- taking "to do everything in his power to carry out the mission for which he had volunteered."

It was laid down that after the landing, the transmitter Libuse was to get in touch with London. If London did not pick up the signal, they would be told by a message broadcast on two successive days in the BBC's Czech-language programme—"The whole world understands your painful silence."

The departure did in fact take place on 28 December 1941 at 2000 hours. Here is the dispatcher's report:

On 28 December 1941 three operations were launched in the course of the same flight, that is to say, 1: Silver A; 2: Silver B; 3: Anthropoid. The three groups were taken by car to Tangmere airfield on the afternoon of 28 December.

At 1230 hours we had been told by telephone that operation Silver A would be carried out. Later this was modified, and the English asked that two additional teams should be provided to take advantage of the flight, for which a Halifax flown by Flight-Lieutenant R. C. Hockey and his

crew had been laid on. Since three groups had been envisaged, this altera-
tion caused no difficulty of any kind.

The three operational groups and their equipment had plenty of room
in the spacious, heated aircraft. Captain Sustr took part in the flight as
dispatcher. Counting the English air crew, there were sixteen men
aboard, together with the equipment needed for the operations.

Log of the mission:

28.12.41:	2200 hours	take-off
	2249	cross French coast
29.12.41:	0042	meeting with enemy fighters over Darmstadt: thanks to the pilot's skill the plane shakes them off
	0132	reach Bayreuth
	0213	the plane fired upon by anti-aircraft guns over the Skoda works and—
	0215	above the centre of Plzn
	0224	drop the group Anthropoid east of Plzn: fly on eastwards
	0227	the pilot gives the order for dropping Silver A
	0256	the pilot gives the order for dropping Silver B: the plane turns back westwards
	0316	anti-aircraft fire again from the Plzn area
	0430	anti-aircraft fire from unidentified area
	0520	anti-aircraft fire from unidentified area
	0716	reach Le Tréport
	0800	reach English coast
	0814	land at Tangmere airfield

The times are GMT. The whole flight lasted 10 hours 14 minutes
and it was carried out by a Halifax flown by a British crew. The average
flying height was 10,000 feet; the drops took place at 900 feet. The
average speed was 187 mph and 120 mph during the drops. Weather:
northwest wind, mist, low cloud and snow over Czechoslovak territory.

After the landing, the pilot informed me that he had dropped the
Anthropoid team in the area Ejpovice–Kysice–Na Pohodnici, about 7 or
8 kilometres south of Plzn, since the designated dropping-zone 3 kilometres northwest of Ejpovice could not be found because of fog. Groups
Silver A and B were not dropped on exactly the chosen places either, as
the pilot was unable to make out the approaches to the Zelezne mountains,

which were entirely hidden in cloud. If he had flown over the cloud he would have lost all touch with the reference points on the ground; furthermore, had he done so, he would not have been able to risk bringing the plane lower, because of the neighbourhood of the mountains, whose tops were invisible. According to his data, he dropped Silver A east of Caslav and Silver B northwest of Zdirec.

No bombing was carried out, as the additional weight of the men and equipment made it impossible to carry any bombs.

The dispatcher continues with an appreciation of the physical behaviour of the parachutists during the flight and immediately before the drops. From this it appears that Gabcik was "markedly superior" to the others. Corporal Zemek uttered a remark far from flattering to those in charge: "It's lucky I'm off at last; I'd have smashed the place up otherwise."

And the report ends: "Sergeant Skacha, on being asked what should be done with his personal belongings, replied, 'Leave them where they are. They are just as safe there as where you think of putting them.' Asked what he meant by that, he only waved his arm.

"The men of Silver A and Anthropoid shook hands with the dispatcher before jumping and said to him earnestly, 'You will soon have word of us: we shall do everything we possibly can.' London, 29 December 1941 ... Captain Sustr."

5

𝕿𝖍𝖊𝖞 𝖜𝖊𝖗𝖊 𝖘𝖙𝖆𝖓𝖉𝖎𝖓𝖌 𝖇𝖞 𝖒𝖞 𝖘𝖎𝖉𝖊

(Vladimir Skacha)

YES, I DID say more or less what Captain Sustr reported. But it happened at the airfield, a little while before we were lined up to get into the plane.

Some time before the flight, they had said we could leave our things at the MDN depot in London, but one of the storekeepers had advised me to put them somewhere safe and to leave them there. According to him that would be better, because in army depots things of that kind might be lost or spoiled, either by the depot being moved, or by the people being changed—to say nothing of the mice.

I did not own many things I valued: just a few photos taken in Africa, France and England, and a few souvenirs and papers. Still, I didn't want to lose them. So I gave them to an English family I knew. When I was officially asked to hand in my personal property at the army depot, I said I didn't possess any.

At the airfield Captain Sustr spoke to me about it again and he said he would put my things into the depot himself if I liked. I laughed and said I'd rather they stayed where they were. I don't know why, but Captain Sustr took it the wrong way and asked me what I meant by that. I brushed it off by waving my hand—it didn't seem to me worth talking about. The plane was waiting and I was thinking about other things.

Kubis and Gabcik were standing next to me; just then the others were a little way off.

At that time the will they made us write at the airfield seemed

to me—what shall I say? Well, anyhow, I smiled and signed
it. I had joined the resistance when I was nineteen. I was one
of a family that was pleased if they could get enough to eat.
That means I owned nothing. I volunteered for parachute training
out of pure patriotic feeling; I had ideals that seem to me exag-
gerated now—the sort you only find in novels. They told us
for sure that the war would be over soon and nobody offered us
the least reward for what we were going to do. And on our side
we never asked for any. I looked upon myself as a soldier who
had been given an order and who could only expect a word of
praise at the most, if he carried out what he had been ordered to
do properly. So I left the trifles I owned to my parents in a will I
wrote on rather humorous lines. Captain Sustr was a brave man
in himself, the sort that's called a good soldier but he hadn't
much idea of people, and I dare say he took what I had written
in the wrong spirit. He was a typical regular officer, and he
thought far too much of his rank. I did not really care for him,
because I'd often noticed that he dodged his responsibilities. If
he couldn't give an exact answer to a direct question, he'd hide
behind military discipline. I thought he was not open and straightforward in the way he behaved towards us, and I did not like it.
Personally, he gave me the feeling that in his opinion I was no
more than a number you add or subtract. He had no notion of
being human.

Our team, that is to say Silver B, was equipped with a transmitter. Each of us had been given a pocket knife, an automatic
with two chargers and twelve rounds, a capsule of poison, a
piece of chocolate, some meat-extract tablets, a few razor blades
and an identity card. These cards were perfectly imitated and
they would have had to be examined in a laboratory to detect
the forgery. All except Zemek's and mine. Our cards were blank
when Captain Sustr brought them to us at the training centre,
where they were filled in and signed and our photos added. All
that was wanted was the stamp, but the stamp Captain Sustr
brought with him was new and it had no ink on it. What was to
be done? Captain Sustr decided to repair his blunder by having
some ordinary ink brought. He spread it on the stamp that he

marked our cards with. The result was a disaster—you could see at first glance the stamp was not right.

The chocolate, the razor blades and the other things they gave us when we left were all specially made and they had no names on them anywhere. If Kubis and Gabcik or anyone else took cans with English labels on them, it could only have been done by hiding them, but I doubt very much that they did.

The clothes we were wearing came from the store of civilian clothing taken from the soldiers of our army, and they were therefore all made in Czechoslovakia. These details were very carefully checked. Only some of the shoes, where there was difficulty with the sizes, were bought in England.

The plane was waiting some way off. It was cold. Captain Sustr came back to us and checked everything again. We had to show him what we had in our pockets.

Up until the last minute before taking off, we had not known that we, group Silver B, were going to fly in the same plane as other groups. Anthropoid, Silver A, and our team had been taken to the airfield separately. It was only when we were getting in that Zemek and I learnt that other parachutists were going with us. We were given orders not to talk to them during the flight— they had the same orders. That's why we never said anything, although we all knew one another well, apart from Potucek. Not a word in the plane, except for "Hi there, boys," and "Good luck." Everything that has been written about our conversations is pure imagination. In any case, there was no question of talking, because of the fact that we were in an unsoundproofed war-plane, that we had rubber helmets on our heads, and that the engines were roaring at full blast.

None of us knew the code name of any group but his own. It was only after the war that I learnt that Gabcik and Kubis were Anthropoid and that Bartos' group were Silver A. Nor did we know anything about each other's missions.

Obviously, we suspected that Kubis and Gabcik were to carry out a killing. Yes, that's how it was, however unbelievable it may seem. It's hard to say now how we came to be so sure. We hadn't been told officially, of course. We had seen that they had a special training programme, and they may have let drop some remarks; perhaps that's what led us to it. Whatever the reason there was the rumour in the rest of the course that they were "out for Heydrich."

I knew them a long while before it ever came to me that I might share such extraordinary moments with them in the same plane. They were both ordinary chaps. Although they were quite unalike, they did have one thing in common—they were both spirited and disciplined. Kubis was a quiet fellow; he would never have hurt a fly. Gabcik, on the other hand, was fiery and enthusiastic, yet at the same time thoroughly sensible. They were inseparable friends. If you were in a tight corner, they were the kind of men you would like to have by you. As soldiers, they felt that orders were orders—no argument. The news from our country, telling us about the tortures and the killing of our people had worked them up to a high pitch. I remember one day I discussed it with Kubis. He shook his head in pain, saying over and over again, "How can such things be possible? How can such things be possible?"

Anthropoid had not been issued with a sending and receiving set: it was only our group and Bartos' that had them. I don't know when the other groups were given the word nor when their members were chosen. As far as I was concerned, it was about two months before 28 December that they decided I should go with Zemek. In the first place I was supposed to drop with Jaromir Sedlak, who came from Tisnov, near Brno. But Sedlak dislocated an ankle during training and he had to be replaced. It was only a little while before taking off that we learnt the code name of our team, Silver B.

This was our mission: "You will be dropped in the Svratouch–Svratka region in Bohemia. With the help of the addresses that will be given you, you will get into touch with the home-based resistance. You will give them the transmitter and the code; after that you will act according to their orders."

To begin with we were to hide at one of the addresses they gave us and there wait for a message that would be broadcast by the BBC: "Each man must relentlessly pursue the aim laid down." This would be the signal for us to go to Chrudim and there meet a liaison agent who would put us into touch with the men who needed us. There were no arrangements for us to help Anthropoid or Silver A.

We winked at one another—clapped each other on the back. The December twilight was falling. Now at this moment, here they were, standing by my side; but in a few hours we were going to say a brief good-bye. Gabcik and Kubis were smiling—a steady, fixed smile. We got into the plane; the door closed behind us.

The flight was far from peaceful, as Captain Sustr said in his report. The noise, the heat, the jangling nerves.

First they dropped Anthropoid; then Silver A. We waved good-bye: they waved back and jumped. We never saw them again. It was said that Kubis and Gabcik found shelter somewhere in Prague. The Silver A team—Bartos, Valcik and Potucek—who had the transmitter Libuse, probably found help and protection in the Pardubice region.

They were all good fellows and brave men, very brave.

6

What is to be done with Libuse?

(*Antonin Novak*)

I NEVER GOT mixed up with anything—what matters is that the potatoes should yield properly and that there should be a good wheat harvest. It's hill country where we live, and it's always cold. You get up thinking, if the weather's better today, we'll have to pour the liquid manure over the fields and mend the cowshed—there's always something like that. Yes, there are members of the Agrarian Party round here; but I myself used to vote for the Social Democrats. Later on, when my son started working in the quarries, he brought home the *Rude Pravo* and then I voted for the Communists. With my bit of a cottage, I had nothing to do with the big landowners of the Agrarian Party. I had to work the fields hard and steady, morning till night.

That day, I'd been to see whether the cold had hurt my corn, but it had snowed heavily, so I was soon on my way home. I was almost at the village when all at once I saw old Knez—though really he was only about forty. I was fifteen years older than him. He was walking slowly, coming back from somewhere or other and wheeling his bike, because the road was slippery. He was wearing his uniform. Knez was in command of our police station.

"Where are you going?" he asked.

We had got to know one another, drinking beer together. I'd seen him once at a Communist meeting. That was before the elections; my boy had said I should go, so I went along with him. There weren't many Communists in our village, but some had come in from the country around, where there were a good many quarries. Knez was there, standing near the door: he said nothing. Afterwards my son told me the other policemen were worse— they interrupted, while Knez kept his mouth shut.

Now and then, as I said, he used to go to the inn. We talked to one another about different things—the weather, the harvest, and more recently about the Germans too. In spite of his uniform, he was a good Czech. We didn't often agree, but we both swore and cursed about the fascists.

"Where should I be going?" I answered. "To the fields, of course."

"I hope you don't wear your legs out. There's snow everywhere, and plenty of it. What more do you want? Your wheat won't freeze."

I jumped the ditch to reach him, and we walked along the road together. Knez said nothing, but pushed his bike along. When we'd gone two hundred yards or so I said to him, "What's wrong? Has something happened?"

"What could happen? No. Nothing. I'm all right."

But it was clear enough to me that there was something on his mind. In Havranek's field two crows were cawing. I don't like the creatures; I pointed them out to Knez and said, "If I had a gun, I'd shoot them."

He smiled. "I've a gun, as you see; but I don't shoot them."

By way of vexing him a little, I said, "That's your business. Maybe you don't know how to shoot."

"That depends on what there is to shoot: there are crows and crows."

"Don't tell me that. I don't understand that kind of talk."

"And if it was men, would you shoot them too?" he asked.

"Oh, I'm talking about crows," I said. Then an idea came into my head and I turned to him. "Have you got any dangerous animals around here?"

He looked at me with an odd little smile. "God knows if they are dangerous. Sometimes you can't tell."

We walked on, and he began to talk slowly. "I have to see to law and order here, you understand. See that nothing happens against the Reich; and yet ... sometimes it weighs me right down. But when these boys ..."

I started. "What boys?"

"How can I put it? There are parachutists here. Have you got anything for them to eat?"

"So that's it, then," I cried.

Knez stopped. "Do you know how to keep your mouth shut?"

"Of course I do. As far as that's concerned, I'm dumb. And we'll find some food, too. What are they doing here?"

Knez shrugged. "You ought to know. Anything's possible. They want information—they ask what's being made in the factories."

"And what do they do with this information? They don't keep it under their hats, that's for sure."

Knez walked on slowly. "No," he said, "and a lot of people know they are here. That's always dangerous. Two or three might keep their mouths shut but now ..."

It was only later that I learnt they had a transmitter they called Libuse hidden in the Hluboka quarry near Dachov, the village next to Hlinsko. And after that at Lezaky. When they came to arrest him, Knez killed himself.

But that evening, after we had met there in the road, I had food ready for him—and a good many times after that, too.

7

The statement of the survivor from Pardubice: 1

(*Vaclav Krupka*)

I AM NEARLY fifty now, and when I look back into the past I have the feeling of having outlived my own death.

It seemed to me that joining the resistance was a patriotic duty. Back in the days when I was a boy, I had seen the armed groups of the pro-Nazi political party, the Ordners, at work. I lived in the frontier region, where there was endless friction between the Czech minority and the Nazis.

In 1937 I finished my studies at the Military Academy. Then came mobilization, and after that Munich and the time of disillusion. Suddenly everything I believed in and thought imperishable collapsed, leaving me utterly at a loss, not knowing what my attitude should be.

I thought of leaving the country and I searched for the means and the opportunity. Together with a few friends, I went to the French embassy at Prague to talk over an escape abroad. You know Sute Brehy, near Tverebechovice, on the Divoka Orlice? That was where we waited for the signal. Then everything went wrong; and then I married.

I met my future wife during the winter of 1940. Six months later we married. I must confess that at that time I gave myself up entirely to my home; nothing else existed for me, and I had peace of mind again.

Our life was happy. Sometimes we would go to see friends or

relations, and sometimes we went dancing or to the cinema. We lived at Pardubice, where I worked at the Eastern Bohemia Electricity Union. All day long I waited impatiently for the office to close and for the moment of going home. Hanka would be waiting for me there smiling, she would ask me my news, I would kiss her, tell her some nonsense or other, and we would both laugh, so happily. Sometimes we went out into the country villages to look for food, because it was wartime and food was getting scarce in the towns. That was how our life flowed along.

I was modelled on the pattern of a young officer of the First Czechoslovak Republic—apolitical, because that was how the Republic wanted its army to be. Certainly, I hated the Germans and I wanted to fight them; but not in any political context— that was something with which I had never concerned myself.

Since the Liberation, I have wondered whether it would not have been better if I had been killed in the struggle. It is not that I have anything at all on my conscience. Yet I wonder what right I have to be alive when all the others are dead.

On Christmas Eve 1941 my wife and I went to stay with friends at Police on the Metuje for the skiing. We sat up late, talking by the fire; a splendid night outside, the kind that is made for lovers; but it was biting cold, and the next day Hanka woke up with a sore throat.

After New Year's Day I went back alone to Pardubice to work at my office. My wife still had a temperature, and she stayed at Police a few days longer. When she came back she went to stay with her people, who also lived in Pardubice and who could look after her properly.

It was at this point that Tatana Hladenova, a friend of hers, went to see my wife and told her that her husband, Franta, wanted to speak to me. Hanka promised to tell me. When I went to see her, she said that Hladena would be coming to our flat that evening to discuss important business. And Franta came. Even before he had taken off his coat he said, "Vasek, we have parachutists here." I stared at him in astonishment, and he went on, "It's true. One of them knows you and wants to talk to you."

"To me? Who is it?"

"Do you remember someone called Bartos?"

"I once knew a Bartos at school, in Pardubice. He was rather younger than me. Would that be the man?"

"You'll see. Come to my place tomorrow. He's staying in our flat for the moment. And above all keep quiet—not a word to anyone."

And Franta left, leaving me thoroughly upset. I walked up and down the room, remembering the time when I had wanted to escape from the Protectorate to carry on with the fight against the Germans. Now here was the struggle within hand's reach. A fight, and very likely a gallows waiting for me at the end of it.

The next day I could not sit still in my office. Every few minutes I looked at my watch, and the afternoon went by even slower. Hanka was no longer in bed; her temperature had dropped, and when I went home in the evening, there she was waiting for me.

"We are going to call on the Hladenas," I said.

Hanka was not particularly surprised. As soon as we got there, Tatana took her into the bedroom so that they could talk and I went into the living room with Franta. Freda was waiting for me there.

I should tell you that his name was Alfred, but when we were at school we called him Freda—an odd diminutive. When he saw me come in, he burst out laughing. "What do you stare at me like that for?"

"Where do you spring from, Freda?"

"I've dropped from the skies."

"What? So you did get away to France?"

"Yes. A friend fixed everything—he was a Czech officer in garrison at Oran. He had a letter sent me from France saying I had inherited a legacy. The Nazis swallowed it; they gave me an exit permit and I left the country in perfect legal order."

"What for?"

"I couldn't tell you that in a few words."

I sat down. It was some years since we had seen one another. As he offered me a cigarette he said, "Have I changed?"

"A little. You've browned, and it seems to me you look rather older."

Hladena sat on the divan. We began talking about more serious matters. Freda Bartos asked me to work with his group, which had recently come from England. He was a First Lieutenant and he had two men with him. But it was only later that he told me that. One of them came to see me, using the name of Tousek. This, I learnt afterwards, was Valcik. The second was the radio-telegraphist Potucek, whom they called Tolar.

"What do you want me to do?" I asked Bartos.

"Several things. My job is to get into touch with Prague, then to send information regularly to London and to get back instructions. I also have to set up an intelligence section. In order to do all this, I need a local helper who can get me identity cards, police declaration forms, work papers, ration books, and that's not all. As for you, you could look after the intelligence, set up meeting places for the people we recruit, and arrange secret letter boxes."

I did not have to ponder it before agreeing.

"Your wife could help us, too," went on Freda.

"I don't like that: it's too dangerous."

"Yet Tatana is with us," urged Bartos. "Women liaison agents attract less suspicion."

Hladena joined Bartos in talking me round, and finally it was decided that both Hanka and I should cooperate. I told Hanka, and she at once agreed enthusiastically.

Shortly after this, Hladena drove Freda and me to my parents' house at Dasice. My father had persuaded a cobbler he knew to sublet Bartos a room. My mother had got him some coal. Freda thought he was better hidden at Dasice, where no one knew him, than at Pardubice, where his mother lived and where he had many friends. I had introduced him to my father as Ota Motycka. My father recognized him, nevertheless; but he promised to keep quiet, and he kept his word.

Some days passed. I came to know Jirka Potucek, the radio-telegraphist. He was somewhere in the Zelezne mountains, and from there he kept in touch with London.

Bartos had given me the task of organizing an intelligence

network. I gave him information on the positions of military units in eastern Bohemia and on the movement of troops towards the front. I found him places where he could have secret meetings and I recruited fresh helpers. Hanka, my wife, was also extremely active.

One day Freda told me about the dropping of his group. After the war I learnt other details. That is how I know that the team's code name was Silver A and that the men were supposed to be dropped near Hermanuv Mestec. Bad luck or the pilot's incompetence brought them down in the neighbourhood of Podebrady.

"How did you get away from there?" I asked Bartos.

"We landed far apart from one another. After a fairly long while I found Jirka Potucek, but we did not come across Valcik. He did not see us either. He took off his jumping overalls and buried them in the middle of a field, together with his parachute. Fortunately for the group, the transmitter and receiver had landed not far from Valcik. He recovered Libuse and carried it as far as the road—he dug a hole in the side to hide it. As he had been told that it was dangerous to stay long near the landing place in case the drop had been seen and the Germans informed, Valcik went along the road as soon as the radio was out of sight. But he did not know where the road led.

"In spite of the danger Potucek and I waited some time, in the hope of seeing Valcik. But he made his way along until he reached a crossroads; there he found that the group had not been dropped at the agreed place, and that he had landed near Podebrady—the village was called Senice, or something like that."

Bartos and Potucek were afraid that dawn would find them in the fields, and that is why they took the same road that Valcik had walked along a quarter of an hour before. They reached the same crossroads; they found the same signpost, and they too were startled by what they read there. Since the village was only a few yards away, they went there. They hesitated over the best place to go—the church or the school—and then decided on the school. They tapped on the window for a long while, and at last a head appeared. After a short explanation, the schoolmaster let them in. They rested, ate, and slept.

Meanwhile Valcik had reached Podebrady, where he took a taxi—it cost him several thousand crowns—and had himself driven to Chrudim. When they left London, the teams had been told of several safe addresses. One of these was the house of a man named Bures, who worked at Chrudim; but when Valcik went there he was told that the Gestapo had arrested Bures some time before—the address was therefore useless. He paid off the taxi and set off alone, on foot, for a village, probably Mikulovice, where he knew another address. In this village there lived a man named Svadlenka, and after Valcik had convinced him that he was not an agent provocateur he took the parachutist into his house. Valcik was in a bad state by then. His legs were giving trouble, and he was dropping with exhaustion and want of food.

Svadlenka, like a straightforward, clear-thinking Czech, then took Valcik to Janacek, a schoolmaster at Pardubice, and all three went by train to Podebrady to recover the transmitter-receiver. At Podebrady they bought a sled and Valcik took them to the place where he had landed. They were lucky enough to find the radio quickly, but not the overalls or the parachute. Probably some inquisitive peasant had been there before them. This made them think that their first plan was too dangerous, so they gave up the idea of taking the radio back to Podebrady on the sled. Valcik and Janacek left Svadlenka at a nearby inn, looking after the well-wrapped-up radio, and left for Pardubice to find a car. Perhaps they looked for Hladena, but they did not find him. However that may be, they turned to the owner of a taxi. It was this man who carried the radio, though without knowing it, of course.

Meanwhile, Bartos and Potucek, who had no idea of Valcik's difficulties with Libuse, set out again, having rested. They went to a village close to Hermanuv Mestec, where the Kostelecky family lived. Bartos knew them, having been to their house several times with a friend, Vera Jungova, who was related to them.

Naturally Bartos did not say where they came from, and Kostelecky put them up. Bartos telephoned Vera Jungova and she came to the village; he told her the state of affairs and she helped him and Potucek to reach Pardubice, where at last they rejoined Valcik.

Freda told me a great many other things. We talked over the days when we were boys together, and then he spoke about his wife during the years after that—his leaving the country for France, his joining the French Foreign Legion and his stay in Algeria; the French campaign, in which he had fought in a re-formed Czechoslovak unit, and his transfer to England after the collapse of the French army. I should add that he had become engaged to a French girl at Agde, where he had been stationed for a while. With strong feeling in his voice, he said to me, "Vasek, if I don't live to see the end of the war, let her know, and send her something to remember me by."

He did not like recalling his early days in England. Many things were not all they might have been: the men were ill-housed and discontented.

As we talked, I came to suspect that Bartos might mean to take to politics once the war was over. But at this point he was essentially concerned with gathering intelligence and trying to get into touch with Moravek's group in Prague. In his work Bartos followed the instructions he received from London, and I know that sometimes he received them straight from President Benes, who signed his messages with the name Svoboda.

One day Freda told me how he had gone through a parachute course, and was thus able to make his mark some time later during British manoeuvres in which he took part. That is how he came to be appointed to the command of the first group of parachutists sent to Czechoslovakia. He often used to speak of England, telling me about the people he had known there. He mentioned a well-known writer he had met, but I do not remember his name.

As I told you, we had taken Bartos to Dasice, where he set up his command post. His room was comfortable, and his landlord, a good sort of man, had not the least idea of what this M. Motycka who lived in his house was really doing. Yet Bartos did not care for Dasice. He said it was not convenient there—the place was too out of the way, unsuitable for maintaining liaisons in every direction. So after a short while he came back to Pardubice; yet he kept on his room in Dasice, telling the landlord that his job as an insurance agent kept him on the move.

It was during this period that Bartos sent me in all directions to make contacts and gather information. My wife travelled too, going to the addresses that Freda had been given in London or that were sent to him by radio. She and I carried out a great deal of concentrated work, and not a day went by without Freda being given fresh intelligence.

Valcik had been taken on as a waiter by Kostal, the owner of the Veselka restaurant in Pardubice.

Potucek? As far as I know, their idea was to find the best possible place for setting up the transmitter. It had nothing to do with me and so I never knew what they decided upon in the end. It was only after the war that I learnt that the original idea of installing Libuse at Bohdanek had been scrapped and that the transmitter was hidden in the Hluboka quarry, not far from the town of Hlinsko. It was all the safer for Libuse to be there, since Karel Knez, who was in command of the nearby police station, knew about it and kept watch.

When the aerial was first put up, London did not answer. The next night they tried again—with no success. Jirka Potucek sent out his messages, but there was no reply from London. No one could tell why. At last, after overhauling the equipment again and again, they found that the damage, which had no doubt been inflicted at the time of the drop, lay not in the transmitter but in the receiver. It was not until Jirka had brought the spare set kept at Pardubice back to the quarry that contact was restored, probably somewhere about 15 January 1942. From that moment on, Libuse sent out an almost continual stream of information.

Our people in London must have wept with joy. The supply of intelligence was assured and the connection with the home resistance re-established. Freda had therefore completely succeeded in part of his mission. That was why one of the first dispatches received from London gave the news that the parachutists of his team had been promoted: Freda became a captain.

The radio link with London made liaison with Prague easier. I cannot tell exactly how the operation was carried out, but I do know that Freda received detailed instructions from London on the subject of the contacts he was to make in Prague. These contacts were probably with the group led by Leon, Captain Moravek's *nom de guerre*, and no doubt Leon put him into touch with Thümmel, whose information, as we now know, was of enormous importance to London. My wife helped establish the liaison. Freda sent her and Tatana Hladenova to Prague-Brevnov together, to call upon Madame Bockova, the wife of an officer who had gone to England. He thought that Madame Bockova knew the path leading to Captain Moravek. But things were not so easy as that. Madame Bockova did not trust my wife, although she and her friend Tatana showed her their identity cards—she said that she was not acquainted with anyone by the name of Moravek. My wife pressed her hard and succeeded in shaking her distrust. It was agreed that a given sentence should soon be broadcast by the BBC to prove their good faith.

Tatana and my wife came straight back to Pardubice and explained everything to Bartos. He told London, and very soon Colonel Bocek himself, under the name of Chodsky, was heard saying the agreed words on the BBC. Now everything was in order. Madame Bockova no longer suspected them of being agents provocateurs and she put Bartos into touch with Moravek. At that time I knew nothing of the part played by my wife; she only told me later.

During this period, and still working with Tatana, my wife helped Bartos in the decoding of messages. Jirka Potucek usually brought us an envelope containing the coded dispatch in the morning—London sent them out by night. He came by bicycle, rang at the door—three short rings followed by one long—said a few words and went away again at once. The strings of figures had to be transposed according to a formula known to Bartos. Once this was done, there was the message in plain language. The deciphering was carried out by means of various books that had been agreed on beforehand in London. I remember having to seek out a collection of poems by Svatopluk Cech—Freda told me that it must necessarily be in the Otto "World Library" edition.

After some time a personal difference between them caused Freda to leave Hladena's house. He came to live with us. I went on going to my office and Hanka stayed at home with Bartos.

Freda knew the head of the Securitas Insurance Company. This friend gave him an imaginary post as an agent in the company; this fictitious official job took almost none of his time and Bartos was therefore able to devote himself entirely to his underground activities. In this way he had an advantage over us, since Hladena, Janacek, Kostal, and the others and I had to carry on with our ordinary jobs, and could only therefore work for the resistance outside office hours. Bartos spent part of his days compiling and keeping up to date a series of dossiers in which he filed all the different material he received—military, political, economic and cultural intelligence.

We became steadily more and more accustomed to the danger. In any case, the greater the risk you run, the less it frightens you. And again, at that point the Germans had not the least suspicion of us. Only once were we alarmed—very much alarmed. We had heard that the German troops were discontented and that there had been incidents at the Pardubice barracks. We sent this information on to London at once. But straight away the BBC repeated it in its news broadcasts, and so exactly that the Nazis might very well have been able to deduce that the clandestine radio was transmitting from the Pardubice region itself. Yet nothing unpleasant occurred, and a few days later we had forgotten our momentary tension.

When Valcik came to see us, everything was gay. He brought laughter with him—he was a good, thoroughly decent young fellow. He used to tell us about the absurd things that happened when he was working as a waiter, and how he would obsequiously offer the Gestapo officers a light, carefully listening to everything they said.

Freda Bartos grew used to living at my place and he no longer troubled with his room at Dasice. Yet our flat was not particularly suitable for underground work. It was on the fourth floor, and it provided no possibility of escape in a sudden emergency. More and more visitors appeared. Bartos had people in whom I did not know, talked with them and often left the house in their company. I remember that Voytisek, the printer at Belohrad, used often to come. Liaison agents arrived from Prague, bringing Bartos information from the capital and from the parachutists who were there.

8

Everyone with clean hands

(Marie Soukupova)

"WELL, MOTHER," cried my husband when he came back from the Wilson railway station, "they're students and members of the Yugoslav sokol." He sounded upset, and as he sat down at the table I noticed that his face was anxious.

"Are you quite sure of it?" I asked, not without mistrust.

"Madame Sramkova told me so, and she asked me to give you her regards. They have to be found somewhere to stay; but they haven't reported to the police."

Automatically I wiped my fingers on a cloth; I'd got back before my husband and had been cooking the meal when he came in. Then I sat down on the sofa and we both thought it over. Yes indeed, where could they stay?

"What a pity we have your mother here," observed my husband. My old mother had been with us since November, and she was not to go home until May.

"What can I do about it? You know her."

There was a long silent pause before my husband went on, "What about the other Sisters?" He was thinking of the other voluntary Sisters of the Red Cross—I had been the president for Prague-Zizkov since 1935—and more particularly of Madame Moravcova, the secretary, and Madame Kaliberova, the assistant secretary. And indeed they were both good-hearted women, always ready to do all they could for the unfortunate.

"Perhaps. We might try, if Madame Sramkova agrees."

Madame Sramkova was the president of the Red Cross nurses

for the whole city of Prague. She lived in Prague-Smichov and her husband taught in a technical high school.

Almost every month, the women in charge from all the districts of Prague met at Sister Sramkova's house. During these meetings we decided upon various special activities. It was in this way, for example, that we collected ration coupons for people who were living secretly in Prague. And back in the autumn of 1938 we had organized different plans in favour of our fellow Czechs who had had to escape from the Sudetenland. With the money we collected we provided them with clothes and linen and organized a Christmas party for them.

These meetings were secret. But as the Moravecs had the telephone and I did not, Sister Sramkova had taken to summoning me by telephoning Madame Moravcova, who then told me. One day I asked Madame Moravcova to go there with me. There were fourteen or fifteen of us, and one woman I did not know—she was a medium whom Sister Sramkova had invited. Madame Moravcova asked her about her eldest son, who had been working at Cakovice when the Germans marched into Bohemia and Moravia and who had vanished without being heard of again. She often cried when she thought of him, and now she said to the medium, "I have a son, but I don't know where he is."

The medium replied, "He is by the sea … in dirty overalls … a mechanic in the Air Force." She also said, "An outrage, a killing, is going to be committed, and many people will lose their lives."

We were struck dumb with astonishment! I give you my word that that is exactly how the prediction was made.

Just as we were leaving, Madame Moravcova said, "If you need anything at all, I am entirely at your disposal."

During the winter of 1942, probably in February, a Sister from Vysocany came to the meeting at Madame Sramkova's. I believe she was called Piskackova, and she told us she needed a place for some young men to stay at.

"Who are they?" asked Sister Sramkova.

Sister Piskackova went red and did not answer. I suppose she must have waited for the rest of us to go before she told our president what it was about. Some days later Sister Sramkova telephoned Madame Moravcova to ask me to meet her at ten o'clock on a certain date at the Wilson station. But just at that time, on that day, I had to be helping a dentist at a school, so I sent my husband to the station instead.

So there we were, both wondering how to house the young men Sister Sramkova had told my husband about, when Madame Moravcova came in and asked us what Sister Sramkova had wanted. My husband told her. At once she kindly said that she would arrange everything for the best, that we were not to worry any more—she knew lots of people and she would take it all on her own shoulders. Her eyes shone with excitement—she looked as though she were flinging herself into the undertaking with great enthusiasm. I had known her for years, and I knew that once she had taken something on, she would carry it through without knowing what weakness meant. When the other Sisters were dropping with fatigue, Madame Moravcova always found fresh strength.

My husband and I helped her as much as we could, and so did the other Red Cross Sisters. Madame Kaliberova took one of the young men to Radotin to have him treated. Organizations like the League against Tuberculosis helped too. And many others. Everyone with clean hands. Many, many families.

9

The caretaker's recollections: 1

(Frantisek Spinka)

THIS IS A DENAR of Boleslav II. In the middle of the obverse is
the Czech royal crown, and on the reverse the lion. Lovely
workmanship! It was the best-known Czech coin—current all
over Europe. In those days the whole world acknowledged the
fame of the Czechs. I often used to think of that in the time of the
Protectorate, when the Germans did their very best to cry down
our past. I can see what you are thinking about the way I talk:
you're saying to yourself, "This old caretaker who is so pas-
sionate about it now, is a collector, a slightly cracked collector."
But these bits of metal you see here on the table tell the glory of
our country in the old days better than anything else. I have a
fine collection. Even the tolar of Ferdinand, struck at the ancient
Javchymov mint. That Ferdinand—he shoved our country around
too; and Lord above, how he exploited it! Just like the Germans,
in the second war. When they came, every single one crammed
himself with whipped cream—you would have thought they
were starving. And after that they tried to stuff us up with their
tales of the superior German race! Concentration camps, yes,
they could do that all right. And torturing people. They could do
that too. A whole family in our building learnt about their
superiority in that line. They were called Moravec and they were
thoroughly decent people. I've lived in this building since 1931
and the Moravecs were here from about the same time. They had
two boys, Mirek and Ata, who were still at school then. They
were good boys—maybe their ball might sometimes drop

where it shouldn't have dropped, but that happens with any boy.

In time, of course, they grew up. Mirek escaped at the beginning of the Protectorate; he was the elder boy and Madame Moravcova wept for him for years—she didn't know what had become of him. He was in our air force in England, and the Nazis shot him down in 1944.

The Moravecs lived on the second floor; they had two bedrooms, a kitchen and a little extra room. M. Moravec worked for the railway and he was pensioned off during the war. He was a thoughtful kind of man who didn't say much, very different from his wife. She had life and energy enough for four: rather a stout woman with brown hair and very kind eyes. You can't imagine how much she did for those boys. For the parachutists, I mean. Why, I remember it as if it was yesterday. I was sitting here at my table, admiring the Vladislav denar which I'd found that very same day—a lovely thing, with Samson on it, fighting the lion. Then there was a ring at my door. I shut my coin box, went to open it, and found myself face to face with Madame Moravcova with a young man standing beside her.

"Can we come in?" she asked.

"Of course," I said.

The young fellow might have been a little more than twenty with blue eyes and fair hair.

"M. Spinka," said Madame Moravcova to me all at once, "can we rely on you?"

I must have looked taken aback for a moment. "Why, certainly," I said at last.

"This is Zdenda; he will often be coming to our flat. If at any time the house happens to be shut at night, you'll open the door for him, won't you? He hasn't reported to the police, you see."

I swallowed. The fellow called Zdenda laughed at seeing me so upset. "We'll play cards together sometimes," he said. "You like cards?"

Madame Moravcova took me by the arm and whispered in my ear, "He's a parachutist. And I've got others. So I must beg you to shut your eyes and see nothing."

"And how am I going to recognize them if they come and ring on my bell when the house is locked up?"

"Our password is Jan. Let anyone in who says that, even at midnight."

"Don't you worry. Everything will be all right. I know nothing and I'll see nothing."

They said thank you and left. Later I learned he was Valcik and he came from Pardubice.

A couple of days later I saw the two other young men. They stayed with the Moravecs for some time. Long afterward I heard they were called Gabcik and Kubis. At that time we called Gabcik, the shorter one, Little Ota, and Kubis, Big Ota.

Madame Moravcova gave me the keys of her flat and sometimes it would happen that Big Ota rang at my door to borrow the keys, because there was no one at home at the Moravecs' and he wanted to rest. And there was another time, when Zdenda was sleeping there. Big Ota could not wake him up by ringing at their door and he had to get the keys from us.

When did all this happen? During the winter of 1942, probably in February. Yes, it was certainly in February, because I remember in March young Zdenda—that is to say Valcik—moved in for good, bringing a dog with him. He often used to go out with this dog, and sometimes he met Zelenka the schoolmaster who lived in a house almost opposite ours. Madame Moravcova sometimes sent me to him with a note or message by word of mouth.

10

The evidence of a woman from Žižkov: 1

(Frantiska Volfova)

IT WAS THAT 27 February that M. Zelenka, the schoolmaster, asked me up to his flat, on the first floor. He was a teacher at Prague-Vrsovice, and I liked him very much. At one time, the Zelenkas had lived somewhere near the frontier, but when the Germans took the Sudeten mountains they had been forced to leave those parts. They had a very pleasant, agreeable son called Jan—we called him Jenda. When the Zelenkas still lived near the frontier and had only sent their son to Prague, Jenda lived with his uncle at Liben. Then, when the Zelenkas moved to Prague, Jenda's father did not want him to change schools, so he went on going to Liben. After the repression that followed the killing, we heard that Jenda had poisoned himself in the Krc woods—though some people said he had blown his brains out.

That day, Zelenka asked me how I was, without really paying attention, walking up and down the room; I sat there in the armchair and waited. At last he stopped in front of me and said, "Are you afraid of the Germans?"

"Me? Why?"

He did not answer, but I could see well enough he had something on his mind. Then all at once he said, "I need a place where some men can stay—where they can sleep and get something to eat. Would it be possible in your flat?"

"Who are these people?"

"I can't very well tell you that. They aren't from here and they can't report to the police. So they can only rely on good, patriotic Czechs."

"All right, then. Send them to us and don't worry; but I must tell my husband about it."

"Of course; and I'll talk to him myself. But you mustn't say anything anywhere. Not a word to relations, friends or anyone."

So they came. They were young and well-mannered. We never knew anything about them. Occasionally they came back late at night and tapped at the window for us to open—we lived on the ground floor. Now and then we played cards until one in the morning, and we listened to the BBC or Moscow to know what was going on in the world. Sometimes they would drop their cards to listen closely; but they never said anything about what they heard.

Once the bigger of the young men, the one we were told later was Kubis, came back about half past ten in the morning, all soaking and dirty. He had been lying in a ditch somewhere, waiting for I don't know what. I gave him clean linen and he changed. As he was taking off his shirt, I noticed that he had a kind of vest next to his skin, with a pistol in it. There was another pistol, hidden in the arm of the shirt. I was terrified. But he comforted me, saying it was nothing—they had a job they were obliged to carry out.

The schoolmaster had said they couldn't stay long in the same place for fear of being noticed by the neighbours. We put them up from the end of February until 11 March 1942. What names did they use when they lived with us? The smaller one called himself Zdenek Vyskocil. We were told afterwards that he was Gabcik. And the bigger one said he was Ota Navratil —that was Kubis.

11

𝔍 was a liaison agent

(*Lida Hajna*)

I WAS JINDRA's liaison agent, and I used to go to various places—
to Prerov for example, or Valasske Mezirici—and bring back
information to pass on to him.

One day in December 1941, a friend of mine named Bilek
asked me whether I would agree to hide a young fellow whom he
called Leon. The Gestapo were after him. I said I would, feeling
it was my duty.

Leon came to my place the evening before the New Year. He
was fair-haired, rather small and thin. For months on end he had
managed to keep ahead of the Nazis; and yet to look at him you
would never have thought it. He wore a little, typically German
green hat with a cord round it and a tuft of badger hair. Later I
noticed that he had lost a finger, which forced him to wear
gloves all the time, even when it was very hot.

Some days after this I took him to a house in Nadrazni in
Smichov, where I introduced Leon as my brother, Jiri Vrany,
to a man who lived there. This was a safe refuge. I saw him now
and then after that, in the spring of 1942. I went there to take him
food and money.

The last time we met was in March, and I remember he said
to me, "They've released Major H, and I suspect they've done so
in order to get at me. I'm going to make sure by arranging to
meet him."

"If you don't trust him any longer, don't go there and don't
meet him," I said.

He shook his head and it was quite clear there was no persuading him. "I have to know how things are," he said.

Those were the last words he ever said to me. He always spoke briefly and to the point; and he had an unhesitating judgment, distinguishing the people he could trust from those who might betray him. He did not know the meaning of fear, nor of indecision; and he always wanted to see everything with his own eyes, however dangerous it was. That is all I can tell you about Moravek. Not long after our last meeting he was surrounded by the Gestapo and he killed himself.

I don't know much more about Jindra, either. As I've told you, I carried his instructions to many places in Moravia and I brought back intelligence of various kinds. Once I brought him crystals for the transmitter and another time I lent him my flat so that he could use it as a rendezvous for people from the country, but I know nothing whatsoever about what they discussed.

I met him for the first time in Podebradova. It was that day which decided my fate. At Jindra's request I got into touch with Zelenka, the headmaster of a school, who saw to the housing of the parachutists. At that time I did not know his real name and I had never seen him before. I never saw the parachutists, and to tell you the truth I knew nothing about them.

At our first meeting Zelenka used the name of Hajsky. This was at the end of the number 10 trolley line, at a place called Ohrada, in Zizkov, in the spring of 1942. Hajsky gave me an envelope containing written information for Jindra. Afterwards, my meetings with Hajsky took place regularly every Tuesday and Friday, at a place where Zizkov runs into Karlin, and always very late in the evening. I must confess that going around at night frightened me. When we missed one another for any reason we used to make a mark on an electric post.

Our meetings with Jindra were also in the evening, near the Zizkov Jewish cemetery. He would come whistling the tune "Boleraz, boleraz" so that I knew it was really him. And once I was there when Jindra had a discussion with Moravek.

On 7 April 1943, that is to say a year after the killing, I was arrested by the Gestapo and questioned about Moravek and

Jindra. I said I didn't know them. After that I was in a concentration camp until the end of the war, without ever having been brought before a court.

That's all I can tell you about my work as a liaison agent. My name is Lida.

12

The statement of the survivor from Pardubice: 2

(Vaclav Krupka)

OUR FLAT became the centre for Bartos' group. Almost every day we assembled and checked the information intended for Libuse, Jirka's transmitter, and we decoded the messages that were sent to us. Bartos gave me a variety of missions. For example, I was to produce a plan of the chemical factory at Olomouc-Lutin, and to find out what was in some cases that had been sent there and that were not to be opened "without orders from the Führer." I succeeded in doing this.

To keep my employer from having any suspicions, I took to being seriously ill. A Pardubice doctor, who knew all about the state of affairs, produced a certificate for my chief, and in this way it was possible for me to leave my work from time to time to carry out Freda's orders.

I remember one day he asked me to take Potucek messages hidden in a tube of the rubber solution used for repairing bicycle tires. At first, as I said, Potucek used to come every morning, bringing us the coded dispatches he had received from London. But later we were afraid that he might attract attention in Pardubice. Since he worked at night, he spent the day sunbathing, and he had gone a splendid brown. Bartos therefore decided that one of us should go and meet him half way, take the messages he had received and give him those he was to send out.

So I told my office that I was unwell, took the bicycle and set

off. On the road from Slatinany to Nasavrky I stopped and went
through the motions of mending the tire. A few moments later
Jirka appeared, coming from Nasavrky; I stopped him, borrowed his pump and at the same time passed him the messages
for London. When it was her turn my wife did the same, though
I believe she handed them over on the road from Semtin to
Bohdanec.

One day Jindra came to our place from Prague to talk something over with Freda. It was then that Jindra and my wife
agreed that in future the liaison should be maintained through her
and a woman called Lida, who would pass her the information
meant for Bartos. Even now I do not know who this Lida was.
In those days it was better not to ask too many questions.

It is interesting to note that the parachutists I met—Bartos'
team, and indeed others, such as Opalka and Dvorak for example
—were convinced that the war would soon be over. They firmly
believed that the Western Allies would invade Europe in 1942—
that was what they had been given to understand in London
before they left on their missions. They certainly never imagined
that in enemy-occupied territory parachutists could remain
undiscovered for years on end. But in London they had been
told that the war would last only a few months longer; they had
gone off to Bohemia convinced that they could survive for this
comparatively short period and that they would be able to keep
out of the Nazis' hands. The very last time I spoke to Bartos he
said to me, "There will be no great difficulty about survi-
ving."

Living with us and being brought face to face with the real
position in the Protectorate, they came to realize that the end of
the war was not so close as they had imagined. For them, this
was like being woken from a delightful dream. At the beginning,
Potucek waved his hand carelessly and said to me, with a broad
smile, "Five more months before the Nazis are done for and
everything is over!"

Meanwhile the winter was going by; the military position
changed only gradually, and the Western Allies did not yet seem
to be concerned with opening a second front. Now it was clear

to these boys that they could only rely on themselves and on their friends in the resistance.

They were young and they loved life. Certainly, they had volunteered; but not for a hopeless mission. They had had the courage to face the enemy, and no one can deny their bravery. But in fact they had been told in London that the end was near. The wholly different reality that confronted them must have weighed heavily on their spirits. And it seemed to me that at that time they were trying to live as intensely as they could.

The development of Bartos, too, seemed to me typical. I had known him before the war, but now I could follow the evolution of his thoughts and opinions almost every day—that is to say, from January 1942 until his death in June 1942. He lived in my house; I shared in his work. And in his case I came to a clear understanding of one thing: the Bartos of June was no longer the Bartos of January 1942. Now he had experienced the atmosphere of the Protectorate, the state of mind of the people who lived there and the nature of their behaviour; all this was very different from what he had been told in London. Being immersed in the real life of a harshly occupied country had matured him.

There were some things he did very well. In others, like everybody else, he made mistakes. He was efficient, full of drive, sometimes hotheaded. He made notes in a red exercise book kept in our wardrobe—this seemed to me useless and risky.

Unfortunately it so happened that some people in Pardubice recognized him. It was hardly surprising. Bartos had lived there before the war and had gone to the Pardubice high school. Growing a little moustache and wearing spectacles was not enough to hide his real identity from everyone. Presently there was a rumour in the town that there were parachutists about.

I believe it was a woman newspaper-seller who recognized my friend. Somebody tried to persuade her she was mistaken— Bartos' own mother, perhaps; but I have no exact knowledge of these events.

At almost the same moment the Gestapo got wind of it. At this time Valcik was working industriously at the Veselka hotel. We used to call him Mirek, although his real Christian name was

Josef. What quantities of names they all used! But they were not really of much value, and in fact it was this new name of Mirek's, this name of Solc, that decided Valcik's fate.

All three of them, Bartos, Valcik and Potucek, had managed to get new identity cards, so it was decided that they should comply with the regulations and declare themselves with the local police. We had blank forms, already bearing the police stamp—it was my wife's friend Helena who had obtained them for us. Some of Freda's colleagues insisted that this would be better; they said the danger of detection was very slight and that the declaration would also have the advantage of getting them ration coupons and tobacco.

And it was exactly at this point, just about the beginning of March, that chance stepped in. The Pardubice police had to send the Gestapo the list of new inhabitants from time to time, and a few of them, picked at random, were checked. For most it passed off perfectly well; but once the Devil begins to interfere... The Gestapo officer who carried out the check that day wrote down the name of Miroslav Solc, waiter at the Veselka hotel, in his notebook. I really do not know whether the young fellow was already a suspect or whether it was mere chance deciding upon a man's life; but the fact is that the Gestapo began to take an interest in Solc.

Later, the owner of the hotel, Kostal, told us how he had been summoned by the Gestapo and questioned at length about Solc— what he knew about him, where he came from, whether he was ever absent and if so where he went.

Kostal did not lose his head and replied that Solc came from Ostrava, where his father had an hotel. The Nazi police were satisfied with this and they thanked him; but after he had gone they telephoned Ostrava. There, of course, nobody knew any hotel-owner by the name of Solc. So the Pardubice Gestapo summoned both Kostal and Solc. Kostal, realizing that things were going wrong, took advantage of the fact that Solc–Valcik was away from the hotel just then to tell him to run for it.

I heard about it all that very evening. At the Gestapo Kostal had had to give a detailed description of Valcik and of what he was wearing. Asked why he had come alone, he said he had just dismissed Solc for breaking a large amount of crockery. We were amazed that the Gestapo had believed this tale, but later I realized that Kostal had been left at liberty because they hoped to make use of him to follow the line right back to the beginning.

It was my wife whom Kostal warned about the threat hanging over Valcik's head. When she told Freda we were at a loss: how should we deal with the situation? We did not know where Valcik was nor what he was doing. At this point the doorbell rang, and by an extraordinary piece of luck it was Valcik himself. Freda gave him his orders and Mirek left. The roads out of Pardubice were watched by the police, but Mala, the schoolmistress, took him out by a side lane and Valcik went to his parents in Moravia, to wait there until a safe refuge could be found for him.

We were very much shaken. This was the first time the Gestapo had broken into our network. Although they had not succeeded in arresting Valcik, Kostal was under surveillance and the Gestapo's attention had been aroused.

At about this time I went to Prague with Bartos on two occasions. He had told me it was vitally important for him to get into touch with someone—afterwards I learnt that this was Leon.

We went to Prague by train and got out at the station; having looked round, Bartos left me and went off to find a man he called Kral, who probably lived in the Vinohrady district. I met Freda later at the Dutch Mill, a café–restaurant on the first floor in Panska. Reproductions of Dutch paintings hung on the walls, and it was the favourite haunt of a great many German officers; this made it a good place for clandestine appointments—as the proverb says, the darkest spot is under the lampshade.

The tables were separated by low partitions, and in each of these boxes there was a radio that the customers could switch on—the music ensured that their talk remained secret. Freda looked pleased and relaxed.

The second time I went to Prague with him, which was some time later, he had a rendezvous at the Julis bar. I did not take part in this meeting.

Sometimes Bartos would go to Prague alone; he could spend the night in Moravek's flat—Moravek had given him the keys. But as far as I know he never used them, because he knew that the Gestapo was on Moravek's trail. For my part, when I was in Prague I slept at my uncle's place or with the Sedlaks, the same people who helped us so much afterwards, when we were gathering the intelligence needed for the bombing of the Skoda works at Plzn.

Valcik sent us word that he had arrived safely in Moravia and that he was in the neighbourhood of Miroslav. This news reached us about 20 March. Shortly before this there had been another unpleasant event, one that might have had tragic consequences. After the Gestapo had chanced upon the track of Valcik in Pardubice they ordered the police registers to be checked throughout the whole region. This step threatened Bartos' security. He therefore changed his identity and registered with the local police at Usti-upon-Orlice under the name of Motycka. Josef Hrdina, one of his friends of before the war, had provided him with a flat in the village. We all went there one day to go skiing with Hrdina. The name Ota Motycka was not invented. It had belonged to a man from the village of Vrdy-Bucice who had died five years earlier. It was with the help of the dead man's papers that Bartos' new identity card was obtained.

Here again bad luck stepped in. It so happened that the policemen stationed at Usti were unusually zealous. When the insurance agent Motycka's form came into their hands they went through the particulars with a fine tooth comb. What happened? On being asked, the Vrdy-Bucice station told Usti that the Ota Motycka in question was dead and buried these last five years. The policemen of Usti at once hurried to the address of the self-styled Motycka to arrest him. Fortunately the nest was empty—Bartos only had this room as an extra refuge in case of emergency.

Their failure induced the police to question the owner of the building, who finally gave them the name of Josef Hrdina. They went to Hrdina's house, and he, not knowing how to get out of it, told them that Motycka was a parachutist and appealed to their patriotism, advising them to forget all about the whole thing. The policemen hesitated, and these few moments of reflection decided the whole subsequent train of events; then they said they would agree, providing that their colleagues at Vrdy-Bucice cancelled their negative report the next day. Hrdina promised them this should be done. What else could he say?

That same evening Madame Hrdinova knocked at our door and gave me a letter from her husband. As Hrdina did not want his wife to know about his resistance activities we had to do a little play-acting.

"You really must come and see him tomorrow," she told me.

So the next day Bartos sent me to Vysoke Myto, where Hrdina worked in the local library. I was to find out everything that had happened and to give him an ampoule of poison. I set out early the next morning. I went to see Hrdina at the library and told him I should be waiting for him at a nearby inn. He came a few minutes later, sat down, and in a bitter tone of voice he said, "We are in a mess, Vasek."

"Why?"

"I've had to promise the Usti police to fix things at the Vrdy-Bucice station. If we don't succeed, I shall have them on my track and they will send on a report about me. You know what that means?"

I knew only too well; but I tried to comfort him. "Don't worry. We'll certainly put it right. I'll go back at once and let you know our news later. Still, just take this poison and keep it on you in case of emergencies. But everything will be all right, you'll see."

To gain time I did not wait for the train—none passed through Vysoke Myto until much later—but set off on foot for Zamrsk, where there were better connections for Pardubice. Every minute seemed precious, and I ran along the road. I was a keen athlete in those days and I went along as hard as ever I could, in spite of the icy layer of snow on the ground. Sometimes I ran myself out of wind, and then I walked, moving my arms to breathe deeply. A few cars came in the opposite direction, and one of them, believe it or not, belonged to my firm. It was an ordinary working day; I ought to have been in my office, and here they found me tearing along the road from Vysoke Myto to Zamrsk!

"What are you doing here?" they shouted from the car, quite astonished.

If the position had not been so serious, I should have been seized with a fit of giggling. My head was spinning and I could feel the sweat pouring down my face and back. My only reply was a wave of my arm and some other gestures that they could make nothing of, and without stopping any longer I ran on.

When I reached Pardubice I told Freda everything; he burst into a furious rage against the police, and I could not calm him down. Meanwhile my wife had gone to warn Franta Hladena, who had a car. When he came we held a council of war. Bartos wanted us to take weapons and go straight to Vrdy-Bucice to silence the policemen, liquidating them if necessary. Hladena and I were doubtful. Bartos insisted. "A report from them would endanger us all. The only solution is to step in at once and with the greatest possible force." Could we not set about it in some other way? we asked. "How could you possibly bring it off?" cried Bartos.

"Let us go to Vrdy-Bucice and see what is to be done on the spot," said Hladena. "Bartos will go into the police station; Vasek and I will stay outside in support. First, Bartos must ask them to destroy all the reports that worry us. And if they refuse..."

We left. Hladena was a very good driver. He used to ride racing motorcycles and he was brilliant. We did not speak. Franta kept his eyes fixed on the road ahead; Freda checked his automatic and then gazed at the landscape.

I do not know how long we took to reach the village; I do not know what time it was when we got out of the car. Hladena stayed in it and kept the motor running. Freda and I got out. If I remember rightly we had attracted no attention. We had taken the number-plate off at the outskirts of the village.

I stood near the police station, so as to be able to cover Freda with my fire if necessary. Hladena was there behind the wheel. Bartos had vanished into the building. I waited, and when anyone passed I pretended to be waiting for a bus, but I never took my eye off the station door.

I was very much on edge; the waiting seemed to me terribly long. Automatically I counted the windows of the police station, and at the same time I had a feeling of increasing tension inside the building. From one moment to the next I expected the sound of shots.

When my nerves were at their highest stretch Bartos walked out, unhurried and relaxed; he glanced round, nodded to me and walked towards the car. At the same moment I felt an immense weariness. My whole body hurt; all at once my legs were as heavy as lead and the automatic I was grasping in my pocket seemed to weigh a ton. Bartos and I got into the car without a word and Franta drove off at once. It was only when we were right out of the village that I said to Bartos, "Well, what happened?"

He smiled. "The policeman watched me coming in, quite astonished. I went straight up to him, told him briefly who I was and why I was using the late Motycka's identity. Then I showed him my automatic and gave him the choice—either he destroyed his report or I wiped him out. I must have had the right ugly look, because he obeyed. Now everything is in order and Ota Motycka can carry on quietly with his second life."

On thinking it over, however, Bartos thought it better to change identities again, and so did Valcik and Potucek. We obtained fresh papers and photographs; then Bartos sent to Prague to ask whether it was possible to provide identity cards to match.

Shortly after, Madame Moravcova (we used to call her Auntie) arrived from the capital. Freda asked her to tell Moravek that we should be bringing him the photographs of the three parachutists who needed fresh identity cards. Auntie agreed and left. So Freda and I went to Prague again.

We spent the night with my uncle at Vinohrady and met Moravek very late that evening in the Chotkovy Sady Gardens. He was shot a few days later on the Dusty Bridge at Prague-Device with the photographs in his possession.

THE HISTORIAN STEPS IN : II

(*The author*)

The liaison between London and the Czech resistance had been broken in the autumn of 1941. London did its utmost to re-establish contact with Moravek's group. That was why, on the night of 28–29 December 1941, Silver A (Bartos, Valcik, and Potucek) were dropped in the neighbourhood of Podebrady. Bartos had been given the mission of finding Moravek.

Meanwhile Moravek and his organization had never stopped gathering intelligence, although he could no longer send it on to London; and still, with the same good fortune, he continued to keep out of the hands of the Gestapo. He could use several refuges in various districts of Prague—Nusle, Smichov, Brevnov. Many members of the resistance provided him with information; and so did Paul Thümmel.

Who was this Paul Thümmel?

On 16 May 1942, writing to Martin Bormann at the Führer's headquarters, Reinhard Heydrich stated that he was a German, born in the Reich in 1902, a former baker who had worked for the intelligence service since 1928. He belonged to the NSDAP and his membership number was 61,574; he had been given the Party's gold badge. To begin with he was one of the Nazi intelligence service's voluntary helpers, and from 1933 he worked for the Abwehr, the military counterespionage branch. In 1934 he became a trusted agent in the Abwehr's central office in Dresden, and the chief of the service, Admiral Canaris, sent him to Prague after the setting up of the Protectorate of Bohemia and Moravia in March 1939. There he was given far-reaching responsibilities, not only for the Czech countries but also for the Balkans and

Middle East. Heydrich noted that Thümmel "was undoubtedly a very good agent, if not the best in the intelligence service in Czechoslovakia."

Under the name of Voral, Thümmel had collaborated with the Czechoslovak intelligence service back in the days of the first republic. In 1937 he supplied extremely valuable information on the Nazis' activities. In 1938 he provided exact intelligence about an attack on the frontier territories (as a consequence of this information the Czechoslovak army was mobilized and rapidly took up positions on the frontiers of the republic). Voral, whose code number was A54, gave news of the plan of Heinlein's pro-Nazi party to blow up the main stand in the Strahov stadium at Prague during the Sokol Congress.

A54 also gave the news that the mutilated republic would be invaded by the Nazi armies on 15 March 1939. When he reached Prague from Dresden, he sent his information to London by means of agreed addresses in Zurich, Stockholm, and the Hague. It was at the Hague, in the home of a businessman named Jelinek, who was born in Czechoslovakia, that he met Czechoslovak intelligence officers from London. After the invasion of the Low Countries contact was lost. In order to re-establish liaison with this invaluable source, the Czechoslovak intelligence service in London decided to get into touch with Voral, or Franta as he was also called, by means of the home-based resistance.

On 29 June 1940 London radioed a dispatch directed to Moravek's group asking for news of Franta. Prague did not reply. On 1 July 1940 London repeated its request: "Once again please answer if you have met Franta. Nothing hitherto has had such importance for our special activities and for the position of us all here in England as the precise and rapid use of this source: a great deal depends on it. Give this the most urgent attention. Mora."

But no reply came from Prague. Moravek's group was having difficulties with the setting up of their secret transmitter. On 11 July London sent out its request once more: "Are you in touch with Franta? We need his information, which has a special importance for us all at this juncture and in view of coming events. Please do this quickly, though with all necessary caution. Regard this as of first priority. Thanks."

London was growing impatient. Why? Intelligence said the Nazis were about to attempt an invasion of England. London needed Thümmel's

information about the Führer's intentions. The next dispatch read:
"*In Prague he lives with Madame (first supplement) who is our man's
mistress although she knows nothing of his activities. Go and see
(second supplement), give the password (third supplement) and ask her
in Czech to be allowed to speak to Franta. Address Franta in German,
with no witnesses present, give the password again and compliments
from (fourth supplement). He is a man of about forty, medium height,
strong features, rather staring eyes. Ask him for information for the
West, and pay him if you can (fifth supplement). Do not ask his name.
Get into touch very cautiously and take care that it is always the same
reliable but well-covered person that deals with him.*"

The next day the continuation of the dispatch reached Prague: "*Do
not confide in him about your own activities. Behave in a friendly way
and agree to his requests for money. He is a colleague of long standing
and very great potentiality and in many circumstances it may be possible
for him to be directly useful to you. It is of essential concern to us to
maintain reliable unbroken contact with him. Take notice of his
suggestions... The number of our people to be told of the situation
must be as small as possible.*"

The supplements radioed the following day were these:

1. *Figarova, 27 Dlouha, L.H.*
2. *H...*
3. *Look out—Pisek*
4. *Voral*
5. *Five thousand German marks.*

The contact was re-established at last. Speaking about it today, the
woman who had to pass on Moravek's message to Thümmel said,
"*Two Czechs I did not know came to see me at my flat. They wanted to
speak to Paul, whom they called Franta. I promised to arrange it.
Some days later the meeting took place in the square of the Old Town.
One of the Czechs came back to my flat for me to take him to Paul, who
was waiting for us in his car in front of the bank. We all three went to
the Hubertus hotel in the village of Jiloviste. Paul and the unknown
man went off together into the forest. They came back about an hour
later, talking in a friendly way. Paul had been distrustful—he had put
on dark glasses—but now all this had vanished.*"

Once the liaison was renewed the radio messages followed one another faster and faster. On 20 July London said, "Ask Franta whether he can let us know in time when the move against England begins."

During August 1940 Thümmel, using the cover-names of Franta, Eva and René, supplied intelligence of outstanding political importance. In a message of 2 August London emphasized this: "As I send this dispatch, Dr. Benes, the President of the Republic, is here in the station, together with his military and political colleagues. From here the President sends you his heartfelt regards and thanks you and your helpers for your accurate, devoted and perilous work."

At last Thümmel announced that Operation Seelöwe, the attack upon England, would take place on 15 September: "It will begin with an assault by 18,000 planes, coming in successive waves and using tear- and irritant-gas. During the air attack the Germans will try to land their army, making use of ships of every kind, high-speed craft and submarines."

It is clear that this exact information enabled Great Britain to organize a vigorous defence. Thümmel told London of the postponement of the invasion. It was easy for him to answer all the questions asked by the intelligence in London and he rendered invaluable services.

Towards the end of January 1941 Franta arranged a meeting with a Czechoslovak intelligence officer in the office of a firm by the name of Kosovka, on the second floor of 4 Njegosova, in Belgrade. The password, Karl Voral-Libuse. The date, 4 or 5 February.

At the end of October 1940, A54 stated that the Germans were preparing a new plan: this was Operation Barbarossa, the attack on the Soviet Union. Later he sent word that the operation was to begin on 15 May 1941. Moravek radioed this to the Czechoslovak government in London; President Benes communicated it to Winston Churchill, the British Prime Minister, who wrote a personal letter containing the news to Moscow. At the same time Moravek informed the Soviet consulate in Prague. The fact that in the end Hitler postponed the date for the attack to 22 June 1941 because of the continued fighting in Yugoslavia and Greece did not diminish the value or the importance of A54's information.

Sooner or later the Nazis were bound to discover that their most secret plans were being betrayed. Some high-ranking officers were arrested and questioned, but the inquiries yielded nothing. When did they start trying to find their betrayer? In his report of 16 May 1942 to Bormann, Heydrich said, "The parachutist [Pavelka] was arrested a few days later. By making full use of the information found on the spot and by decoding messages, we learnt of the existence of an important Anglo-Czech agent named René and identified him on 27 February 1942 as Paul Thümmel, the Haupt-V-Mann at the head of the Abwehr central office in Prague."

The parachutist Pavelka was arrested on 25 October 1941; this means that Heydrich was aware of the existence of the spy René at that period. Heydrich's letter also gives the exact date at which they identified Thümmel.

But before this Thümmel had given the Czech resistance valuable help; he told them of the Nazis' informers, warned them of the people and the addresses being watched by the Gestapo and of the arrests that had been decided upon.

Then a tragic event occurred: during the night of 4–5 October 1941 the Gestapo, guided by their radio-detection teams, discovered the last of the resistance's transmitters. The two radiotelegraphists were surprised while they were actually sending out messages: one, Jindrich Klecka, killed himself as he was being arrested; the other, André Regenermel, was taken. The Nazis' success once more broke the connection between London and Prague.

Meanwhile Thümmel continued to supply information, but Moravek was no longer able to transmit it to London. That was why London sent Silver A to the Protectorate, under the command of Bartos, whose mission was to find Moravek and through him, Paul Thümmel.

Our witness from Pardubice has given us a detailed account of how Bartos at last succeeded in getting into touch with Moravek by means of Madame Bockova, who was deeply distrustful to begin with.

In a dispatch dated 11 February 1942 Bartos told London, "*Bockova found, but remains inactive. She knows neither Ota nor Vlk. I feel that both the military and political organization [of the home resistance] are in a state of total confusion.*"

A few days later, on 16 February, Bartos advised London, "*. . . the teams you send should be amply supplied with money and properly dressed. A small-calibre pocket-automatic and a briefcase—hard to* *find here—would do very well. The poison should be carried in an appropriate smaller tube. According to the possibilities, drop the teams in districts other than those to which they are to go. This makes the task of the German security organizations harder. The greatest difficulty here is finding work. No one will take on any man who has no work papers. Those who do possess them are found jobs by the labour office. The danger of forced labour is much greater in spring and it is therefore impossible to commit a greater number of secret agents without increasing the risk of the whole system's being discovered. That is why I think it more profitable to make the utmost use of those who are here and* to limit the number of fresh arrivals to the lowest possible figure. *Ice."* (Our emphasis.)

Unhappily the London authorities did not follow the advice that Bartos sent them over the signature Ice, the last letters of Pardubice.

At the beginning of March Bartos radioed that he had found a group that knew Ota, that is to say Moravek. He asked that an agreed phrase should be broadcast by the BBC to give them confidence; this was done on 5 March 1942. And on 14 March Bartos was able to radio, "As a consequence of my information of Saturday and with the help of B personal contact with Ota has been established." Now the information that Moravek received from Thümmel could reach London once again, and the Czechoslovak intelligence service in London replied, "By achieving contact with Ota you have carried out one of your main tasks, that is to say the renewal of liaison with the home organization and the beginning of your cooperation with it. Your conduct has been brave, intelligent and well-conceived. I thank you for it and express my gratitude."

Everything seemed to be in order once more. But, in fact, Moravek had been given the photographs of three parachutists by Bartos. He in his turn was to entrust these documents to his colleagues who provided false identity cards. He made an appointment with them for 21 March.

And that was the tragedy.

As we have already said, the Nazis unmasked Thümmel towards the end of February. It seems that Moravek was unaware of this, but he knew that he was himself in danger. He pointed this out to London in his dispatch of 14 March 1942, in which he said that the interrogations of Vlk were a grave threat to Franta's position. He spoke of a traitor who "*may bring about the end of our supply of information.*" *Franta had made up his mind to stay until the last moment, but he was thinking of escaping to Switzerland or Turkey. The last dispatch of 20 March— the day before Moravek's death—stated that Franta was travelling. This "travelling" might mean "taken." That day Thümmel had already been arrested. For the third time.*

The first time was on 13 October 1941, when he was taken into custody by the Gestapo. His confrontation with Colonel Churavy (Vlk) produced no result. Churavy stated that he did not recognize Thümmel as the Franta–René whom he had met. On 25 November the Gestapo, having found no direct proofs against him, had to let him go.

But the Gestapo inspector Abendschön carried on with his investigation. Thümmel admitted that he was acquainted with Moravek, but he said that he used him to learn about the activities and connections of the anti-German resistance. The Gestapo insisted on being told where he hid. Thümmel was forced to comply and he gave them an address; but the flat was empty. It was obvious that Moravek had been warned.

In February 1942 Thümmel was once more placed under arrest. This time Abendschön was in possession of documents proving that the Haupt-V-Mann was hiding certain things both from the Abwehr and the Gestapo. Thümmel defended himself by asserting that he was preparing a far-reaching operation for the Abwehr and that for this purpose it was essential for him to say nothing about his contacts with Moravek until the moment he could uncover the entire illegal resistance network.

This confident statement made the Gestapo hesitate. They set Thümmel free on the condition that he should help them capture Captain Moravek. Thümmel was obliged to arrange a meeting with him in an arcade in the Wenceslas square in Prague; but Moravek did not appear.

Thümmel, at liberty but still under surveillance, was ordered to arrange another rendezvous. So that he should not be able to leave and warn Moravek, a member of the Gestapo by the name of Scharf spent the night in his flat. Franta managed to get out by the window and meet Moravek.

It was now clear enough to the Gestapo that their suspicions about the head of the Prague Abwehr were sound. He was ordered to ask Moravek to come and see him at his flat, where he would be arrested. Thümmel agreed, but alleging that Moravek would only agree to come to his flat if he went to meet him at the streetcar stop, he went out. He came back alone, saying that Moravek could not come that day but that he would the next.

Abendschön understood the game, lost his patience and arrested Thümmel once more, for good and all. This was 20 March. The next day Franta was no longer able to warn Moravek and the tragedy reached its climax.

Heydrich wrote to Bormann, "By means of the interrogation of a prisoner [of the resistance] we learnt that one of Moravek's liaison agents was to be in a park in Prague at about 1900 hours on 21 March 1942." Heydrich had the park surrounded before the appointed time. His men waited: would the agent come?

He did come and he was arrested in spite of a desperate resistance— he could neither use his weapon nor escape. Questioned there on the spot he admitted that he had come to fix a rendezvous with someone at 2200 hours, as Moravek could not be there at 1900 hours.

Now let us recall Leon-Moravek's last conversation with Lida, the liaison agent who had found him a refuge in Prague-Smichov. He said he had an appointment at 1700 hours. With whom? The place where they were talking was quite near Thümmel's flat.

Moravek, fearing treachery, may have sent his agent to change the time of the rendezvous. Or did he wish to ascertain whether the appointment for 1900 hours had been betrayed to the Nazis?

In his report Heydrich states, "At about 1915 hours, when my men were preparing to leave with their prisoner, Moravek suddenly appeared from a sidestreet."

Moravek tried to come to his friend's help. Shots were exchanged. Moravek fired fifty times with his pistols but, according to Heydrich's report, without hitting anyone. On the other hand, still according to Heydrich, the Nazis wounded Moravek in the calf and the lower thigh. The report states that he was hit ten times, and that seeing he could no longer escape, he killed himself. In his last attempt at getting away he lost his bunch of keys and the briefcase holding the photographs of the parachutists.

There are other versions of Leon's heroic end. According to one, Moravek and his liaison agent were on their way to Thümmel's flat—Thümmel had been arrested the day before—when suddenly he noticed that they were surrounded by the Gestapo. Moravek tried to jump on to a passing streetcar; the Germans opened fire, and the rest of the account is the same—Moravek's suicide and the seizure of the briefcase.

In another version the liaison agent, a man called Rehak, went to Thümmel's house alone; but not finding the agreed sign, a chalked circle on the pavement, he turned back. It was then that the Gestapo attacked and captured him.

A man who witnessed Moravek's suicide states that as he was walking along late that afternoon he suddenly saw a man jump on to a moving No. 20 streetcar, pursued by two others in plain clothes who fired at him. The man on the trolley fired back, but they hit him and he then killed himself with his own pistol, quite near Dusty Bridge. Madame E.P., who was passing by on her way home from her office, gave an almost identical account.

Such was the end of that courageous partisan Leon or Ota, whose real name was Captain Vaclav Moravek. Paul Thümmel was imprisoned in the fortress of Terezin; he was kept there in a cell for three years and then shot just before the end of the war.

How did the Moravek–Thümmel affair affect the fate of the parachutists? It directly threatened Bartos' group. The Gestapo now possessed the men's photographs; their names were unknown, but on the back of the prints the Gestapo found the address of the studio in Pardubice where the photographs had been taken. The Nazi police machine therefore turned in the direction of Pardubice.

13

The chemistry teacher's account: 2

(Ladislav Vanek)

THE POSITION grew worse. The Gestapo were following the trail that led to the Bartos group. That was why "Auntie" Moravcova went straight to Pardubice to give the news of Moravek's death and to warn them of the imminent danger that was now threatening Silver A.

Valcik was the only one the Pardubice Gestapo recognized from the photographs. They remembered the waiter from the Veselka restaurant who had vanished, and presently a placard appeared on the walls, describing the alleged Miroslav Solc and promising a reward to anyone who gave information leading to his arrest.

The Nazi police had gathered no other clue about the men whose photographs they found in Moravek's briefcase. They suspected that they were parachutists, but that was all they knew.

Bartos had sent Valcik to Moravia, and it was agreed that later he should go to Prague, where it would be easier for him to pass unnoticed. Valcik had already stayed with the Moraveks at an earlier stage, but now it was a question of finding him a refuge for a considerable time. Bartos and Potucek were also being hunted; every Gestapo office in Bohemia and Moravia had been sent their photographs and had been told to search for these unknown men.

Valcik changed his appearance, dyeing his fair hair and growing a little moustache, which he also darkened. His first contact with Prague was the schoolmaster Zelenka, who took him to

Madame Moravcova; Valcik was now called Zdenda. The Moraveks' flat had become a centre of underground activity and now no parachutist could stay there for any length of time. Auntie therefore entrusted Zdenda to a friend, a railwayman. At this point Kubis and Gabcik were busily making their preparations for the killing, and it is understandable that Valcik, now in Prague and anxious to make himself useful, should have helped them. He was found a nominal job as a commercial traveller for a firm named Topic which made *objets d'art*, and this allowed him to move about the town freely.

Almost every day the three young men, Kubis, Gabcik, and Valcik, went out in the direction of Panenske Brezany, where Heydrich lived. They examined every clump of trees on the road, every curve and every ditch. Heydrich had decided to rebuild the chateau of Panenske Brezany, formerly Jewish property, for himself and his family, and it was said that in doing so he spared "neither the marks nor the Jews"—the prisoners who had to work there. His wife Lina was cruel to them.

The various possibilities for an attempt on Heydrich's life were carefully studied, and from this study three plans emerged. The first was an attack upon Heydrich's private train. There would be men posted to give sufficiently early and precise notice of the train's departure, so that the parachutists would be able to attack it. The engineer, who was in the plot, would then pull up, and the railwayman on duty would take advantage of the confusion to throw a bomb into Heydrich's compartment. This plan was dropped for two reasons: it relied too much on chance, and, even more important, the engineer and railwayman who had promised to help were taken from the special train and transferred to other duties.

The second plan was centred upon the road leading to Panenske Brezany. That was why the parachutists went there so often that in the end they could have walked its whole length blindfolded. Zelenka–Hajsky suggested providing them with a very strong cable, possibly even of steel, and to stretch it across the road immediately before Heydrich's arrival. With the car suddenly stopped by the cable, they would be able to take him by surprise.

They found a suitable rope and tried it out, but there was always something unsatisfactory about it. Furthermore, the country round Panenske Brezany offered not the least possibility of hiding or of getting away. For those who carried it out, an attempt in this place would certainly have meant suicide. Kubis and Valcik often discussed it together, and later they talked it over with Valcik. They settled the duties and positions of each man, and agreed on the way they would try to escape. They looked for a car that could be standing at some distance with its number-plates removed, waiting for them. On the other hand there was the likelihood that the alarm would be given after the attack—given by telephone. Would not this mean the immediate sealing-off of Panenske Brezany and its neighbourhood? And in that case would the car have time to get out of the district? The whole thing might easily end very badly.

Lastly there was a third solution. If the attack were carried out in a densely populated place, the young men would have time to get away and they would soon be out of sight. There would be a panic; the streetcars would stop and it would be easy to escape in the turmoil.

It was obvious, even for one who had not studied it, that any attack on a straight road, with Heydrich's car travelling fast, might easily fail. Heydrich travelled every day from Panenske Brezany to Prague, so they looked for a turning in the road that would compel the chauffeur to slow down, thus giving them a fair chance. If you look at a map, you will see that the only spot fulfilling these conditions is the curve at Prague-Kobylisy, where V Holesovichkach Street makes a sharp angle. This is in the suburbs of Prague, where a whole network of narrow streets is lined by little houses. No barracks and no police station in the neighbourhood. In short, the place seemed specially created for the parachutists.

They examined it again and again, and finally said they were satisfied. It was decided that on the appointed day they would go there on bicycles leaving them near at hand, in the direction of their flight.

One very important thing remained to be settled, and that was the exact times at which Heydrich left Panenske Brezany and reached the Castle in Prague. The young men could not watch the crossroads every day and all day. They had to know precisely when the Protector left his house, what time he reached the Kobylisy turning, and how he was escorted. The resistance set about looking for someone who worked in the Castle and who would know these things.

Nerudova Street goes straight up from the Mala Strana Square to the Castle. The part under the Castle walls is called Uvoz; they are all old houses, and one of them, a watchmaker's shop, belonged to Josef Novotny. Novotny had worked in the Castle for years, looking after the clocks. Nothing could have been better. The Germans did not think his work important enough to replace him with one of their own people. Novotny therefore often went to the Castle, on the pretext of repairing watches and clocks, and he kept his eyes wide open. He repaired watches belonging to the German officers and employees for nothing; they were very pleased with him, never supposing that the good-natured watchmaker carried off valuable information every time he left the Castle. Thus it was possible to draw up a timetable of Reinhard Heydrich's day and his regular movements.

Josef Novotny was even called upon to carry out a repair at Panenske Brezany, and he took advantage of this to bring more useful intelligence. Novotny was one of the organizers' best helpers, and it was he who brought the news that Heydrich would be leaving for the Führer's headquarters on 27 May. All this information was collected by Zelenka–Hajsky.

There was another man inside the Castle who helped the parachutists. His name was Safarik. He worked on the maintenance of the Castle buildings, and he too communicated his information to Zelenka.

And so that strange spring of 1942 went on, filled with preparations and some degree of nervous tension. The resistance had a great task ahead of it.

14

The evidence of a woman from Zizkov: 2

(Frantiska Volfova)

"He met with a dumb man, Blaha," says the Czech proverb, and my husband used to say that about M. Zelenka. The schoolmaster could hold his tongue better than most people. We used to meet him in the street sometimes, but he behaved as though he had nothing much to do with us. He would say good day, ask how we were, and then walk on. He did not want the young fellows to go to his flat, so it was at our place that Kubis and Gabcik met him, sometimes with Valcik.

Once he came to our flat without having made any arrangement. I don't remember now just when it happened.

"M. Volf," said Zelenka to my husband, "would you do something for me?"

"Why not?"

"I want you to go to the Castle."

"The Hradcany Castle?"

"Yes. To see a M. Safarik who looks after the repairs. You must ask him if he remembers the schoolmaster who used to teach him at school. When he says my name, tell him I'd like to speak to him and fix an appointment for us. Please do this for me—it's important."

My husband agreed, asked for a description of the man and then went to the Castle. But he had no luck there; they told him the handyman was ill, and gave him his address, somewhere in Vokovice.

In Vokovice all he found was Madame Safarik. Her husband had had to go for a medical check at the Castle. Employees had their own doctor in the second courtyard of Hradcany. There was nothing for it but to go back again. This time he found Safarik.

My husband asked Safarik whether he could manage to come to the Mala Strana Square, because his old schoolmaster wanted to talk to him. They settled the day and the time and separated. When M. Zelenka heard this he was very pleased and he thanked my husband heartily. I don't remember what day the meeting took place, but I do remember that Zelenka wanted Kubis and Gabcik to go with him.

Spring came. Now and then M. Zelenka would bring someone we didn't know to sleep at our place and then send him off the next day. Once, when Madame Moravcova had come to fetch one of them and I was making the bed, I found a pistol under the pillow. I didn't dare touch it in case it went off; but my husband said to me, "Why, you stupid thing, you have to press on the trigger to fire; otherwise nothing happens." So I wrapped it up in a handkerchief and took it to Madame Moravcova. I believe that boy's name was Bublik.

Another time—it must have been Easter or 1 May—Zdenda–Valcik came to our place and said, "I've brought you a guest, a friend of mine."

I made them coffee and M. Zelenka left Zdenda's friend with us for some days. He limped, probably because he had hurt his foot dropping from the plane. This newcomer used the name Zelinka. I used to mix his name up with the schoolmaster's. When we got to know one another better he told us how his group had separated. He landed in a meadow where horses were grazing, and he stayed there without moving for quite a while so as not to give the alarm. And he had no idea of what had happened to his friends. He had brought a great deal of money—about 45,000 marks. He put the notes out on the table for M. Zelenka and they made a fine great heap. M. Zelenka's brother worked in a bank, and it was he who changed the money into Protectorate crowns.

This Zelinka—later we learnt that his real name was Svarc—wanted M. Zelenka to give him something to do. But the schoolmaster told him to get better first. So he took care of his leg, and when he could get about better we took him for a walk in the park at Vitkov. He put a small advertisement in the *Narodni Politika*. "Lost, at the Black Beerhall, a ring," or something like that. The Black Beerhall is a restaurant in Prague.

Zelinka went through the small advertisements in the paper regularly, and sometimes I used to help him look for one about a violin, something to do with buying or selling it; but I couldn't tell you what it was supposed to mean.

Some time in May Kubis came to fetch Zelinka–Svarc. They often had to change lodgings so as to avoid suspicion. Later Kubis told us that Zelinka had gone to stay in a flat not far from Charles Square. He had a sister who lived here, in this part of Prague; he saw her now and then and he came back to see us too.

Of course, we were frightened all the time those days. It was no small matter, but we didn't think we could shirk it.

No. No, I don't know anything about the men who were with Zelinka–Svarc.

15

The joiner's statement

(Frantisek Safarik)

YES, OF COURSE I knew M. Zelenka, the headmaster. How could I possibly not know him? He was my teacher in the fifth year at school. I went to school at Liboc, near Prague, and he was a master there. It was only later that he moved away to the frontier zone.

I remember how he used to play soccer for the *Liboc Star* and how he used to keep us on the go in class! But then the years went by; I became an apprentice joiner and I didn't see Zelenka again for a great while. Not until the winter of 1942.

In those days I had a job in the Castle at Prague, working as a joiner and repairer. I used to repair the furniture and make anything that was wanted; and then one day as I was walking across the courtyard I saw Zelenka. He was rather thinner and his overcoat hung loose. He cried, "Why, I had you at school!" And he asked how I was getting along. What could I say? I was getting along like the rest of us. The Huns were here; bad times had come, I said.

Zelenka agreed. Then he started sounding me. What did I think of the situation? And of Heydrich? He questioned me like in exams at school. I said to him, "What are you after?"

The headmaster laughed. He was saying thou to me in the familiar way and he told me to do the same.

"That would never do. You're my teacher," I said.

But Zelenka said I was to behave as if I was his brother-in-law, and then I could say thou to him. "Come and have a glass of beer," he said.

After that he went off, but presently I met him again. And he began going on about the situation again—something had to be done, and the man who did us most harm was Heydrich. He ought to be put out of the way, he said.

That frightened me. "Hold on a moment," I said. "You're forgetting I have a little girl. And the Germans don't know the meaning of pity."

All he said was, "Well, think it over. You can help me, my boy; no one will suspect you."

My job was with the furniture, so I could go anywhere in the Castle. I thought it over and told him all right—that I'd be a swine if I didn't help.

Then one day a man came to the Castle. I happened to be in the doctor's waiting room and this man asked me if I remembered who used to give me lessons at school. "Why, Zelenka," I said. So we knew where we were. He gave me an appointment to meet these parachutists. First it was in the Mala Strana Square, and Zelenka came with Gabcik and Kubis. After that I saw them in the little park behind the museum and then another time at the pub called the Three Cats.

They always wanted to know when Heydrich reached the Castle and at what time, and who went with him when he left in the evening. And I told these boys I didn't like it—the whole thing stank of the graveyard. But they calmed me down. The one from Moravia said, "Listen, Franta, don't say a word at home. All you have to do is tell us where Heydrich goes; and you only have to help before it happens. When we get him, you won't be in it at all."

They used to go about with girls and I told them to look out—these girls might get them into trouble. They said I needn't be afraid; they went with them because it was less obvious than going about alone.

Once I showed the paras where Heydrich got out of his car every day. They talked it over: they could hide behind the corner of the house and fire from there. But I said to them, "You

could never escape from the Castle. It would be impossible."
So they went to look at Nerudova Street, down under the
Castle; there's a good corner there. And they had a look at the
curve in the road near the Liboc cemetery—Heydrich had to go
along it to reach the airfield.

They wanted me to tell them about his times. So I took what I
found out to Zelenka in Zizkov; but that's at the other end of the
town—it was too far from Hradcany. I told the schoolmaster
he'd have to manage it some other way; I couldn't get to Zizkov.
He arranged for the girls Kubis and Gabcik went out with, to go
and live just under the Castle in Letenska Street.

I went there as often as necessary. I tapped at the window, it
opened, and one of the girls took the envelope. Now and then
there was a parachutist standing there behind her. I never said a
single word and I hurried off again straight away. Inside the
envelope I always wrote the times: for example *9–5 with* or
without. The figures meant the time Heydrich had reached
Hradcany and the time he had left. The words with or without
meant whether he had come with an escort car or without.

I don't remember now how many times a week I took an
envelope to that window.

It was only long after the war that I heard that these two girls
were called Kovarnikova and Soukupova, that they were sisters
and that the Germans had executed them both. They never
revealed anything, so they saved my life.

I don't know anything about Gabcik and Kubis' friends. I
didn't know there were any other parachutists here, that their
groups had names, or that other teams had been dropped in our
country in spring 1942.

I never did anything except keep an eye on Heydrich to see
when he came and went, and I took that information to Letenska
Street. That's all.

THE HISTORIAN STEPS IN : III

(*The author*)

At this point we should make a survey of the various groups of Czecho-slovak parachutists sent by London to the territory of the Protectorate of Bohemia and Moravia.

The first parachutist, Riedl, was dropped by mistake at Landeck, in the Tyrol. The second, Pavelka, a former student in the faculty of letters, was arrested by the Gestapo in Prague on 25 October 1941. Papers that they found at his lodging told the Gestapo of the existence of the agent René, who was later to be identified as the Haupt-V-Mann Paul Thümmel of the Abwehr. After the Nazis closed the Czech schools and universities on 17 November 1939 as a reprisal for the students' revolt, Pavelka spent some time at Brno as a working-man. He left Brno and on 31 March 1940 escaped from the Protectorate; crossing the frontiers illegally he reached France and eventually arrived in England.

After Pavelka, the men of Silver A were dropped—Bartos, Valcik and Potucek; those of Silver B—Skacha and Zemek; and those of Anthropoid—Gabcik and Kubis. All on 29 December 1941 and all from the same aircraft.

Anthropoid landed near the village of Nehvizdy and the group was lucky from the start. As early as 4 January Piskacek and Novak, warned by a member of the Sokol, reached the spot, got into touch with Gabcik and Kubis and helped them to make their way to Prague. According to Vasek Khodl's notes, which have been found, they arrived in the capital as early as 8 January 1942. Some days later, on 12 January, Kubis went back to Nehvizdy to hide the parachutes and the equipment better. After that, with the help of Inspector Kral, they must have spent a short time at Plzn.

Silver B did not succeed in carrying out its mission. Just as Kubis and Gabcik had luck, so the men of Silver B had none. The addresses they had been given in London turned out to be useless, and their transmitter broke. In the end Skacha was found by the Gestapo, shot and wounded. When his wound was healed he was deported to the extermination camp at Mauthausen. As for Zemek, he managed to join the Partisans in the autumn of 1942.

The statement of the survivor of Pardubice has shown us how the men of Silver A established themselves in that town.

In the spring of 1942 a second wave of parachutists followed—the groups Out Distance and Zinc. Both were dropped on 28 March. They will have an important place in our account.

Both these groups were the victims of an error in dropping. Zinc came down near Kbely in Slovakia, then a so-called independent state. There were three men in this team, First Lieutenant Oldrich Pechal, Sergeant Arnost Miks and Corporal Vilem Gerik. Pechal had the Gestapo after him for a long while; he succeeded in crossing the frontier of the Protectorate, where he was finally betrayed, tortured and put to death. Miks was shot near the castle of Krivoklat during the night of 30 April–1 May 1942. As for Gerik, he gave himself up voluntarily to the Gestapo and supplied them with very valuable information.

What of the Out Distance group? Its leader, Adolf Opalka, will appear again in the following pages. So will Karel Curda, but in his case for not very creditable reasons. The third man of this team killed himself when he was surrounded by the Gestapo.

In all there were several dozen teams of parachutists who took off from London for the Protectorate. Generally speaking these groups were given names associated with the chemical industry: Antimony, Barium, Calcium, Carbon, Potash, Glucinium, Wolfram, Bauxite, Platinum, Diamond, etc. They usually met with great difficulties after their landing. Because of the circumstances of their flight—the great distance that had to be covered, the aerial navigation techniques then in use, and the enemy's defences—they were often dropped hundreds of miles from the agreed point. But the local addresses they were furnished with before leaving were restricted to that given region.

Most of the missions these teams were given had to do with intelligence rather than armed combat. Generally speaking it was a matter of getting into contact with a resistance movement, collecting information and sending it back to London by radio.

It seems that of all these groups only two were given a specific task: Anthropoid (Kubis and Gabcik) were to liquidate Heydrich (K. H. Frank had been thought of in the first place), and Tin was entrusted with the killing of Emanuel Moravec and other notorious pro-Nazi collaborators.

Like Anthropoid, Tin was made up of two men, Jaroslav Svarc and Ludvik Cupal. Svarc was hurt on landing and a family in Prague-Zizkov looked after him. His companion Cupal, having landed in the neighbourhood of the town of Trebon in southern Bohemia on 30 April, went to the south of Moravia, where he was found by the Gestapo. He was wounded in the fight that followed, and he poisoned himself so as not to be taken alive. That is why the attempt on the life of Emmanuel Moravec, the Minister of Culture in the pro-Nazi government of the Protectorate, did not take place.

Why did London send so many groups of parachutists into the Protectorate so early? The answer is simple. The first parachutists dropped there at the end of 1941 were filled with optimism. Following their chiefs' opinion they believed that the end of the war was close at hand. Here it is worth recalling that on 28 October 1941 Allied aircraft, flying over the territory of the former Czechoslovak republic, dropped tracts entitled The Message of the British and Czechoslovak airmen on the occasion of 28 October, *saying "There is one consolation that may comfort you in your brave resistance. You are not faced with three hundred years of slavery, nor with three. Perhaps one at the very most!"*

And this was in 1941.

It is not surprising that the parachutists too believed that the short-term war was not going to last long. But as their stay in the Protectorate grew longer, so their illusions were eroded by contact with the harsh realities that they saw with their own eyes in their occupied country, and they realized the extent of the gap between London's sanguine appreciation of the situation and that of the patriots who had stayed in the country or returned to it. Headquarters in England, becoming aware of the contrast, sent other groups in order to strengthen its own influence. This is proved by a dispatch sent to Bartos on 11 February 1942: "If our view of the organization of the home resistance is correct, it is vitally necessary to stimulate it from abroad by all valid means. It was with this intention that we have sent and that we shall continue to send groups of parachutists into the different regions of our country; their missions will include intelligence activities on the one hand, and on the other effective cooperation in the setting up of our national resistance. It will be necessary for you to take the required steps for establishing and maintaining liaison with these groups in order to send London the results of their intelligence and resistance activities and in order to be in a position to convey our orders and instructions to them." A later passage gives the various passwords these groups had been given to enter into contact with Bartos, including that which Kubis and Gabcik were to use.

Another dispatch from London said, "Acquire Svatopluk Cech's poem Enthusiasm. *It will be used to set up the code. We will give details as soon as you let us know that you have the poem." This confirms the statement of the survivor of Pardubice.*

Contact between Bartos and Anthropoid was established at the beginning of March 1942 by means of an address in Plzn. Bartos informed London on 5 March and stated that "the group is working at a large farm on the outskirts of Prague and living illegally in Prague."

Towards the end of the same month—28 March—the teams Out Distance and Zinc were dropped. They too were to get into touch with Bartos. As soon as the agreed small advertisement appeared in the Narodni Politika *they were to meet at the address given in the paper.*

The different teams made use of a variety of small advertisements. These were usually concerned with the purchase of dictionaries, encyclopedias, musical instruments, etc. It was laid down that members of a group who had been separated during the dropping should use the same system.

If we look over the back numbers of the Narodni Politika *for this period, we find in the Books and Music column the following advertisement, which was published on the 1, 2, 5, 6, 7 and 8 May 1942:*

Wanted: a Czech dictionary. Offers to Jan Vojtisek, Lazne Belohrad 354 or to offices of this paper.

From Vojtisek the path led straight to Bartos. London had been given Vojtisek's address by a Czech teacher who escaped from the country and who reached England. It was radioed to Bartos, who sent Hanka, the wife of the Pardubice survivor, to Belohrad. She succeeded in establishing contact with Vojtisek, whose house then became a rendezvous for parachutists.

On 9, 12 and 13 May 1942 the Narodni Politika *published another advertisement:*

Wanted: Czech–German dictionary, two separate volumes. Jaroslav Lukes, Bernartice no. 39.

The Gestapo's final report on the killing stated that the parachutists had nine places where they could shelter at Bernartice near Tabor, and one at Belohrad. Later Bernartice was razed to the ground: it suffered the same tragic fate at the Nazis' hands as Lidice. Jan Vojtisek was arrested and put to death; so was Jaroslav Lukes; so were twenty-two other inhabitants of Bernartice.

Other small advertisements appeared. These were inserted by parachutists who were trying to find one another. This, for example, was published by the Narodni Politika *on 12, 13, 15, 16 and 17 May 1942 in the Lost column; it was put in by Svarc–Zelinka of the Tin group:*

An old ring with the initials J.S. lost
at the Black Beerhall 30.4.42.
Information to Familiale, c/o this paper.

Svarc was searching for his lost comrade Cupal, but he searched in vain—Cupal was hunted down by the Gestapo and he killed himself.

In spite of all these disguised signals on the part of Zinc, only Miks managed to reach Bartos at Pardubice. Gerik gave himself up to the Gestapo because the addresses supplied in London were of no help and because he did not succeed in getting in touch with any underground organization—finally he decided to turn traitor. The third man, Pechal, fought to the end—hunted, wounded, tortured, he never lost his courage.

Contact with Pardubice provided support for Opalka and Curda, the Out Distance team. On 14 April the underground transmitter Libuse told London that the Kral team, that is to say Opalka, had got into touch with Bartos.

During the night of 28 April 1942 two other teams were dropped in the Protectorate: Bioscop (Kouba, Bublik, and Hruby) and Bivouac (Pospisil, Coupek, and Zapletal), both being intended for sabotage. Their drop was a complete success, but for greater security they hid their equipment in the forest near the castle of Krivoklat.

In March and April 1942 seventeen Czechoslovak parachutists were dropped over the territory of the Protectorate. Among them were heroes and traitors, fervent patriots and opportunists. Each of these men's lives had its own orientation, its own highest point, moment of crisis and termination. The orientation was the same for all—the instruction in England, the arduous training, the airfield and the take off, the tension of the waiting and of the flight, the drop in the hostile night. From the moment they touched the ground of their own country their fates diverged, taking on different forms. The final outcome set them far apart, and in spite of appearances they were in fact separated by a distance as great as that which lies between courage and cowardice, heroism and treachery. Pechal was put to death; Miks was shot near Krivoklat; Kolarik committed suicide; Cupal and Kouba took poison; Zapletal ended in Mauthausen; Gerik went to the bank every month to receive the reward of his treachery.

What of the others?

The names of Kubis, Gabcik, Opalka, Valcik, Svarc, Bublik, and Hruby will have never-dying fame: they were brave and courageous men. Karel Curda's will not be forgotten, either.

History, at least, gives no rewards for treason.

16

The statement of the survivor from Pardubice: 3

(Vaclav Krupka)

YOU ALREADY know how tragically it ended, the business of those photographs—the photographs of the three parachutists Bartos and I took to Captain Moravek in Prague. Valcik disappeared from Pardubice; Bartos stayed there alone; sometimes Potucek, the radiotelegraphist, came to the town.

In the spring of 1942 more men were sent into the Protectorate. In London each team was given certain addresses, and they were supposed to go to them once they had been dropped over occupied territory. At the same time these addresses were radioed to Bartos, and we expected the fresh parachutists to appear at our flat. The password agreed upon was Alcazar; and if no one came within a week after the date set for the drop, Freda Bartos was to give my wife the addresses so that she could check them. It was a dangerous job, with the Gestapo moving about in every direction. It was agreed with London that there should also be another way of getting into contact with the parachutists, and this was a small advertisement in the *Narodni Politika* giving an address, which was usually that of Vojtisek, the bookseller at Lazne Belohrad where the teams were expected.

My wife went to fetch the parachutists at the Vojtiseks' place and brought them back to us at Pardubice. The first to come in this way was Kral—a splendid man from every point of view. He stayed with us a couple of days and then we sent him to the

Moravecs in Prague; their flat had become a kind of transit centre, a base from which the parachutists moved on to other lodgings. It was only later that I heard that Kral was the *nom de guerre* of Captain Adolf Opalka.

After Kral had gone to Prague we waited for another parachutist, but we waited in vain; he gave no sign of life and nobody knew anything about him. Freda gave my wife various addresses and she went to find him; but every time she came back empty handed.

She had to go right out to Moravia, into the neighbourhood of Uhersky Brod, but there she found that the address we had been given had been useless for some time—it was the house of a man who had been arrested by the Gestapo. She even went to look for him in the Bucklov forests, but the whole region was ringed round by the Germans and the police. She was lucky enough to get out, thanks to a Czech policeman who showed her the way and let her cross a railway bridge. He told her that the Germans were hunting for parachutists hidden in the woods and that they had caught one and shot him. We supposed that he was the man we had been looking for. Later we found out that it was Pechal's team that the Germans had discovered.

At last the man we had waited for so long knocked at our door in Pardubice. This was Curda. At that time he went by the name of Vrbas. It so happened that I had gone to Prague with Bartos that day and my wife was taking advantage of our absence to spring-clean the house. She had gone out for a few minutes and the only person Curda found was the charwoman, scrubbing the floor. She told my wife that a man had been looking for us—an odd, frightened-looking man. When he came back he gave the password, Alcazar. He told my wife that he came from Vojtisek, that he was called Vrbas, and that he was the man we had been trying to find for the last month. He seemed nervous and uneasy; my wife gave him Hladena's address, so that he should not have to spend the whole day wandering about the streets.

When we returned from Prague that evening he came to the house again. Bartos and I talked to him, and to tell you the truth he did not make a favourable impression at all. He hesitated as he spoke and he stammered a little; but the really serious thing was that he appeared to be thoroughly frightened.

"It's a month now that we've been looking for you everywhere," I said.

He replied that he had been staying with relatives.

"And did you see our advertisement about buying a dictionary?"

"Yes, just the other day; that's why I'm here."

We sat down. After a little while he began to talk rather more openly. He said they had told him all manner of things about the Protectorate in London, but that the facts were quite different. He was right, of course. But what were his conclusions? He said one of his relations had been drafted into the Protectorate government army and he was quite happy there; so why, asked Curda, did the occupying forces have to be opposed? The more he talked the less we liked him.

He even spoke about his life in England, telling us more than all the other parachutists who had ever come to us. We realized that he was too talkative by far and that we should have to try to do something about it. Bartos and I had a brief conference and then we wrote out rules of conduct and practical instructions for the work of a parachutist in the Protectorate—how one should behave, what could be done and what was forbidden; we added all our experience and advice and the next day we told Curda to read the paper carefully and to sign it. He took his pen and calmly wrote his name. But he never obeyed our instructions.

That night he slept in our flat. He did not see Bartos' mother, nor did Freda go to see her. But she often came to our place, and this distressed us because it was too conspicuous and, above all, very dangerous.

Bartos gave Curda–Vrbas some work to do and decided to send him to Prague. Not one of us was capable of imagining the tragedy this man would bring about. As I have already said, we did not like him—we thought him a coward; but would they have dropped him if he had not been trustworthy? But what does trustworthiness mean? And what is the meaning of cowardice? Take Curda, for example. He had done well in training, he was a good shot, he had passed his final examination, he had made a number of drops after that, and then he had set off. How can you delve into a man's heart? And what guarantee could they have in London that this man would not turn traitor?

Ata Moravec came to Prague and took Curda away. I never saw him again.

I have tried hard to remember the exact dates when Opalka and Curda came, but I cannot recall them. I do remember that my wife brought a "student" from Vojtisek in Belohrad—this was probably the parachutist Kolarik; and then still later, towards the end of April, another parachutist turned up. We called him the little gipsy. This little gipsy was supposed to bring us poison and spare parts from England for the transmitter. When he landed he hid them in fields near Krivoklat Castle, not far from Prague.

Later I saw a piece in the newspaper saying that a parachutist had been shot in the Krivoklat forest—that was at the beginning of May 1942.

17

The caretaker's recollections: 2

(Frantisek Spinka)

DID YOU KNOW that John of Luxemburg was the first Czech king to strike gold coins? He was copying Florence when he did that. I've got a silver piece of his period. At the top, next to St. John's head, there's a little lion, the Czech lion, the symbol of our country.

You often find portraits of saints on the old silver coins: St. Wenceslas, St. John or St. George. And now I'll tell about what happened a week after St. George's Day, 24 April.

I was sitting in the kitchen, resting, and then all at once somebody rang at the bell. My wife opened the door—it was Zdenda and Ata, Madame Moravcova's sons. They came into the kitchen. They were tired out; Zdenda sat down on the sofa, sighed deeply and said, "Well, Landlord, here we are."

He often used to joke like that. He knew perfectly well I was only the caretaker, but he would call me Landlord for a laugh.

"What's been happening to you?" asked my wife—she was easily frightened.

But Zdenda—that is to say Valcik—let a few moments go by before he answered, "Ask Ata."

I looked at young Moravec, sitting there next to Zdenda. He looked exhausted. "What's wrong, Ata?"

"Well ... we had no luck," he began. He stared at the floor, his head in his hands, then he leant back against the wall and told us that one of the men who had been dropped not long before had hidden the equipment he brought somewhere in the fields near the castle of Krivoklat. He'd hidden it where he landed. So

Zdenda and Ata had been given the job of bringing it all back to Prague. To help them find it, two parachutists went with them, Kouba, one of the team that had been dropped there, and Miks. Miks had come to the Protectorate with Gerik, who gave himself up to the Gestapo before the killing.

"We set off," said Ata. "I knew my way more or less, because we spend the holidays in those parts. To get there quicker we took the train as far as Zbecno, and from there we went through the forest, Zdenda and me from one side and the others from the other; according to our sketch-map we ought to have ended up by meeting. We crawled through the bushes and down into ditches and just when we thought we had succeeded without anyone seeing us, a policemen with a rifle got up in front of us. He asked to see our papers. I showed him mine; he looked at them, stared at me, and told us to get out quick, because the whole neighbourhood was ringed round and watched by the Germans and the police."

"Go on, Ata," said Zdenda—but Ata said nothing.

"Now Ata's afraid the policeman will remember his name and report him. It could turn out nasty for all of us."

I thought for a few moments and then I said, "You can rest easy. If he'd wanted to do you any harm, he'd have done it right away; he wouldn't have warned you and let you go; he wouldn't have told you the Germans were there too. Oh no, he must be a good Czech."

Then Zdenda said to young Moravec, "You see that wooden crate, Ata? The Huns might knock it about so hard it would begin to talk; but if that happens to you, you mustn't say anything, not a word, you understand?"

Ata nodded, turning pale. I looked at Ata, and I was afraid for him. After this they went off, tired though they were—they must have gone to get some sleep. The next day I learnt what had happened to the two others, Kouba and Miks. They had had bad luck too—even worse. They had run into the police who were watching the place where the things were hidden; but whereas Ata, thanks to Valcik's coolness, had shown the policeman his papers, Miks had pulled out his revolver and fired.

Look, I've still got a cutting from the paper of that time. Here:

CTK Prague. On 30 April 1942 at about 22 hours the Kladno police caught two criminals red-handed; the men, of Czech nationality, intended to perpetrate outrages by means of explosives. They were taken by surprise and they opened fire at once. In the ensuing struggle Sergeant Ometak was killed and Constable Kominek seriously wounded. One of the criminals was shot. The acting Reichsprotektor has given orders that the widow of Sergeant Ometak, killed on active service, should be generously provided for. The acting Reichsprotektor has expressed his particular gratitude to the wounded policeman; and the SS Obergruppenführer Reinhard Heydrich has rewarded the carter who helped to find and catch the criminals. It was thanks to his presence of mind that it was possible to take the adequate steps to prevent the outrage that had been planned.

That was the official account. As we read it, Madame Moravcova and I thought it over carefully. She was frightened—she kept thinking about that policeman who had checked her son's papers and who might have reported him.

He never did. Believe it or not, I met him later, towards the end of the war. In 1945 he came here, to look at the house—I mean the house where the Moravec family had lived.

Kouba, the parachutist who went with Miks, managed to get away. The paper speaks about a carter. It was probably he who found the parachutists' things in the field and told the authorities. People also say the Gestapo sent the traitor Gerik to identify Miks' body.

It's very hard to say whose fault it was—maybe the carter's. If he had kept his mouth shut, the Gestapo and the police would not have been there. But what do we know about him? Perhaps someone saw him just as he came across the hidden things, and that would have forced him to tell the authorities.

Or perhaps it was poor Miks' fault. If he'd shown his papers like Ata instead of bringing out his revolver, maybe they wouldn't have started firing—maybe the police would have let him go. But it might have been even worse—the police might have arrested Kouba too. He was saved. But for how long? With arrest hanging over his head, he killed himself, you know. He killed himself on 3 May, three days after the business in the Krivoklat forest. But you can't go on asking yourself the same questions forever—what might have happened if someone had done this and someone else the other. To put it in a nutshell, Miks was shot and the Gestapo confiscated the equipment brought from London. That's a fact. And another fact is that I saw that Ata, Madame Moravcova's son, was frightened. And I said to myself, how will it all end if he's arrested and tortured by the Germans? Will fear and love of life be stronger than other feelings or not?

My wife said nothing: she washed down the stairs every week, and now and then someone would ring at the bell and say "Jan" and we would let them in as we had said we would. Once a young lady came from a great way off, from Moravia. She wanted to see Kral, the one whose real name was Opalka, but he was busy and they could only talk together for a few minutes.

And sometimes a captain used to come to the Moravecs' to see Zelenka–Hajsky. I don't know his name. I never asked people their names.

A very pretty young lady came to the house, too. Later Madame Moravcova told me she was a liaison agent from Pardubice. And to leave nobody out, there was a schoolmistress— she came from Pardubice too. She came to see Zdenda (Valcik), and she brought him a suitcase full of food and other things. She rang on our bell and said, "Are you the caretaker of this house?"

"Yes," I said. "What about it?"

She leant nearer me and said, "Jan."

I didn't know what to do, but I answered "Janovice." When I didn't know the person who gave the password Jan, you see, I was supposed to answer "Janovice." That's what Madame Moravcova had asked me to do.

The young lady smiled and told me she had rung on the Moravecs' bell, but there was no one in. "And at our place they had told me that if I found no one at home, I could speak to the caretaker, who knew everything."

"Well, I don't know everything, but please come in."

She left the suitcase with us and then we went to look for Valcik. I knew he'd be somewhere in the Vitkov park. It was a fine day, and the young lady was wearing a light-coloured coat that suited her very well. We reached the hill and I saw Valcik sitting on the grass, just over the railway tunnel. He was looking down, and there on the training ground the SS were learning to march in step. When the girl saw him she said "Thank you" to me and ran to him. I went home, and that evening my wife asked Zdenda if that pretty young woman was his sweetheart. He laughed and said, "No, Madame, I haven't enough time for that." He told us this schoolmistress was a splendid girl and that it was she who had helped him get out of Pardubice when it grew too hot for him.

Zdenda had a dog, too. It was a magnificent German sheepdog, and he called it Moula. He had to go off somewhere, and speaking in such a persuasive way that nobody could have said no, he said, "Landlord, look after my monster, will you?"

The dog slipped under the table and waited for his master there—sometimes he had to wait a long while, too. My wife told Zdenda he ought to give the dog to someone else, because he had no time to look after him, but Zdenda wouldn't hear of it.

It was about this time that Madame Moravcova bought a bicycle from a family living near Teplice and put it into the garage of the house next door. M. Janecek, a taxi-driver, used to look after these garages. He was a fine man, a Communist, and he knew how to keep his mouth shut. He had known Valcik since the mobilization in 1938. He often used to say to me, "You'll see how things change here, after the war. We'll have the republic again. It'll be *our* republic, our very own republic!"

I must confess I didn't pay much attention to my coin collection in those days. People were risking their lives—how could I play about with old bits of metal?

I'd almost forgotten to tell you about another interesting event. In April, before the Krivoklat business, Madame Moravcova came and asked if we would let some young men sleep in the house. "They won't make a noise; no one will know anything about it."

"Let them come," I said, "and we'll have everything ready for them."

We lent Ata the key to the fifth floor, where there's a little attic—no one ever went up there. These boys left some small boxes in the attic and their briefcases. And grenades too, it seems.

Madame Moravcova told me they had to leave the next morning and then in the evening they were all to meet at her place. She asked whether we had any friends or relations at Plzn, where these young fellows could sleep in safety. In those days my brother worked as a warder in the Bory prison at Plzn, so I gave her his address.

When they came back from Plzn they were all very tired and depressed. They gave us their map of Plzn and their papers to hide. Among these papers there were some birth certificates from the district of Caslav. No, wait a minute. They may have given us all these things before they left. There, I'm beginning to forget, you see. Yes, and together with their papers they also gave me a hat; and according to the label inside it had been bought at Pardubice.

Madame Moravcova was a very fine woman. She did every-thing for those young men—for the paras, I mean. She washed, ironed, and mended their clothes and hurried all over the town looking for food for them and the things they needed. She travelled, gathered information, and sent it on. A real heart of gold. There were some other ladies who helped her. Madame Kaliberova, for example—she often came here. She was a fine woman too, careful and brave. I've been told that all these ladies got to know one another in their Red Cross work. Madame Moravcova was the secretary, I think.

Once, about midnight, my wife opened the door for Big Ota and said to him, "Well, and how's the work? Going along all right?" She knew nothing about it—not the least suspicion of what they were getting ready for. She just said that for something to say.

Big Ota smiled. "You'll have news of us presently, Madame," he said.

My wife told me she felt a thrill of horror. What were these young men up to, we wondered? I thought perhaps they were going to blow up a factory, or something like that.

One evening the parachutists went to see the Kalibers. The talk was all about politics—what else could you talk about during the war?—and someone mentioned Heydrich's name. At that Little Ota broke in, "Ha, ha, that's my job!" saying the word job in English.

After the killing Madame Kaliberova told me about that evening, and she told me what the English word meant.

That's about all I remember of what happened in the days before the killing. Now and then Zdenda–Valcik came to see us and have a chat, but he never told us where he was living, and we never asked. Madame Moravcova must have found him lodgings somewhere.

18

A railwayman's recollections

(*Vladimir Tichota*)

MADAME MORAVCOVA found him lodgings with us. In those days I was working at the railway central office in Prague, transport inspectors' department.

One day in March 1942, at about ten in the morning, one of the inspectors I knew came to see me and asked me to come out of my office into the corridor. There he said to me, "Would you like to meet a lady?"

I thought it was a joke and I said, "Do you mean to introduce me to your sweetheart?"

To my astonishment he remained serious. Shaking his head he replied that he was talking about the wife of a retired inspector, Moravec—about a thoroughly trustworthy woman.

The moment he said "trustworthy" I felt there was something odd. I said I had nothing against meeting this lady of his. Straight-away my friend took me to his office, where there was a woman waiting for us. She was rather tall and stout; her expression calm and determined. You might almost say dynamic. When I came in she stood up and gave me her hand. "I am Moravcova," she said, simply.

I introduced myself in my turn. The talk that followed only lasted ten minutes or a quarter of an hour. Madame Moravcova wasted no time: "I am looking after some young men who have not been declared to the police. Now I need lodgings for one of them. You need not be afraid. He won't bring you any trouble; he's perfectly straight."

"Are you certain he's not a German agent provocateur?"

"There's nothing wrong with him; you can set your mind at rest."

"I'll agree on one condition—that no one should know anything about it. Could you bring him to our house yourself?"

"Yes, Monsieur. If it suits you, we'll come this evening at eight o'clock."

I said yes.

When I got home I explained the whole thing to my wife, and she got a bedroom ready for our unknown guest at once. There was a divan, a little bookshelf, a wardrobe. That evening, at five past eight, Madame Moravcova came, together with a young man.

I looked at him closely. He was of a medium height; his black hair—too black—clashed with his blue eyes.

"This is our Zdenda," said Madame Moravcova as she came in.

We gave them coffee and cakes. Zdenda had no luggage at all, only a briefcase. He was wearing a short overcoat, greenish, if I remember right. From that evening on he lived with us. I gave him the key to the flat and we agreed that when he had shut the door behind him he should put it in the little sand box that had to be there according to the regulations, in case of fire in an air raid. I did not want him to have the key in his pocket: a little while before the police had gone from house to house showing a bunch of keys and trying to find the person they belonged to.

Our guest was a taciturn man; he did not look for conversation. He said good morning and good night and thank you and so on. He was often out. My wife and I both went off to work very early in the morning; he went out after us, but he came back later. One evening, four or five days after his arrival, he tapped at the door of our bedroom and came in. We sat down and talked a little. We talked about the war, of course—what else was there to talk about in those days?

He did not tell us why he was in Prague. Later—I can't remember the exact date—he casually mentioned that his friends and he had been dropped from English planes. Up until then I had not known where he came from, whether from the East or the West.

Gradually we came to know how he lived. He took to coming to see us every evening before going to bed; he would sit down and talk. We did not interrupt, we did not ask questions: we listened. He told us he had been parachuted and that he had landed near Podebrady. He had not found his companions, and they had looked for one another a long while before they managed to find the right contacts. He never said that his real name was Valcik nor that he had worked at the Veselka restaurant at Pardubice.

One evening he asked me whether now and then he might bring a friend who would sleep in his room. I said yes. From the photographs that I only saw after the end of the war, the other young man who slept in our flat must have been Gabcik.

When Zdenda had been living with us over a fortnight he said he would like to change his quarters for a while, so as not to compromise us unnecessarily. I went to see a friend called Antonin who lived at Prague-Branik. He had a big garden with a hut in the middle of it. I told him plainly what it was all about and he agreed.

Valcik and I made an appointment at the Bulhar streetcar stop so that I could show him how to get there. It was Zdenda who suggested the place, as he had something to do in the Zizkov district, near the trolley stop. I got there at two o'clock in the afternoon and he joined me a few minutes later.

We did not speak to one another. He knew he had to take the same trolley as me and get out where I did. A No. 21 came along and we set off. It was a fine day, I remember, a really sunny, charming spring day. Zdenda looked out at the street and the sun lit up his hair. Suddenly I realized that the roots of his black hair were fair—it was dyed. If a Gestapo man appeared it was possible that he would notice it, and that might be tragic. I beckoned to Zdenda. We got out at the next stop.

"What's the matter?" he asked curiously.

"Zdenda, your hair's dyed, and it shows. Come along with me to a barber I know; he'll cope with it."

He agreed and we went to Karlin—my friend's shop was there, just opposite the theatre. He had been arrested by the Gestapo, but his son was carrying on the business. I told him what we wanted and he asked Valcik to come upstairs to his flat, and there he re-dyed his hair. Then we set off again for Branik.

Antonin was waiting for us. He showed Zdenda where he could always find the garden keys—on the street side you had to push your hand into the hedge and feel for a little hole where the doorkey was hidden. He showed him the key to the hut, too. This took about twenty minutes, then I left and Zdenda stayed. He lived in the hut for a few days and then he came back to us. After that he went to spend the nights at Branik or some other place. He used to walk about the streets of Prague as though he were travelling for the firm of Topic, who made *objets d'art*. He carried their catalogue in his briefcase, and he used to joke about it.

From time to time Madame Moravcova came to see him at our flat, but she would only stay ten minutes, say a few words and leave.

The weeks went by. May was coming and we had agreed with Valcik that he would move to another railwayman's house in the district of Hanspaulka. Was he still using the hut at Branik to sleep in? I don't know at all. Our watchword was, ask as few questions as possible.

One day I went to the Hanspaulka hill with him. The whole district was full of flowers; in the suburban gardens the cherries and lilacs were heavy with blossom. He walked along, delighted—his hair black as coal and a little black moustache under his nose; all he had was a small briefcase. He told me he had seen his mother again, for the first time in years and years.

My friends lived in one of these little houses; they had a daughter and two sons, and the eldest boy was then in a German prison—the Gestapo had arrested him for underground Communist activities. The other boy was a painter. They got a little room ready for Valcik; then we shook hands. I left, and I never saw him again.

I was very fond of him: he was a brave, unassuming man.

Straight and very careful; a man who obeyed the rules of underground resistance, the kind of man you could work with.

I remember another experience I had with him, in April. One evening he asked me whether I knew Plzn well.

"Of course I do, Zdenda. Why?"

"Do you know where the Tivoli restaurant is?"

I took a piece of paper and drew a map. He looked at my sketch and I could see he wasn't pleased.

"What's the matter, Zdenda? Isn't it clear enough?"

"Oh yes. But—well, I don't know the town, and if I ask the way too often I may be noticed."

"When do you want to go?" He told me the date. "All right, Zdenda, I'll arrange things so as to be able to go with you. We'll go by the same train, but in different carriages. We'll get out at Plzn and you'll follow me. I'll lead the way."

He was very pleased and he accepted my offer. On the day, we left by the seven-twenty and reached Plzn about ten in the morning. I set off from the station in the direction of the Tivoli, with Zdenda following me twenty yards behind. I had to admire him—he was perfectly easy and natural. When we reached the restaurant I saw a man walking up and down in front of it, and he joined Zdenda. So it was a settled rendezvous. I went to see my relations and that evening I travelled back to Prague by the eight-fifty. Zdenda stayed in Plzn.

The next morning I learnt why he had gone there. I was eating my breakfast when the radio gave the news that English planes had bombed the Skoda works at Plzn, but without hitting them. I said to myself, our guest was certainly mixed up in that. I was sorry that according to the radio it had not been successful. I knew nothing about the details of the raid on the Skoda works. When Zdenda came back he looked angry—he was obviously put out. So I was sure the bombing had failed.

19

𝕎𝕙𝕒𝕥 𝕒𝕟 𝕒𝕣𝕔𝕙𝕚𝕧𝕚𝕤𝕥 𝕜𝕟𝕠𝕨𝕤: 1

(*The author*)

EVERY OLD document has its own particular odour. You may well laugh, but they say that a real archivist can take up a document and tell what century it belongs to by the smell. A man's memory can make mistakes, either by chance or on purpose; but records are trustworthy. Or more exactly, they almost always tell the truth. Here we have some very interesting documents on the bombing of the Skoda works at Plzn in 1942: they are the radio dispatches that passed between our resistance in London and that in the Protectorate by means of a clandestine transmitter. The first, sent from London on 14 April 1942, speaks of the intention of bombing the Skoda works as from April and gives the Silver A team (Captain Bartos' group) missions to ensure the success of the operation.

On 18 April, Bartos' transmitter, Libuse, tells London that preparations for the bombing will be made as from 20 April. Subsequent dispatches state that the parachutists Valcik and Kubis will set fire to a cowshed and a stack of straw to guide the planes. Other documents show that the parachutists Opalka and Curda were also to take part in the operation.

It was agreed that on the appointed day Dvorak's 8th Slavonic dance would be played during the BBC's German-language programme. The departure of the planes would be confirmed by the words "Have patience; the day of revenge is approaching" spoken by the announcer during the Czech programme at 1830 hours.

The Slavonic dance was played on Saturday 25 April 1942. The four parachutists were at their posts.

Libuse's next dispatch gives the result of the bombing. Two farms burnt by the parachutists; a few people arrested on suspicion of having set them on fire; the workers who had prepared the destruction of the factory's most important equipment bitterly disappointed. The final outcome of the raid, zero.

Libuse's dispatch of 5 May 1942 again speaks of the great disappointment of the parachutists, the partisans, and the workers. It insists that in such cases pilots who know the region and the position of the works should be chosen.

It was not until April 1945, a few days before the end of the fighting, that a great Allied raid almost entirely destroyed the Skoda works, which had provided Hitler with a positive arsenal throughout the war.

20

The statement of the survivor from Pardubice: 4

(Vaclav Krupka)

I WAS NOT at Plzn during the raid on the Skoda works, but I shared in the preparations for it. In April my wife and I went to see the Moravecs in Prague and there we heard some very disturbing news. One of the parachutists had given himself up to the Czech police of the Protectorate and they had handed him over to the Gestapo. We now know it was Gerik; but at that time it worried us, all the more so since we had not expected anything of that kind.

From the time we first joined the resistance we had realized the danger and the risks of our underground work; we had sometimes discussed them; but we had never foreseen that the parachutists might turn traitor. Only wholly reliable men should have been chosen for missions of that kind.

Leaving the Moravecs, we went to see the Sedlaks. The wife had Jewish relations, and the Germans were after her for that fact alone. She was a very courageous woman. My wife acted as liaison agent between Pardubice and Prague and sometimes spent the night with her.

Sedlak, too, was of the same stamp, staunch and loyal; he was a technician and he was working on the plans for a new Skoda factory to be built near the town of Hradec Kralove. So it was possible for him to provide us with very valuable information on the Plzn workshops. The head offices of the Skoda works were in

Prague, and it was there that he had his office. He gave me information on the potential production and on orders for war material, and I handed it on to Bartos to code and radio to London.

Sedlak gave us important intelligence for the preparation of the raid—the site of the anti-aircraft batteries, the position of the mock buildings that had been put up to mislead observers in the aircraft about the local geography, the situation of the most important war material workshops, above all those where prototypes were being built.

That was not all we did for the success of the raid. Long before, I had been carrying out one of the tasks Bartos gave me: I obtained meteorological instruments—no easy matter in wartime—set them up on our balcony and took readings every day on wind, weather, and so on.

We waited eagerly for the day London would choose for the attack. One week went by, then a second, and then at last London broadcast the agreed signal. That night we gathered round our radio; we were all keyed up, hoping that everything would go as planned. It must succeed, said Bartos. Through Sedlak we knew that the workers in the factories had been warned of the danger and that they had even prepared to sabotage the machines and above all to destroy the essential equipment; they meant to do it during the chaos that would follow the raid. But the Prague radio gave no news whatsoever.

Next morning Bartos sent my wife to Prague to get exact information about the results of the bombing. She came back thoroughly upset, bringing a letter from the parachutists. Valcik and the other men were disappointed and furious; Valcik bitterly criticized the organizers of the raid. We all of us, including Bartos, utterly deplored the farce London had made us play.

You must not be surprised: these young fellows had risked not only their own lives but the lives of dozens of other people. So we could not understand. What was the point of it all? What was the use of all this extreme danger?

But we had to go on working in spite of our doubts, in spite of the questions no one could answer. We searched for intelligence, prepared radio messages, decoded the replies and the orders.

At the beginning of May, Bartos left for Prague. There he met Vanek, the chemistry teacher. When he came back he told me that he had had a discussion with Vanek, that things would have to be postponed for a while, and that he would ask for a change in the person aimed at; he spoke of a dispatch beginning with the letter H and I imagined that it concerned Hacha, the so-called President of the Protectorate. I know he sent this message, but I do not know whether he received a reply.

After his journey to Prague Bartos fell seriously ill. He had rheumatoid arthritis; he was unable to walk and he had to stay in bed. Just imagine the situation: the commanding officer confined to his bed!

I don't know what the other parachutists were doing at that time. I had not seen Valcik since he left Pardubice. At that point I knew nothing about the existence of Kubis and Gabcik, nor that they were going to Panenske Brezany every day.

Bartos tried to get up, but he could not manage it. And my wife carried the radio dispatches; she had lost weight, but she did not complain. That is how we lived through May 1942. The storm was coming nearer; but fortunately we knew nothing about it.

21

The account of the schoolmaster of Dejvice

(*Josef Ogoun*)

I AM FAMILIAR with all the works of Palacky, the historian, and with Jirasek's historical novels; and I know the Czech poets, Jaroslav Vrchlicky, Julius Zeyer, Jan Neruda, and Sladek. I love the history of the Czech people and above all the period of the Hussite movement—the finest period in the nation's history! Oh yes, indeed; our people's ancient splendour is something that makes men hold up their heads: it raises their souls.

But I also read Tacitus and Caesar. Thanks to them I have a better understanding of the German mind, and that is why the conditions in which we had to live after the invasion of our country in 1939 did not surprise me. As far as I was able I tried to help those who were fighting against German Nazism.

At the beginning of 1940 Cerny, a student at the Charles University in Prague, who had been hunted by the Nazis since November 1939, that is to say since the reprisals against the students of the great teaching establishments, came to us. His people had been arrested by the Gestapo and his perilous road brought him to our flat, where at last he found shelter. He was a Communist; but to tell you the truth, I for my part never asked anyone what party he belonged to. He was fighting the Germans; for me that was enough—it was decisive.

Cerny was convinced that Russia would win in the end, but he thought the war would be a long one. In this his opinions differed from those of Kubis and Gabcik, who lived with us after he had gone. They asserted that the war would be over towards the end of 1942 at the latest.

I remember that once Cerny came to our flat—at that time he was no longer living with us but in the district of Kosire—and he brought about five dozen eggs, flour and butter, for our parachutists. I have no idea where he found all this food.

And now I will tell you about Kubis and Gabcik: I saw them as men who were about to avenge the Czech nation, and that is why I helped them.

Towards the end of April 1942 Madame Fafkova came to see us. Her husband was Petr Fafek, accountant to the Czechoslovak Red Cross and later to the Masaryk League against Tuberculosis, a serious, straightforward man—one of those brave and unassuming patriots who take no count of their own labour or their anxieties, never weary, always ready to make sacrifices for the nation. And his wife: she too was one of our heroic women. For a while their daughter Rela had attended the classes I taught at school—she was an excellent student—and it was at that period we came to know the Fafeks.

Madame Fafkova told us there were two young men living with them who were not declared to the police. It was only later that I learnt their real names, Kubis and Gabcik. They had been at the Fafeks' for the whole of April and now it was necessary to find them another place. Madame Fafkova asked whether we could take them in and look after them both during May, because the nature of their mission did not allow them to live separately. I did not know what their mission was, and probably Madame Fafkova did not know either. My wife and I agreed to house them, and they came.

How shall I describe them? Although two men may remember the same thing, both will see it in a different light. So I do not claim for myself the merit of an exact and complete description.

Both conducted themselves faultlessly, like disciplined soldiers who are thoroughly trained for the missions they have to carry out. They were intelligent, and they were prepared for the ultimate sacrifice. You must understand me when I tell you they believed in what they were doing; they were deeply convinced of the justice of their struggle for the Czech nation, hideously tortured by these twentieth-century Teutons.

They never said what they had done or what they were doing, where they had lived, what they were to do or what they wished to do. It was only later that I heard—though without being able to verify it—that several plans for an attack on Heydrich had been worked out. It appears that there were at least three: they had wanted to take Heydrich alive in the neighbourhood of Melnik, and they had meant to carry out the attack where the road curves near the Kramar villa, not far from the Chotkovy Sady garden; but in my opinion these are only hypotheses based on certain remarks they may have made, and no one said this until after the killing, after their death, when people were thinking of them and talking about them.

For my part, I can assert that they never talked about their plans. Sometimes during a conversation there might be a few words about their training before they came here, but never a connected account. They taught my sons wrestling and certain particular grips—what do they call it nowadays? You certainly have other terms for the sport.

They paid great attention to the ways of the house. Neither the caretaker nor the other tenants could suspect that we had guests of that kind. The only one who knew was our neighbour, M. Kriklan, and he helped us get clothes, shoes, and food for them. His son was friendly with our boys and he often came to the flat. So we were obliged to let his father become one of our group.

The Fafeks had two daughters, Rela and Libena. The two parachutists had been comfortable there; the family was very fond of them and sometimes one of the Fafeks would come to see them at our flat—but I will tell you about that later.

They were quiet and unassuming. When Madame Fafkova came to arrange about their staying with us—and it seems that they had gone to the Fafeks from the Moravecs—we said how sorry we were that we did not have enough food to entertain them well, what with the war and the Protectorate, you know.

And Madame Fafkova replied, "Don't worry about that at all. They will be happy with anything you can give them."

Madame Fafkova had a very high opinion of these young men, and she would have consented to an engagement between Gabcik and her daughter Libena. Here I have the date at which Kubis and Gabcik came to us: it was 10 May 1942. My memory had put it at the beginning of the month. They left towards the end of May.

There was one other man who knew they were living with us and that was Uncle Hajsky—Zelenka, the schoolmaster. And it was he who said that we should never mention them to anyone at all, apart from Madame Moravcova.

Zelenka–Hajsky was wholly dedicated to the nation's cause, a man filled with courage and hope. He watched over these young men with extraordinary care and anxious kindness; he not only saw to housing them but he also looked after all their needs. I remember one day he came to our flat, and smiling broadly he brought a little parcel out of his briefcase. My wife opened it— pork chops! Just imagine that, in wartime. Zelenka said the young men liked them and that my wife should cook them with cumin seeds. Sometimes we used to talk a little, but he never said that he was looking after other parachutists, yet there were others living in Dejvice, our district. It was only after the war that we learnt about them—a confirmation of his exemplary prudence.

Gabcik and Kubis, in their turn, were very fond of Zelenka–Hajsky, and they did not disguise their gratitude. They felt they could rely on him entirely, and Gabcik was particularly attached to him—it appears that Zelenka upheld him when important decisions were to be made.

Gabcik was an interesting man: rather short, powerful, quick in his movements. He had brown eyes and brown hair brushed back. His lightfooted, easy way of walking made me think of a dancer. He told us his name was Zdenek Vyskocil and he showed us an identity card with his photograph and the same name. He talked quickly, speaking in Czech; but as I had taught for three years in Slovakia I recognized his accent, particularly by the length of his syllables. After the war I wrote to his father, who lived in Slovakia, and he sent me the personal account that his son had drawn up in London in 1941. At that time he was in the infantry and he was asking to be transferred to the Czech air force in England. In this account Gabcik wrote:

I was born on 8 April 1912 at Poluvsie in the district of Zilina. Trade: fitter. I went through primary school at Rajeske Teplice; then four classes of upper primary school and two in the technical apprenticeship school at Kovarov, in the district of Milevsko. On 1 October 1932 I was drafted into the 14th Regiment at Kosice: I passed out of the non-commissioned officers' school at Presov with distinction. Having finished my obligatory military service with the rank of corporal I stayed in the Czechoslovak army as a regular non-commissioned officer. After three years I was transferred at my own request to the Zilina military factories.

After the occupation of the Czechoslovak Republic I was posted to No. 5 depot at Skalka, near Trencin, as storekeeper. Having spoiled mustard gas by pouring acid over it and having also inflicted damage on German army property, I was obliged to escape from Slovakia on 1 May 1939.

I left for Cracow in Poland, where I joined the Czechoslovak military group. From Cracow I was transferred to France, where I joined the Foreign Legion. After the declaration of war I was drafted into the Czechoslovak army that had been formed in France. At the front I had the rank of sergeant attached to the officer commanding the machine-gun platoon. In the course of the Czechoslovak unit's first action at the front I became the commander of the platoon. I reached England with the last convoy that left France. On 15 December I was promoted company sergeant-major. On 28 October 1941 I was awarded the Czechoslovak military cross. At present I am attached to the officer commanding the 3/1 Company.

In civil life my trade is fitter. I have asked for my transfer because I think I could make better use of my technical qualifications in the air force. I said to myself that I too should like to help the Czechoslovak cause as much as I could, to contribute to our victory and to that of the Allies.

In making this request I understand that my admission to the air force will mean the loss of all the advantages arising from my

service in No. 3 company of the First Infantry Battalion ...
I should be glad if I could carry out the duties of gunner. For all
these reasons I beg you to give my request a favourable reception.

Such was the request of Josef Gabcik, infantry sergeant-major
in the Czechoslovak army in England. Subsequently he went
through a parachute course; and finally he became a gunner too.

I should also add that Josef Gabcik had two brothers and a
sister. His father was poor—for a while he had worked in America,
and he had returned just before the declaration of the Second
World War. After Josef's escape his family had no news of him.
He was very cautious, and even during his stay in Prague he
never wrote to his people.

And what of Kubis?

He had papers in the name of Jaroslav Navratil. He was
somewhat taller than Gabcik, perhaps two or three inches. He
had broad shoulders, a rather large head, and very kind eyes.
A well-built man who held himself very straight. His speech was
slower than Gabcik's, almost hesitant. I was ill and I had to stay
in bed the day they arrived. They came to my bedside, and at the
first words that Kubis spoke I said, "You are a Moravian!" He
was astonished that I should have detected it. "And from the
region of Trebic, too," I went on.

He nodded, saying that another man had already guessed
where he came from by his pronunciation. How could I have
failed to recognize him, since I too am a Moravian?

Straightaway we agreed on what we should say in case of an
arrest. I told my sons that our guests were the children of distant
relations who had gone to the Argentine long ago, and that I was
their uncle. I advised the parachutists never to return to the house
together, to signal first by whistling an agreed tune, and to give
two rings on the bell. In case of immediate danger they would be
warned by the window curtain being in a certain position; and
if possible we should put another sign at the front door.

They slept in my room, Gabcik on a cot and Kubis on the sofa.
All they had were their briefcases and the clothes they were
wearing. In the briefcases they brought their pyjamas and some
weapons, nothing else.

As soon as they arrived they asked to see over the whole flat: they looked at every detail of every room, paying particular attention to the doors, windows and skylights. They looked pleased, and one of them observed, "It would be easy, out through here, even with no rope."

Everything they did was orderly. Before going to bed at night they carefully arranged their clothes on the chairs beside their beds so as to be able to seize their weapons with a single movement in case of need.

When they came they asked us to wake them at a quarter to six every morning. They said that at six either the one or the other went off in search of information. I do not know what it was about—whether it was intelligence or orders. In those days we were living in Prague-Dejvice, near the Castle. Perhaps they went to see one of the people who worked there to hear news of Heydrich. They might also have gone to see Captain Opalka. He too had found shelter in our district, and it appears that he was the commanding officer, that is to say the head of all the parachutists in Prague at that time. But an event that occurred immediately before the killing goes against this supposition. My wife told Kubis and Gabcik that while they were out Opalka had come to see them. He had mistaken the floor and had very nearly gone to look for them the next storey up. Gabcik became very angry: it was the first time I had ever seen him in that state. "Why does he come here?" he cried. "I've told him I don't want any visits. Let him look after himself; I know perfectly well what I have to do."

From this it may be inferred that the young men were not under Opalka's orders; but these are only my inferences. I think Gabcik did not want anyone to interfere with what he was doing. He had been given his orders and he wanted to carry them out, whatever the cost. Besides, Opalka's group had only been dropped towards the end of March, that is to say three months after Anthropoid—the Gabcik and Kubis team.

The young men took turns with their morning duty, Kubis one day, Gabcik the next. Kubis would wake his friend and say with a laugh, "Today it's the little one's turn." This never irritated

Gabcik. They were real friends, and they shared everything they were given.

The day before the killing there was a meeting at our flat, with a great deal of animated discussion. Zelenka–Hajsky came, then a man I did not know. It was probably the boys themselves who opened the door for Valcik or Opalka. After the talk our young men seemed anxious and on edge. Zdenek, that is to say Gabcik, went out at once: Jarka–Kubis stayed in the flat. A few moments later Libena, the Fafeks' daughter, came with some cigarettes for her fiancé. "He's not here," said Kubis.

Libena hesitated for a moment and then gave them to Kubis, saying, "Listen, Jenick, you mustn't smoke them all." That was how we learnt that Kubis' real name was Jan.

Gabcik and Kubis smoked, but never in our house. This was out of consideration for my state of health and because they did not want the smell of cigarettes in the flat: none of our family smoked and if a visitor were to come or if there were an unexpected check on the household the smell might give their presence away.

It was a strange evening, that of the day before the attack. Kubis looked out of the window at the Castle and said, "I'd like to know how things will be tomorrow, just at this time."

"Why, what's going to happen?" asked my wife.

"Oh, nothing, Madame," replied Gabcik.

A little later Kubis took his grenades out of his pocket and did something to them. After the killing he told us he had shortened or removed the metal bands so that they should explode in time. Kubis was a calm, thoughtful man. The next morning, 27 May 1942, he saw my son Lubos anxiously going over and over the subjects for his school-leaving examination. He said to him, "Take it easy, Lubos; you will pass—you will certainly pass. And tonight we'll all have a party to celebrate your success."

Gabcik was at the door; he turned and whispered, "Don't worry if we are not back as usual: we have a great many friends and maybe we shall stay with them."

And so they went out. Earlier than usual. In the street they looked up at the windows of our flat for a moment. A few minutes later my son left too, to sit for his examination. The sun rose and it looked as though it were going to be a beautiful day.

"Where are our young men going today?" I wondered, remembering their strange meeting of yesterday. All the time they had been with us, nothing of that kind had ever happened in our flat.

My wife went out shopping. I walked slowly through all the rooms: yes, everything was in order—not the least sign of our guests. I stopped in front of my bookcase, looking at the rows of volumes: there was Bezruc, with his poetry of revolt, next to the dreamer Sramek and Tolstoy and my beloved philosophers, my favourite Tacitus.

On the pavement below I caught sight of our neighbour, the one who knew all about our young men. That day Gabcik was wearing an overcoat borrowed from Marcel, his son.

At the moment I looked out of the window the young men were probably already waiting at the Liben turning; but nobody had told us about it. And the hands of the clock were moving towards the hour of the killing.

22

The chemistry teacher's account: 3

(Ladislav Vanek)

THE OPERATION, that is to say the killing, should have taken place on 28 October 1941. But this was impossible, because the parachutist who was supposed to cooperate with Gabcik was injured in training. During that period the Czechoslovak government in London radioed a message to the political headquarters of the resistance in Prague asking for full preparations for the attack, and for a national rising; but I only heard of this later.

In the autumn of 1941, then. But the political situation in the Protectorate was wholly unfavourable for action of that kind.

In January 1942 I met Kubis for the first time, and when I was talking to him I learnt, either by chance or by deduction, that he and another man had come to carry out the operation. Kubis told us that there were several teams of parachutists in the Protectorate, and that "Jozka," the commanding officer, wanted to see me. The first meeting with Bartos, who used this cover-name of Jozka, took place at Captain Prochazka's flat at 23 Kodanska, Prague-Vrsovice, in the middle of February 1942.

I had several other interviews with Bartos. At that time Valcik was already in Prague, and Kubis and Gabcik were actively preparing to carry out the order received from London. We talked the matter over, and it seemed to us a very perilous undertaking. We were of the opinion that the Nazis would take their revenge—that they would punish the Czech nation. But what could we do? The young men asserted that their mission was perfectly clear: they were to organize and carry out the killing. They were soldiers, so they could not find fault with the killing, or discuss its point or lack of point, its timeliness or its untimeliness. At the most, they might think it over; but they could do nothing against an order they had been given. But what if the Nazis were to react with hideous atrocities?

It was towards the end of April, if I remember rightly, that I sent a message to Bartos through Valcik, saying I should like to see him in Prague. I wanted to explain the situation to him, study all the problems, and state our views on the subject. I hoped he would understand us.

Again we met at Captain Prochazka's flat—according to my recollection it was on 26 April. Opalka had come back from Plzn and Bartos was able to talk to him too.

Gabcik came with Bartos. Our discussion was very tense and urgent. I said that in our opinion neither the moment nor the situation was favourable for the attack. "Just picture to yourself what will happen afterwards: the Germans will arrest our people, torture them, kill them."

Bartos listened to what I had to say without a word; then, having considered, he agreed. At this point Gabcik spoke. "The killing is necessary," he said, "and for my part I shall obey the orders I have been given."

Bartos spoke to him sharply; Gabcik left; and Bartos and I decided to prepare a radio message for London in which we should explain our views on the killing. It was to be a dispatch drawn up by Bartos, and he was to let me have a copy.

The message ran roughly as follows:

At the request of the Jindra movement, which you authenticated on the night of 30 April to 1 May and which is in contact with one of our liaison agents, we send you this dispatch, upon which we are in entire agreement. Judging from the place and from the preparations made by Ota and Zdenek we believe that although they do not speak of it they are now getting ready for the killing of H. This attack would not be of the least value to the Allies and it would have serious and unforeseeable consequences. It would threaten not only hostages and political prisoners with shocking reprisals but also thousands of ordinary people. Its consequences might include the complete suppression of all underground organizations. It would then be impossible for the resistance to be useful to the Allies. For all these reasons we beg you to give orders through Silver A for the killing not to take place. Danger in delay: give the order at once. If for international political reasons the action is nevertheless essential, pick another person to be killed.

As "another person" we thought of Emmanuel Moravec, minister in the Protectorate government.

This dispatch was sent to London at the beginning of May—perhaps on the fourth. I felt calmer once it had gone, being sure that London would understand our position.

But I was still worried, and I thought it would be useful for this dispatch to have the support of the UVOD, the central home resistance organization. I spoke to Arnost Heidrich, one of its chiefs; I told him of our reasons; I lent him the text of our message, and he drew up another dispatch in almost identical terms. That is why even now some historians believe that it was the same message. In fact there were two.

What were the differences between them? In the text written by Bartos the parachutists Ota and Zdenek are named; the UVOD message uses the pseudonyms Strnad and Vyskocil. And the last passage is different. It was Bartos who added it, as he told me later, so that the Anthropoid team, Gabcik and Kubis, should not be left without a mission. The first text ran: "If for international political reasons the action is nevertheless essential, pick another person to be killed." The UVOD message ended: "If a gesture is required for international political reasons, choose a Quisling: E.M. for example."

The UVOD message was sent by the same transmitter, Libuse, about 12 May 1942. I do not know who passed the text to Bartos; neither do I know which member of the UVOD was in touch with him at that period.

There is one passage in the 4 May dispatch that may not be understood: "which you authenticated on the night of 30 April to 1 May." This is the explanation: the Jindra resistance movement had acquired many new members at that time; the movement had to be reorganized and confidence established. At our request the BBC had broadcast an agreed phrase or watchword in its Czech-language programme. In this way the new members could feel sure that everything was in order and that our resistance abroad knew about our work.

We waited with the utmost impatience for the reply to our messages. When I look back on it now I see we acted with the best possible intentions but that we forgot one important factor—London was dealing with matters and events far more important than ours. What weight could a request or a warning from a resistance movement in the Protectorate have in London's eyes?

Since I had no means of establishing direct contact with London, it was impossible for me to insist upon an answer. And all we could do in that critical period before the attack was to wait, wait.

But Gabcik had not the least desire to wait; and he had no patience either. He was convinced that we were afraid; he did not understand the reasons behind our request for a postponement of the killing. Perhaps this was in his character; perhaps in his deep belief in the necessity for carrying out orders. He had been given an order, so why should he dilly-dally?

As I told you earlier, according to the first plan the attack was to take place near Panenske Brezany, where Heydrich lived. The village runs along a valley, with one castle at the top and another at the bottom. Heydrich and his family lived in the lower castle; it was surrounded by a large park with fine trees in it. In the nearby forest he had laid out a race course: in short, he was setting up his racing stable in the Protectorate.

He went to Prague every day. His car came to fetch him at the castle gates; then it drove through the village, climbed the hill, passed the second castle, which also belonged to Heydrich, and then went through a dense copse about a hundred yards in depth before reaching the fields. There an escort car waited for Heydrich's and drove with him as far as Prague Castle. The road is straight, with a few rows of pear or plum trees running along it; a little farther on it forks and joins the main road to the city.

The parachutists had exact information about the movements of Heydrich and his chauffeur. They often went to Panenske

Brezany, and they chose this little wood for their attack on the Protector's car.

Gabcik heard that we had asked London to change his orders, and he persuaded Kubis to act without our agreement and before the arrival of the answer to our message. About 15 May 1942 I met Opalka in the evening, and he told me that Gabcik was determined to carry out the order at any cost. I grew angry, saying that we were waiting for London's reply and that if the order were changed ... "No," I said to Opalka, "they cannot carry out the attack like that. They must be persuaded to go on waiting."

Later Opalka told me he had bicycled to Panenske Brezany the next morning and that he had persuaded the young men not to undertake any action. You may ask why Opalka did not speak to them in Prague the same evening. Why did he go to Panenske Brezany—a far more dangerous proceeding? There are two possible answers: either he did not know they were living with the Dejvice schoolmaster (and I did not know it either, at that time), or he went there and did not find them at home. But at all events they did listen to him and we went on waiting for London's reply.

It never came. The order was not changed. During the last days of our waiting I had a talk with Zelenka–Hajsky, who told me an interesting thing: Kubis and Gabcik had disclosed that about 20 May they had received a radioed message in a code known only to them. Bartos, who had sent it to them by the Pardubice liaison agent, was unable to decipher it. And it appeared that this message contained a confirmation of the order—that it said the attack on Heydrich was to be carried out.

I never saw this message, and when I asked Zelenka about it later he admitted that he had not seen it either. So I do not know whether it exists, and if it does exist, I do not know its text.

All that remained for us was to take note of it. The intelligence network we had in Prague Castle told us that Heydrich's duties in Bohemia and Moravia were shortly to come to an end; that he would be sent to France; and that on 27 May he would leave for Berlin in a special plane for an interview with Hitler.

Everything showed that the moment for Gabcik and Kubis was coming closer—that it was beyond recall.

The parachutists' preparations reached their final point. A decision had to be made. At a meeting arranged in the Dejvice schoolmaster's flat, where the young men were living, Gabcik stood firmly by his orders: London had not changed them, and therefore he was going to carry out his mission. Zelenka–Hajsky upheld him in his stand. What were the results of this meeting? The date for the attack was fixed: 27 May 1942. Opalka told me the outcome of their discussion—he had not been able to make the parachutists change their minds. Zelenka also spoke to me about it.

Since Heydrich might have valuable and important papers in his briefcase, it was to be seized if possible. Gabcik was to open fire and Kubis to remain in reserve, using his special grenades only in case of absolute necessity, so that the papers in the briefcase should not be destroyed.

The Liben turning was finally chosen as the most suitable place for the attack. The parachutists were to go there by bicycle, leave them, and pick them up again for their escape after the attack.

Valcik was to wait somewhat farther along the turn to signal the coming of Heydrich's car with a mirror. The Protector usually left for Prague Castle fairly early in the morning; but since he had to go to Berlin that day he might set out either earlier or later. This had to be taken into account.

Members of the resistance were posted in the streets by which Gabcik and Kubis were to make their escape after the attack; that is to say the streets of the Kobylisy, Liben, and Karlin districts. It was Piskacek who attended to this. They did not know beforehand what it was about; all they had from Piskacek was a brief note stating where they were to be stationed. Ruzicka, for example, received a scrap of paper saying "Come to the Rokoska corner between 9 and 10 and keep your eyes open. If you see a policeman there, try to attract his attention by asking him some question or by talking to him."

Among our people, Hejl was to be in the middle of the town,

Filipek in the Invalides in Karlin, Oktabec in the Liben Palmovka. Piskacek, Strnad, and Novak were also posted in Liben.

What a beautiful day it was! A perfect May morning. Everything urged one to leave the city and lie in the fresh green grass with one's hands behind one's head, eyes closed against the brilliance of the spring sun.

Reinhard Heydrich (second from right) with SS chief Heinrich Himmler (fourth from right), at Hradčany Castle, Prague, 29 October 1941. (*Camera Press*)

Heydrich (right) and Karl Hermann Frank in the courtyard of Hradčany Castle on the day Heydrich assumed command of the Nazi "Protectorate" in Prague, 28 September 1941. (*Camera Press*)

The last photograph of Heydrich, taken the day before his assassination in May 1942. He is pictured attending a concert at the Wallenstein Palace in Prague with his wife, who was pregnant at the time. *(Camera Press)*

Heydrich's car after the assassination, wrecked by the bomb thrown by Jan Kubis. *(C.T.K.)*

a. Adolf Opalka

b. Jan Kubis

e. Jan Hruby

f. Josef Bublik

c. Josef Gabcik

d. Josef Valcik

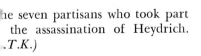

he seven partisans who took part
the assassination of Heydrich.
.T.K.)

g. Jaroslav Svarc

The church of St. Cyril and St. Methodius, where the seven parachutists took refuge after the assassination. *(C.T.K.)*

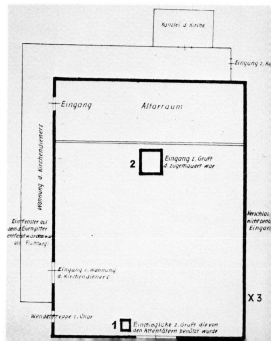

Kanzlei d. Kirche

Eingang z. K

Eingang   Altarraum

Wohnung d. Kirchendieners

2 Eingang z. Gruft
   d. zugemauert war

Ein Fenster aus
dem d. Eisengitter
entfernt worden war
als Fluchtweg

Verschlos.
nicht ben
Eingang

Eingang z. Wohnung
d. Kirchendieners

X 3

Wendeltreppe z. Chor

1 Einstiegluke z. Gruft die von
   den Attentätern benützt wurde

The crypt of St. Cyril and St. Methodius where the partisans hid from the Nazis. The arrow marks the hole through which the partisans entered the crypt. *(C.T.K.)*

Map of the church of St. Cyril and St. Methodius. The entrances to the crypt can be seen as follows: 1) the entrance used by the parachutists and the priest—a hole through which they climbed, using a ladder; 2) the main entrance to the crypt, with the staircase covered by a heavy stone slab; 3) the small window facing the street. *(C.T.K.)*

A mattress blocks the window as the Nazis try to smoke out th
partisans. *(C.T.K.)*

The partisans succeeded in pushing back the hoses with the help of a ladder. Karl Hermann Frank ordered one of the firemen to grab the ladder and the picture shows the moment at which he succeeded in dragging the ladder from the crypt. *(C.T.K.)*

The interior of the crypt after the battle. *(C.T.K.)*

Objects belonging to the partisans, found in the crypt. *(C.T.K.)*

The bodies of the parachutists who committed suicide lie on the sidewalk in front of the church. *(C.T.K.)*

The broken windows of the church after the battle. *(C.T.K.)*

The partisans tried in vain to find an underground passage to escape from the crypt. *(C.T.K.)*

The identification of bodies on the pavement outside the church. The man marked by an arrow is Karel Curda, the parachutist who betrayed his comrades. *(C.T.K.)*

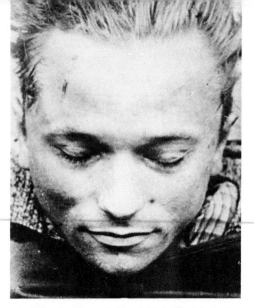

The bodies of Josef Gabcik (above)
and Jan Kubis (below), the killers
of Heydrich. *(C.T.K.)*

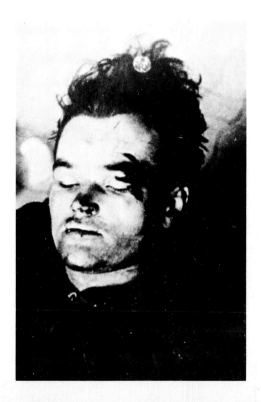

The SS group responsible for the capture of the partisans, photographed near the church. *(C.T.K.)*

In September 1942, a military tribunal in Prague sentenced to death the priests who had helped the partisans. *(C.T.K.)*

Heydrich's last journey through Prague. The funeral was held in Berlin. *(Camera Press)*

23

𝕿𝖍𝖊 𝖏𝖔𝖚𝖗𝖓𝖊𝖞

(*The author*)

HE FINISHED his breakfast and stood up. Tall and thin; high cheekbones; deep-sunk eyes aslant. He pushed away the newspapers that he had read before the meal—they were brought from Prague every day.

He took a few steps and looked out of the window; the big Mercedes—an open sports model—had just arrived under the castle porch. "Klein is prompt," he thought, looking at his watch. It was a few minutes past nine.

The big garden and enormous trees surrounding the house were still wet with dew. "At home," he thought, "there were magnificent old trees by the high school." Home meant Halle an der Saale: he was born there in 1904, and went to school there. Ever since his youth he had adored military uniforms and giving orders. After the First World War he had enlisted as a volunteer; then later he had transferred into the navy. Bohemia had nothing but lakes, alas. Lord, how many things he had missed here. Klein, the chauffeur, in his SS Oberscharführer's uniform was standing there at ease by the car. He could go on waiting: Heydrich had to get his papers ready and say good-bye to his wife and children.

The morning sun lit up the leaves and the lawn; round the great park gates the dew was drying off. The guard was relieved, the tramp of soldiers sounded on the sanded walk.

"Where is Klaus? Where are Heide and Zilke?" he wondered. And aloud he called, "Klaus! Klaus!"

Heydrich waited for a moment, then with a gesture he moved to his desk; he looked through various papers, took his briefcase and thrust some documents into it. Once again he looked round the room and at his desk so as to forget nothing. He ought to have been at the Castle already. Where was Lina?

Lina. When he remembered her, in his mind's eye he saw a slim woman. She used sometimes to wear riding breeches in those days: she was young then and he was a lieutenant in the navy of the Reich. Now she had borne him three children, and presently there would be a fourth. He ought to forbid her to go riding.

"*Vater!*" His daughter Zilke was calling him. She looked in through the open door and caught sight of him. Heydrich took up his briefcase and in that voice of his which sent a shiver down one's back he said, "Where are you all?"

"Outside. In the garden. Herbert has been showing us how to load a revolver."

He took her hand and they left the room. "Have you seen your mother?"

"She's waiting below."

They walked down the stairs. Klein came to attention, but Heydrich took no notice of him; he was looking for his wife. There she was on the lawn, looking closely at a huge ash. "These trees are completely useless," she said. "Have them cut down."

"I'm going. What have you got against them?"

"We could plant fruit trees here and sell the wood of the others."

"Don't worry about it now. I must go. Where are Klaus and Heide?"

At that moment they came running. The Heydrich family went off for a stroll in the park. Klein sprang to attention again: Herbert Wagnitz, Heydrich's senior warrant officer, said something to him. A second car pulled up at the entrance. The castle was a big square building with a balcony and a little balustrade. From the nearby village one could hear the sound of geese, the clucking of hens; but the village square was empty—at moments like these all the people vanished behind their doors and their closed windows.

At moments like these. Moments like these because the Protector was about to leave his castle. But just now he was walking about the lawn where his children had been playing. Klaus wore shorts and the dagger of the Hitlerjugend in his belt. Lina followed them slowly, slashing the high grass and trying to cut off the heads of the daisies with the riding crop that she always carried. The sun shone and Klein, the chauffeur, began to feel hot. The Mercedes stood there, gleaming in the sun. The clock above the balustrade had just struck ten. Ordinarily they should have been on the road by now. Or at the Castle. At last the Heydrichs came back. The park gates opened wide.

"All ready?" The SS Oberscharführer clicked his heels. Heydrich got in beside the driver and nodded. The car moved off, gliding smoothly through the gates; the sentry sprang to attention, the Mercedes turned left onto the road and here were the first houses of the village. Heydrich set his briefcase on his knees.

The road was empty. Having run through the village it climbed a hill, turned, passed across a little plain, turned again, reached the second castle and then plunged into the forest.

The sound of the leaves was like music. How good it smelt, the scent of spring and greenness. A few little yellow flowers dotted the roadside; the trees were still a tender green.

The car ran between the fields. Klein was silent, his eyes fixed on the road: he was expectant. But Heydrich was in no mood for conversation. He looked at the trees along the road, all white with blossom: the first flowers were beginning to fall on the grass. Then he opened his briefcase and leafed through his papers.

The car turned on to the main road, running faster now. A few old men sitting in front of the houses got up and vanished indoors as soon as they saw the big dark Mercedes approaching in the distance.

"We are late." Klein nodded. "When shall we be at the Castle?"

"At ten-fifty, Herr Obergruppenführer."

"Drive faster." He loved speed.

The trees along the road sped by, merging into a grey line, green at the top; and over it all the sky was blue. The minute hand of his watch was on the quarter: fifteen minutes past ten.

"I told you to drive faster. I don't want to have to say it again." His voice had grown sharp. Klein bowed his head. Klein always bowed his head—he was all obedience.

At this speed one could no longer read the names of the villages on the signposts. Sperling, Zdib, Unter-Habern: clumsy German versions of Czech names. Houses, trees, and the empty sky raced away behind them.

The Protector was on his way. The Protector was on his way to the castle of Prague.

He was thirty-eight and at the height of his power—men trembled at the sound of his name. The houses along the road were closer together; now they were a continuous line and the fields gave way to little gardens all brilliant with the cheerful flowers of spring; green hedges or railings painted white or blue; and down there, rising above the hollow, rose a smoky haze—the city of Prague.

Prag-Kobilis, said the signpost, giving the German name for the Kobylisy district. Heydrich sat straighter. He stretched and looked appreciatively at the pure blue sky. He thought with real pleasure of the flight to Berlin. The low houses grew closer and closer together—here and there one with an upper storey. The road became a street, a badly-surfaced street with holes that jolted the car.

Perhaps he was travelling along this road for the last time. The Führer had once spoken of the possibility of his being moved, probably to France. Yes: he would be able to set things in order there, too. He would know for sure this afternoon. What about Himmler and Bormann? How would they receive him in Berlin? He glanced at his briefcase.

Now Klein slowed down: he had to drive more carefully here. Sometimes a cyclist darted from a side street, an old woman made as though to step off the pavement, a little boy or girl ran straight across. Klein knew the road well—in a hundred yards he would have to turn to the right. He must brake and slow down to twelve miles an hour and take the sharp corner. He looked at the speedometer: the needle still showed twenty-five. Gently he took his foot off the accelerator; passed a streetcar; there was one car in front of them, but apart from that nothing, nothing anywhere. Leaning against a tree a young man was combing his hair and playing with a little pocket mirror—how it gleamed. You could make signals with it for fun. "We did that too, when we were boys," reflected Klein. "We used to flash into the little girls' eyes, and how we laughed when they got angry."

And here was the corner: the same as every other day.

Just as Heydrich's car went into the turn a streetcar came in the other direction, ringing its bell: its halt was at the crossroads, and it pulled up. A few people got out: a woman was about to cross the road, but at the last moment she changed her mind and stopped in the middle to let the Protector's car go by. The trolley slowly moved off: Klein had to slow down again.

A splendid May day. In the gardens of the suburban houses the lilacs were in full bloom, and there to the left a gardener's flower beds were a blaze of colour.

At this instant Klein suddenly caught sight of several men standing motionless on the pavement on the right-hand side of the road. All at once one of them began to run across the road. "Hell," exclaimed Klein. "He might have set about it earlier." His foot pressed hard: the brakes screamed. Heydrich looked angrily at his chauffeur. But before he could open his mouth something happened that neither had expected.

A young man dashed from the right-hand pavement and leapt into the road a few yards ahead of the Mercedes, which was already in the turn. He flung his raincoat aside: Heydrich gave a start—the man had a weapon in his hand. Klein gripped the wheel harder: should he accelerate, knock the man down? If only someone would tell him what to do. A hundredth part of a second and Klein swerved towards the pavement; but the man aimed carefully and Heydrich knew—yes, he was quite certain the automatic was pointing straight at his chest.

Murder?

The sweet scent of the lilacs: Klein opened his mouth. It was thirty-one minutes, perhaps thirty-two minutes past ten: but who troubles to count the minutes when one second means life or death and this fellow is aiming at Heydrich's chest?

Gabcik pressed the trigger.

24

The turning

(*The author*)

THEY WALKED fast that morning, after they had left the house where the Dejvice schoolmaster lived. "We have a great deal to do," said Josef Gabcik.

The sky above their heads was light blue, pure, cloudless. They took the streetcar at the stop near the Dejvice level crossing. People were hurrying to work, and in the streetcar they read books or newspapers. Jan found a place and Josef sat opposite him. They no longer spoke.

For a long time now they had known just what they should do on this day. They knew every step and every movement they would have to carry out. They had briefcases in their hands, and Gabcik folded his raincoat carefully over his knees.

The streetcar moved slowly. Kubis looked at his watch. They had to cross almost the whole city to reach Zizkov. At last they arrived at the garage, took their bicycles from Janacek's place, bade him good morning and asked him what he was going to repair that day. Janacek knew the two young men well: sometimes, when they came to take their bicycles they used to chat with him, being interested in cars; but that morning they were in a hurry.

They rode away from the garage. Just as though they were going to work. Then they went to Vysocany to see Madame Khodlova. The day before they had called on her brother, Jaroslav Smrz. They had made an appointment with him for today.

They fixed their briefcases to the handlebars. They were

carrying two bombs in one of them and an automatic Sten gun in the other, hidden under some grass in case of an unexpected superficial check.

Mama Khodlova was surprised. They only said a few words— thank you for all you have done: we often think of you: you have been so kind.

"You haven't come to say good-bye, surely?"

"Oh no, Mama," replied Kubis cheerfully. "We'll drop in and see you again soon. Maybe even today: will you be at home?"

"Why, of course. Do come."

They left, remounted their bicycles and continued their journey. Valcik was waiting for them at the streetcar stop at the bottom of the turning.

"Any news?"

"No. Opalka is up there already. I've got my mirror and I'm on my way."

Near the stop there was the Bulkova hospital. Girls got out of the streetcar with their coats over their shoulders: under the coats their nurse's uniforms could be seen.

The clock was just about to strike nine. They reached the turning.

There is an important crossroads here. The downhill road running southwards from Panenske Brezany to the centre of Prague forks at this point: to the right it carries on down to the Vltava; to the left it slopes away to the district of Liben.

Every day, Heydrich's car took this right-hand turn and drove on towards the bridge. The corner makes a sharp angle, and the visibility is still further reduced by a hedge and some trees.

Kubis and Gabcik stopped near the hedge. Gabcik leant against the low garden wall. Kubis remained standing on the pavement to watch the passing cars. They fell silent.

They were a few yards from each other. Shielding it with his folded raincoat Gabcik carefully drew out his Sten gun, hidden up until now in his briefcase. He knew all the motions by heart— could carry them out with his eyes closed: he knew exactly what screw to tighten, how to load the weapon. The grass got in the way, tangling between his fingers. Why had he put it there? There was no need for it.

Kubis held his briefcase in his hand. It contained two special grenades, two little bombs. He would not need them, he knew; you could be dead certain of Josef with his Sten. But if by some chance. There were countless chances that might cut across their plan, so carefully, so scrupulously worked out. Heydrich might have his escort with him, the escort in another car. If that were to happen, Kubis was to look after the second car. If Heydrich was travelling alone, Kubis was only here in reserve. He felt a certain envious feeling towards Josef. He did not hold it against him—they were friends—but in a corner of his heart he said, "How I'd like to be in his place, with a Sten under my raincoat." He knew just what he would do. He would lean against the post and the moment the dark car with its little swastika flags began to turn the corner he would leap out in front of it and open fire. But he was only waiting here as a reserve, a safety measure. He would have to stand and watch the whole thing, and perhaps his being here would be pointless. Just stand there, without being able to do the least thing.

Were they drawing attention to themselves? No: people were coming and going, and no one seemed to be taking any notice.

How the time dragged! Kubis could not bear it. He wiped his forehead.

In the old days, when he had worked at the Vielmovice brickyard, he had been as hot as he was now. He worked close to the kiln, and his hands were all cracked and split. The worst was when they had to empty the kiln. The bricks were still hot and they burned; he covered his hands with rags, but nothing was any good. And the dust! He had it in his hair, in his eyelashes, it turned his skin whitish and all rough.

His father had been right when he told him the brickyard was a cruel, hard job and that he would do better to take up his own trade. "You'll be under cover, in a room with doors and windows: what better could you ask? Working in the brickyard, you'll wear yourself out in the sun or the rain, and all for a starvation wage."

His father was a cobbler. Kubis could see him sitting there forever on a low chair near the window with pairs of down-at-heel shoes all round him and the whole house smelling of cobbler's wax. To begin with he had liked that smell; but then the older he grew the more he hated it. When his mother died his father married again, and they moved to a new house. In the end Kubis had several half-brothers and half-sisters, as well as his own.

It was better on the land. He had worked for a good many farmers and he knew how to plough, reap, tend the threshing machine, look after cattle; but then later his father decided to go back to Vielmovice and there was no farm work to be had there, only the brickyard.

Kubis darted a questioning look. Gabcik understood its meaning: he too knew that Heydrich should have been here long ago, but what could they do?

"We've got to wait: he must come."

"But what if he's taken another road?"

"Impossible. He has to go to the Castle, they're waiting for him there. It's only when he's been to the Castle that he goes on to the airfield. Go on, get back to your place."

Kubis went back. He sat hesitantly on the low wall, trying not to attract too much attention. A van went by and the driver glanced cheerfully at the two young men. A No. 14 streetcar stopped just by them; then another, a No. 3.

Kubis' patience was ebbing away. Maybe he ought to count the streetcars as they went by. How was all this going to end? They had talked it over the day before with Gabcik. Obviously, they were risking their heads. They would like to get away alive, of course, but...

Who could tell what might happen? If Heydrich's escort did come with him, that was the end: it was death. They would have to run, leap on the bicycles leaning against the wall not far away, and pedal hard, hard, hard. But Josef was a crack shot. In the training course he had always been among the best. He was a cool-headed, deliberate man. When he opened fire, no one would be left alive in the car. He glanced at Josef, whose face was tilted to the sun, as though he meant to tan himself.

The same van moved over the crossroads.

It was past ten. Ordinarily Heydrich should have been in sight long ago. He was late today. Kubis broke a twig from the hedge. There was said to be an experimental institute in the middle of the garden. Once again he examined the road: he saw Valcik leaning against a tree, admiring the blue sky. Oh, this waiting. On the opposite pavement there was Opalka, walking up and down. He pretended not to know his companions.

Kubis felt his briefcase: yes, the bombs were there. Would he need them? He had checked them yesterday evening, and Gabcik had cleaned his Sten. Now he was holding it under his raincoat: his hands were damp and he felt a drop of sweat run down his forehead. Ten past ten. Opalka crossed the road. Kubis too joined Gabcik. "What do you think about it?"

"Suppose Valcik signals him this minute? Get back to your place. Quick!"

"And what if he doesn't come?"

"He'll come. He must come," said Opalka.

Kubis sighed and moved off. He was wearing a dark striped suit and he was hot, very hot. His brother Rudolf, who lived at Trebic, had made it for him; Kubis had gone to see him not long ago. Another trolley went by; some people got out. Two men walked towards the entrance to the experimental institute, the others towards the nearby hospital.

Twenty-nine minutes past ten.

Kubis looked at Valcik and all at once he saw a flash. Yes, Valcik had straightened from the tree and he was signalling with the mirror in his hand. Kubis felt his heart give a leap. No, no: he must stay calm. He turned towards Gabcik and Opalka. "He's coming!"

Gabcik smiled—a sardonic smile. He looked at his coat: everything was in order. Then he remembered a forgotten detail. He had borrowed a beret and put it in the briefcase. A pity: he would have liked to put it on now so that no one should see the colour of his hair. But it was too late. Kubis leant against the telegraph post: yes, at that moment a car appeared in the turning. A woman was sitting by the driver: Kubis stared at her hard. "She has no hat!"

If he could cry "She has no hat," it would mean that today Heydrich was travelling without his escort.

"Josef, look!"

Gabcik saw it too: he nodded. In this instant nothing mattered. He forgot the fear and the hours and days that had gone before. He knew just one thing—Heydrich was coming! At last he was coming.

A streetcar rumbled up from the direction of the bridge. Was this a piece of bad luck? The stop was close at hand: there would be a lot of people. Opalka came running across the street. Kubis leant against the post. It was half past ten. The Mercedes was there; and inside it, next to the driver, Heydrich. Heydrich the tyrant, with his expressionless face and his fishlike eyes. At that instant Gabcik leapt into the road, flung aside his raincoat, and gripping his Sten gun he aimed straight at Heydrich. He looked into the fish-eyes: he was cool, sure of himself: it was a second that lasted forever.

The killing!

The car was three yards, two yards from him. The chauffeur was staring—he did not understand what was happening yet. Desperately he grasped the wheel: there was nowhere for him to escape. And at that moment Gabcik pressed the trigger.

Nothing. Silence.

The Mercedes ran on; Heydrich reached for the pistol in his belt. He was very pale, his eyes fixed on the man standing there in the road, rigid, astonished at having a jammed Sten gun in his hands.

Kubis! It was his turn!

He moved with lightning speed: whipped open his briefcase, took a bomb. He felt the familiar shape in his hand, dropped the case with the other in it, and threw the grenade.

The little object soared into the air like a bird. Gabcik, recovering from his total shock, threw down his useless weapon and fled. Kubis looked up at the sun and the blue sky: yes, the bomb was flying. This lasted no more than a second: the car ran on, moving ten yards, twelve yards farther off. Heydrich rose in his seat, shouted something to Klein; and the sun shone and still the people in the street suspected nothing at all.

Thirty-two minutes past ten. The little object fell. The explosion.

The attempt on the life of the acting-Reichsprotektor, Reinhard Heydrich, had been carried out.

25

The first woman's evidence

(*Marie Sochmanova*)

I'VE PLENTY of time, I said to myself; all I have to do is to get there at eleven so they'll take me before noon. I was going to the Bulkova hospital for my mud baths; my rheumatism was giving me pain and this mud was a great relief. They covered me with it up to the neck, and very odd it looked, I thought. But what was I doing on that 27 May 1942? Why, yes, I remember now: that day too I was going to Bulkova.

I had to stand in the streetcar—it was a No. 3—and we were jerked about all the way from the Vltava. I thought about my baths and then about my son Mirek; the day before we had done his arithmetic homework together, and the master might very well give him good marks.

The streetcar went slower and slower up the hill; it really crawled. Then at last we came to the stop and I got out. There, at the big crossroads I generally used to change streetcars; I crossed to the other side and waited for a No. 14, which stops just outside the main gate of the Bulkova. I know very well it's only a little walk, but my rheumatism hurt me and I preferred to take the streetcar.

So I got out and began to cross; then when I'd taken three steps I suddenly saw a car coming round the corner, a car with little flags coming down the hill. "Let it go by," I said to myself; because I could not walk quickly, you see, on account of my rheumatism.

I stopped almost in the middle of the road and waited: the car was ten yards away. The driver looked at me, and I looked at him. On the pavement the other side I saw three men—yes, there were certainly three of them—and all at once one of them began to run across the road towards me, but at the same time he cut straight across the car so it had to brake and this—no, I shan't tell you how old he was or what he looked like—this man just darted across the street and disappeared somewhere behind me. The car slowed down and at that moment the second man there on the pavement jumped out right in front of the hood; he had something in his hand—it was only later that I heard it was a pistol or something of that kind—but the whole thing only lasted an instant, maybe one minute, and then suddenly the third man swung his arm wide and there was a terrible great bang.

There was a great deal of smoke all round me and there was dust and sweepings in my eyes; only it wasn't dust or sweepings either, but the stuffing of the car seats.

I felt a stabbing pain in my right leg. It was dreadful. There was blood running all down my leg and a German jumped out of the car and began firing at these men and then there was another German holding his back and trying to fire too, but he was staggering about and he couldn't manage it. The first German began running, firing at these men and they fired too and then one of them went off on a bicycle towards Liben and the other ran up the hill towards where the car had come from.

As for me, I walked slowly towards the No. 14 stop: I said to myself, "Don't you interfere; it was Germans in that car." I waited at the stop and when my streetcar came along I got into it to go to the hospital—my leg was hurting me dreadfully. There was no longer any question of baths; they gave me an anti-tetanus injection and treated my wound, and they asked me what had happened and I said some Germans had been firing at the crossroads. I rested a while and then went home.

That afternoon I learnt that I had been a witness at an attempt on Heydrich's life and that frightened me, particularly afterwards when the radio said they were looking for an eyewitness of the attack who was a lady and who had been looked after at the Bulkova.

Yes: I had forgotten to tell you it was a bomb splinter that had wounded me. It hurt a great deal, even in the streetcar, and the man had said, "Madame, what's the matter with you?" There was a pool of blood in the streetcar, and the blood came from my wound.

I was afraid of going to the police; I thought they'd forget me. But then they broadcast again on the radio saying the lady wounded during the attack was to go to the Gestapo. I didn't go and at dawn the next Monday, about half past four, there was a ring at the bell; I opened the door and there were two Gestapo men. And they said I had to go with them and why hadn't I come and they had been looking for me. And we went to the Pecek palace—that was the Protectorate Gestapo's place—and they slapped me, saying I belonged to that gang and I was in league with these criminals over the whole thing and I said "But I've got rheumatism and what's more articular rheumatism" and that they ought to look at my appointment card with Dr. Prerovsky who was looking after me and then they'd see I was put down that day, 27 May, for my treatment.

They left me in their prison for six days; they questioned me several times and I always said the same thing. The sixth day they let me go, but I had to sign a paper saying I would never tell anyone what they had asked me or anything they'd done to me during the questioning. I signed the paper, of course, and that was the end of it.

I don't remember anything else now. There were three men on the pavement; then there was the bang; and lying there on the ground there was a briefcase, a coat and something else, and a bicycle.

26

The coal merchant's evidence

(*Jan Zavazal*)

WELL, BOSS, if you want to know, this is how it happened that morning. In my little shop here I sell coal, Kladno and Ostrava briquettes, and that morning I was pulling out my cart and then all of a sudden *boom*, like a clap of thunder.

Hey, I said, I'm frightened but I'm going to see what's going on. Up there a car was turning the corner and a man had thrown a grenade or something like that at it; a second man had meant to fire but the gun hadn't gone off, they told me. One of the boys had jumped on a bike and escaped, but the other had run this way. My wife was scared and she went and hid in the shop; but I stayed there on the pavement. This boy ran along Na Zapalci with Heydrich's chauffeur after him, both of them firing at one another like in a western. Here, at this crossroads, the young man stopped; he probably didn't know where he was any more. Then suddenly he saw the butcher's shop. I must tell you about this butcher's shop. It was a little place and you went into it down some steps. The butcher was called Brauner: he had a relation who worked for the Gestapo. And this young man, all out of breath, saw the shop and darted in. How could he have told the butcher was a fascist?

Brauner came out of the shop and looked round and at this moment up comes Heydrich's chauffeur and a carter with him. They say the chauffeur had seen him in the street and forced him at pistol-point to run after the young man along with him. Brauner pointed to the shop, to tell them he was inside.

And now it all began again. The chauffeur sheltered behind a little post in the garden and blazed away like mad. But the man hidden in the shop opened fire too and he fired better than Heydrich's chauffeur because the next moment the chauffeur fell, holding his leg. He had a bullet in his thigh. The young man came out of the shop and started running again with the carter and Brauner the butcher after him—the chauffeur had given Brauner his revolver, but he didn't know how to use it.

And the boy ran along this street towards me: I made myself small. A young man, good-looking, his hair dishevelled: he went right by me and vanished between the houses. They sent for me to the Gestapo afterwards and there they said to me, "Why didn't you catch hold of him, you bastard?" and I said to them all I had was my bare hands and he had a revolver.

27

The second woman's evidence

(*Milada Matulova*)

IT WAS A marvellous spring day with a lovely clear blue sky and everywhere the scent of flowers. My husband had gone to the office and I took a collection of poems and went into the garden to sunbathe. We lived not far from the corner where the attack took place.

I sat down in the middle of the trees and the flowering shrubs, and I dozed a little; the poems were odd—I could not really see what they meant—and I was warm in the sun. It was lovely: here at least you could feel you might forget the war and all the unhappiness it had brought us.

And then at that moment I heard a great explosion: it brought me straight back to reality. I jumped up and ran out of the garden onto the pavement—a woman is always curious—but I saw nothing: no smoke, no fire.

In the turning, at the corner, there is an experimental institute; so my first idea was that there had been an accident there. But then I saw a woman who came running from the corner crying "Oh God, oh God! Our Heydrich, our Heydrich." I asked her what had happened and she said there had been an attempt on the Reichsprotektor's life and he was probably dead. A woman who lived in the next-door house said "Thank God."

The next day the Gestapo arrested her whole family and they were all executed for approving of the attack. This woman who told us all about it—she was Heydrich's chauffeur's wife and they lived in the house over the way—went and denounced her.

People were coming and going along our street; up the hill we heard a few shots, but from our place you can't see as far as the corner. At that moment Gabcik came running from the side street. How best to describe him? Rather short, staring eyes, a revolver in his hand pointing in front of him, his tie flying in the wind: he was out of breath. At that time I had no idea of his name, of course, and I didn't know he had taken part in the killing, but that came to my mind at once. His strange look drew your attention. Brauner's butcher's shop was in the street he had just run along, and afterwards people said there had been a positive gun battle between him and Klein, Heydrich's chauffeur.

For a few seconds Gabcik stopped there at the corner of our street and it seemed to me he didn't know where to go on running—he stood for two or three seconds perhaps. He looked up the hill and he must have realized that he was right by the place of the ambush—that he had turned a circle in escaping. Then he set off again, running down the hill along the streetcar tracks. I could still see him as he went round by the inn, but then he vanished among the surrounding gardens.

All what I am telling you now took place in a few minutes. Probably between five and seven. I was trembling, I was so upset: in no mood for poems or sunbathing any more. My morning was spoiled and I didn't know what to do. I went back into the house, dreadfully tense, and I picked a telephone number to tell someone what had happened; and I don't know why, but it was my shoemaker I had at the end of the line. I talked to him without thinking—I was frightened—and later he told me he thought I had gone out of my wits.

And there was another thing. At that time a "half-German" lived in our house. Her son was in Hitler's army, and she was a Nazi sympathizer too. An hour or two after the killing she came back from Liben, where she said she had been buying shoes at Bata's. When she came out of the shop she saw a young man on a bicycle ride up, his face all covered with blood. He left the bicycle outside the shop and hurried off. She waited to see what would happen, and a few minutes later a girl came running for the bicycle and disappeared. This German woman said the man must certainly have been someone who had taken part in the attack and she hurried away to tell the German authorities. The next day the Gestapo came to the house and questioned her about the girl and the bicycle. Later, K. H. Frank had a reward and a medal given to her.

Perhaps it was because of her denunciation that the Nazis learnt about Kubis' escape by way of Liben, his stopping in front of Bata's, and the business about the bicycle. Later they called in all the Liben girls for questioning.

28

The first driver's evidence

(*Karel Duben*)

"OH YOU get lost," I thought; but what could I do? I'd had to stop. I looked around. There by the curb, a Mercedes all knocked about; people staring at it; an accident, maybe. This woman who had stopped me calls out, cross and excited, "There's just been an attack. Here, in this very place."

"An attack?"

"Yes. And you must take the Herr Protektor to the Bulkova hospital."

"Me? But I can't. You can see for yourself the car's full."

"Then you just empty it. Quick. He's wounded."

"You go to hell," I thought; but if I didn't do it they'd arrest me straight away. But then again, driving Heydrich—how do you like that? My friend was sitting next to me; I looked at him; he shrugged. So we got out, precious slow. I had a car of my own, an old Zetka, and in the back we had boxes of sweets. During the war we used to make a kind of drink with sugar and yeast—quite strong it was. The shopkeeper who got us the yeast wanted us to carry his boxes of sweets in exchange. That's why we were going from Troja to Kobylisy, and on the way this bit of bad luck was waiting for us. "Go slow," I whispered to my friend.

He thought the same. We opened the door and began to unload. Like a film in slow motion. Opposite us there was the Mercedes. Right by it, a group of people. Heydrich was leaning against the car. He was pale—holding his side with one hand. A blonde, the one who'd stopped me, was fussing round him, bleating something in German; but he might not have known she was there. I didn't see the boys who brought it off. They escaped right away; but they were brave men. Heydrich, the bastard, had deserved all he got.

We were unloading the boxes when all at once a two-cylinder Tatra came up. A little van. The blonde stopped it too. Maybe she liked the look of it better; anyhow, she told us it would be the Tatra that would take Heydrich to hospital, and we'd better hurry.

What a bit of luck, I thought. What a prime bit of luck. I gave my friend the nod, we reloaded as fast as we could go, and we shot off.

29

The second driver's evidence

(Frantisek Sitta)

It was a diabolical piece of bad luck. In those days I worked for Holan's, the transport firm—had been with them since about 1941. Before that I drove for a furrier in Vysehrad. At Holan's I drove a three-ton van, a little thing, an oil-driven job.

That day, 27 May, a floor wax and polish firm had hired the van. In the morning I went to their depot and we loaded the Tatra; a man who worked for them got in next to me and we went off to deliver the stuff. We had to take it to several shops in Liben and Kobylisy.

To begin with we went over the crossroads where the attack was to take place. The boys must certainly have been waiting there, but who could have known? We went down towards the river and there on the right was a little shop where we delivered part of our load. Then I drove towards the bridge; I turned there and we went up again by the same road. Two hundred and fifty yards from the corner we stopped in front of a hardware shop; their man went in to show the delivery notes and I helped to carry in the goods, little crates of floor wax. And just as we were finishing the job there was a huge bang.

"A truck's burst a tire," I said.

"Oh no, it was louder than that," said their man, as though he knew anything about it!

The road goes winding down to the river, so we couldn't see the top. We calmly shut the van, carefully stowed the few little crates we still had left, and then sat down while their man looked at his papers to tell me where to drive next.

"Up to the top now," he said. "After the turning we'll unload the rest."

Ignition, slip into gear, and we move off. We'd gone a hundred, a hundred and fifty yards up the hill when all at once I saw a fair-haired woman running and shouting to me to stop.

"What's up?" I say to her.

"Murder!"

"Well, what of it?"

"You must take the Herr Obergruppenführer to hospital."

"And why me of all people?"

"Your van's empty."

You won't believe me, but at that moment my head seemed to have nothing in it at all. I began stammering something about I didn't know if it was comfortable enough—we had crates of floor polish on top—it wasn't right to take the Protector on bad-smelling crates and she ought to look for something else; but all this got me nowhere. This German woman shouted, "Hurry up! Jump to it!"

Meanwhile a policeman was helping Heydrich towards our van. He tried to walk upright; he couldn't manage it; but proud to the bitter end, you know.

"Put him in by the driver," said someone.

He looked at me like a tiger that's just been wounded, and very slowly—it must have hurt him, because he kept holding his back with one hand: blood was running from it and his uniform was torn—very slowly he got in and sat by me. He was tall and had to bend his head to get in. The wax firm's man and the policeman sat behind, on the crates.

Then we set off, Heydrich holding his revolver in one hand and his briefcase in the other: he held it tight against him all the way.

Yes, there's something else I forgot to tell you. I said how at the moment of the attack we were coming up the hill—that is, in the opposite way to Heydrich's Mercedes. After the argument with that blonde I had to turn to get near his car, so now we were facing the other direction.

We went down the hill. He kept his mouth shut, and so did I, of course. I was scared, as you can imagine, with this Protector sitting next to me with blood running from his back and a revolver in his hand. Who could tell what crack-brained ideas might come into his head?

At that moment I realized that the shortest road to the hospital was by way of the crossing. So I turned and we went up the hill again. Heydrich noticed it, sat up a little straighter and shouted, "*Wohin fahren wir?*"

I don't speak much German, but I understood that—I understood he was asking me where we were going. But I couldn't remember how you say hospital in German. Now I knew perfectly well it's *Krankenhaus*, but the way I was then I couldn't remember it and all I did was to shrug. Heydrich shouted out something else in German and pointed his revolver at me. Fortunately at this moment we were back near the place where I'd had to take him and the blonde was still there. I stopped the van; she ran over when she saw us and he began to mumble something to her.

"Where are you going?" she said to me.

"I had to turn at the bottom of the hill. The quickest way for the Bulkova is by here—we turn right at the crossroads."

She translated my reply, and he said something else to her.

"The gentleman can't stay there beside you," she said to me. "It's too low."

"Your gentleman can go to hell," I thought. "I'd like to toss him in the ditch, the bastard."

I got out and the policeman helped Heydrich. We put him flat on his stomach in the back among the crates of wax and the tins of polish—it must have stunk. He asked us to give him his briefcase and the wax firm's man threw it in by him. Heydrich covered his face with one hand and he kept holding his side with the other.

The policeman sat by him on a crate; the other man by me. After that nothing much happened. We reached the hospital and handed him in. He looked in a bad way, yellow as a lemon and hardly able to stand.

30

The doctor's evidence

(*Vladimir Snajdr*)

THAT DAY I was on duty in surgery—a great many cases. The Bulkova at Liben is a big hospital and work goes on almost all the time. About half past ten I went to my room—there were two of us on duty, Dr. Puhala and I—because some freshly-laundered curtains had been brought for me and the nurses were arguing about how to hang them.

So I went into my room and all at once there was the sound of an explosion. We looked up, surprised, and by way of a joke I said, "Murder!" We laughed; nobody had the least idea that what I had happened to say was so near the truth. Then I went to the lavatory, came out, washed my hands, and went back; and at that moment the head nurse, Sister Sophie, appeared. She was frightened and quite beside herself. "Doctor! Doctor!"

"What's the matter, my dear Sophie?"

"He's sitting there on the operating table."

"What of it? Is he going to fall off?"

"You're always joking, Doctor. But there he is, looking round him, and he's as white as a sheet."

"Almost a corpse, then?"

"No, no—I'll never survive this. He looked me through and through."

"Who did?"

"Heydrich!"

I stopped and looked at Sophie. She was trembling and gasping;

175

her eyes staring. She couldn't finish a single sentence; she had to lean against the wall.

"Wait a minute. Who did you say is in the operating room?"

"The Protector. Heydrich!"

"And what's he doing there?"

"He's got a hole in his back."

I swallowed. I asked no more questions—in any case there was nothing to be got out of her—and I hurried to the operating theatre. Just as if he had done it on purpose, Puhala was not there. Heydrich was alone in the room, stripped to the waist, sitting on the table where we carry out the first examination.

I greeted him in Czech; he raised his hand but did not answer. I took forceps and a few swabs and tried to see whether the wound was deep. He did not stir, he did not flinch, although it must have hurt him. Meanwhile a nurse had telephoned Professor Dick, a German, asking him to come to the operating room.

At first sight the wound did not seem dangerous—unfortunately. Sometimes, you know, doctors find themselves in a complex situation. How should I explain it? Take this case, for example. Since I was a decent Czech I was delighted that Heydrich should be in a bad way. All it needed was for him to have been wounded a few inches lower down, in the kidneys, or for the spinal column to have been affected and everything would have been straightforward. But since I was also a doctor my duty was to cure, not kill. But should you cure fascists? He was a murderer: and killing a tyrant is an act that benefits mankind as a whole. Before I could make up my mind Professor Dick hurried in. He was a German doctor who the Nazis had appointed to our hospital.

"What's the matter?" he asked. It was only at that moment that he caught sight of Heydrich. He cried "*Heil!*" clicked his heels and began to examine him. He tried to see whether the kidney was touched: no, all seemed well for Heydrich. And the same applied to his spinal column. Then he was put into a wheelchair and taken off to the X-ray room. Heydrich tried to behave courageously and he walked from the chair to the X-ray machine by himself.

The X-ray showed something in the wound, perhaps a bomb

splinter. Or a piece of coachwork. In short, there was something there inside. Dr. Dick thought the splinter was in the chest wall and that it could be extracted by a simple local operation. We had an operating room in the basement for operations of that kind. Dick tried it, but without success. The patient's state called for a fullscale surgical operation: one rib was broken, the thoracic cage was open, a bomb splinter was in the spleen, the diaphragm was pierced.

"Herr Protektor," said Dick to Heydrich, "we must operate."

Heydrich refused. He wanted a surgeon to be brought from Berlin.

"But your condition requires an immediate operation," said Dick. They were speaking German, of course.

Heydrich thought it over and in the end he agreed that Professor Hollbaum, of the German surgical clinic in Prague, should be called in. He was taken to the aseptic theatre: I was not there; I had to stay in the room where the instruments were sterilized. Dr. Dick was the only one who helped Professor Hollbaum during the operation. The wound was about three inches deep and it contained a good deal of dirt and little splinters. Karl Hermann Frank, Hacha—the President of the Protectorate— and members of the government waited in the corridor outside the operating room.

After the operation Heydrich was taken to Dr. Dick's office on the second storey. The Germans had emptied the whole floor, turning the patients out or sending them home; and they transformed the dining room into an SS barracks. They set up machineguns on the roof and SS, armed to the teeth, paced about the entrance below.

No Czech doctor and no Czech member of the staff was allowed on the floor where Heydrich was. I tried to go up there to ask how he was doing; I said I was on duty and that I was looking for Dr. Puhala, but they told me openly that I had no business there.

So I have no exact information on Heydrich's condition after the operation. Perhaps they had to remove his spleen. I did not see him again. But Dr. Dick said that he was coming along very well. His death surprised us all. Up to the last moment of his life, not one of the Czech doctors working at the Bulkova knew the truth.

There was one thing that attracted our attention. The quantity of morphine that was used would have been enough for several patients. Even the nurse who delivered the doses thought it odd. It is possible that there was a morphine addict among the German doctors; but that is a matter for the police.

I do not remember the briefcase. He might have had it with him somewhere, but I really never saw it and I know nothing about it. They say it held important papers and information meant for Hitler, but journalists often see more in these things than eyewitnesses.

During the last days of Heydrich's life we lived in a kind of dream. Every day visitors appeared, wearing black uniforms, the cream of the SS with bunches of flowers; his own doctor flew in from Berlin; Frau Heydrich came to see him.

Up until 4 June, the day of his death.

"Septicaemia," they said. Blood transfusions could do nothing. Professor Hamperl, head of the German Institute of Pathology, and Professor Weyrich, head of the German Institute of Forensic Medicine, drew up a joint report on their medical conclusions. Among other things it said, "Death occurred as a consequence of lesions in the vital parenchymatous organs caused by bacteria and possibly by poisons carried into them by the bomb splinters and deposited chiefly in the pleura, the diaphragm and the tissues in the neighbourhood of the spleen, there agglomerating and multiplying."

That is all I can tell you.

31

The recollections of the gardener of Panenske Brezany

(Vaclav Kraus)

HERE, AT Panenske Brezany, we had news of the ambush before noon. Frau Heydrich and the children were just going to have lunch when Sergeant-Major Wagnitz told her. I wasn't there at the time, but according to what they said, she was calm and unmoved. Ice and calculation, that's what she was made of. Grasping and unfeeling, too. Later, when the bus bringing the Panenske Brezany soccer team back from a match one Sunday ran over her son by pure accident—this happened long after Heydrich's death—do you know what that woman did? The boy—it was Klaus—lay in a lead coffin in the Castle hall, surrounded by bunches of chrysanthemums. After the service he was buried in the park; and at the moment he was being lowered into the grave she told us to sell the chrysanthemums to the Prague florists! She made quite a bit of money out of it.

I'm a man and there are a lot of things I don't give a damn about; but for the moment I felt a shiver run down my back.

And there were plenty of other things. In the Castle corridors there were splendid great antlers: she sold them to a button factory. The old trees round the Castle? Yes, she had them cut down, sold the wood for a good price, and instead of the ash trees she had apples and pears planted, saying there was good money to be made, selling the fruit.

I don't think I ought to tell you any more about her, although

I remember lots of other things like that. I had to work for them; that's why I know so much.

Heydrich owned the two Castles at Panenske Brezany. As well as me, there were two maids, a cook, and a major-domo. It was usually Czechs who were given these jobs. Now and then we used to listen to the foreign radio in the evenings, but you had to take great care.

For my part, I went there as gardener and odd-job man. When they put in central heating I had to see to the stoking of it, and in the time I had to spare from everything else they turned me into a baker. Yes, a baker.

There were ten or twelve SS soldiers living in the house near the entrance to the park: they were a bodyguard for Heydrich and his family.

I remember the day of 27 May 1942 very well: it was like a real madhouse here. That morning, I had been working in the garden of the other Castle, the one at the top, where the Heydrichs had their kitchen garden. I washed the vegetables I was to take to the kitchen and brought them back here. When I reached the park gates I saw Heydrich's car; it had just left the house and it was coming towards me. The Heydrichs insisted upon being saluted the Nazi way, that is to say by putting your arm up, and we did all we could to avoid meeting them. I just had time to hide behind a huge rock near the entrance to the park so as not to have to salute and I reached the Castle when his car was on the way to Prague.

Another car stood in front of the Castle door. Herbert Wagnitz, Heydrich's sergeant-major, was talking to the driver. From our point of view, this Wagnitz was not such a bad fellow. He was an SS, yes, to be sure; but you could talk to him. He didn't shout, and as far as we were concerned he behaved like a human being. He saw I was carrying all these vegetables and he asked if they were for the kitchen. "Where else would I be taking them?" I thought; but aloud I said, "Yes, sir." And seeing he was in a good mood I added, "Tell me, are you going along with the Herr Protektor?"

"Sure," he said, straightening his uniform.

Sometimes when Wagnitz went to Prague, he let me ride with him as far as the upper castle; so I asked him, "I just have to give these vegetables to the cook and then I've got to go back to the Castle up the hill—I have a lot of work to do there. Would you take me with you?"

Wagnitz nodded. "All right. But hurry up."

I went down the passage—it was pleasantly cool there—and took my vegetables to the kitchen. Then I meant to go, but the cook wanted to get something else out of me or else she started telling me a story, I forget which; but anyhow, I stayed there longer than I had thought.

At last I got out of the kitchen and reached the front door; but Wagnitz wasn't there. He'd gone to look for something, and the chauffeur and I had to wait for him. A few minutes later he came back and we set off.

It was a lovely day—sunlight and young green leaves everywhere. We went through the village, climbed the hill, and after a few more turnings there we were at the Castle. I thanked him and his car went off to Prague. I don't know whether Wagnitz was supposed to go to the airfield or to join Heydrich at Prague Castle. Anyhow, he set out very late, and that's why Heydrich's car reached the corner where the ambush was waiting for him without his bodyguard.

I worked in the garden all that morning and about noon I went back; and when I reached the lower Castle I heard all about it. Heydrich's wife was expecting a baby and her maid was afraid something might happen to her—hysterics or worse. But she was a hard woman. All she did was to utter a few insults about the Czech nation and then she held her head even higher than usual.

Even at a moment like this, she didn't forget moneymaking. Heydrich's funeral was at Berlin: she only sent her two sons. They went in a special plane. The maid packed their bags and Frau Heydrich looked after the vegetables that were to be sent to Berlin, because she was afraid we might forget them. Yes, the vegetables travelled with the boys in this special plane for Berlin.

In 1945, when things were beginning to go badly, Himmler

came here, tired and unshaved; they shut themselves up in a room. I don't know what he told her, but the next day she had a car turned into a kind of caravan; she had geese and chickens killed, and she added a few sacks of wheat and potatoes to the load. Then at the beginning of April she set off with the children, the governess, and Wagnitz for somewhere in the west. Before she left, she sent for us and said she'd be back in six weeks.

Why now, to begin with I thought I was only going to talk to you about him—he was a hard, rough man—but there's so much I remember.

32

The evidence of a woman from Žižkov: 3

(Frantiska Volfova)

THE DAY of the attack my husband was alone in the house when Kubis arrived. He was wearing a blue railwayman's coat, and he lay down on the sofa, tired out.

"What news of the little man?" he asked my husband. "Have you heard anything?" It was Gabcik he called the little man.

"Yesterday, after the attack, he went to the Zelenkas," said Father. "He borrowed a raincoat from the mother and gave her a bunch of violets. Then he went to the Fafeks."

Kubis was wounded; he had little splinters buried in his skin, particularly in his chest, and my husband took tweezers and pulled some out. He dressed the places with sterilized surgical cotton, and lent him a vest so that blood wouldn't stain his shirt. Then he called M. Zelenka, but they had hardly said more than a few words to one another before the bell rang. It was Svarc.

Kubis told them all about the attack, saying that Valcik had been a little slow with his signal and that they had almost missed Heydrich's car.

"Where are you going now?" asked my husband.

"Don't worry about that," answered the schoolmaster Zelenka. "I've already arranged something for them. But lend them warm underclothes. It will be cold there."

Later, when everything was over, we saw in the paper that they had taken shelter in the crypt of a church. M. Zelenka told us that the first to go there was Zelinka–Svarc. He went the same day he had come to see us, the Thursday. The others followed him on Friday and Saturday. The last to join them was Opalka: he went some time after Sunday.

It's hard to say where Kubis and Gabcik were during the night of Wednesday to Thursday, that is to say the night after the attack. Maybe with the Fafeks. When Kubis went away after his talk with M. Zelenka, he left a grenade with us, so as not to have it on him. To begin with my husband hid it in the sand bucket you had to have outside the door; later we put it in the cellar. We also hid it in a shoebox, in the bedside table and under the bath. Finally, in May 1945, after the liberation, we handed it over to the authorities.

33

A second railwayman's recollections

(*Frantisek Sulek*)

I HAD PLENTY to worry about in those days; my eldest son Miroslav had been arrested because of his secret Communist activities—his group printed and distributed tracts. The Gestapo had a special section for the Communists alone and they were treated with extraordinary harshness; so wherever we went all we thought about was our son.

To begin with he was shut up in the Terezin fortress, then in the prison at Budisin, and then at Bayreuth: my wife was bitterly unhappy; we waited for letters from him—in short, we lived between hope and despair.

We have two other children. Our younger boy was born in 1921, so he was twenty-one at the time of the killing, and our daughter was twenty. I used to work as a railway inspector at Kosice in Slovakia; then in 1939, after the occupation of the republic, I was transferred to Prague, where I carried on with my job. If you have been in the same concern all your life, you come to know a great many people, and I had lots of friends among the railwaymen. Inspector Pouba, a fine man, came to see me one day and said, "Do you know Alois Moravec?"

"Where does he work?"

"He's an inspector."

I thought for a moment, and then it occurred to me that he must be the man from Bratislava. "Why do you speak of him?"

"He has to find a lodging for someone who is not registered with the police. Would it be possible in your house?"

I asked my wife and she agreed; so the next day I told my friend we were ready to take this unknown man in. We had a fairly big flat in a little house in Hanspaulka. We prepared a room with a bed, a wardrobe and a few other small pieces of furniture. Mirek came to our place about the middle of May. We did not ask where he had been living before or what he was doing in Prague or whether he was here alone or with friends. He did not speak about it and we asked no questions. When he was at home he often used to come into the kitchen and help my wife.

It seemed to me that he would draw attention anywhere. He had blue eyes and jet-black hair and a little dark moustache—he was always good-humoured.

"You'll be noticed," I said to him, one day.

"What ought I to do?"

"Don't come to the house by the bus: we all know one another in the district and the neighbours will soon see that you're living with us. It would be better to get out at the streetcar stop and walk the rest of the way."

He followed my advice. I was often away, travelling, and my wife stood in queues to find something for us to eat. I don't know where he went, but sometimes he came back late at night. Our children were very fond of Mirek; he was only a little older than they were. And then there came that day in May—it was a Wednesday, if I remember rightly. That morning Mirek went out very early without telling us where he was going. Towards noon a friend of my daughter's ran in to tell us there had been an attempt on Heydrich's life. My wife took fright, thinking of our son in prison, yet she saw no connection between our guest and the attack. But when Mirek came in he looked very strange and she said to him, "Mirek, don't you know something more about this attack on Heydrich?"

He looked at her closely. "Is he dead?"

"Not yet. But what about you? Were you concerned in it?"

"What an idea! I am much too soft-hearted." But he smiled, and my wife saw he was not speaking the truth. "Is there anything you need?" she went on.

"Could you go and see people to hear what is being said? And please may I have some very strong coffee?" And then he asked whether he might have a bath, because his legs were painful, the result of a long walk, perhaps.

My wife made him his coffee and then went out. When she came back, Mirek was writing a letter. He asked her to give it to Madame Moravcova, in Zizkov.

"Now?"

"Yes; as soon as it's finished."

A quarter of an hour later Mirek gave her his message and she left. She had to go right across the city, but when she got there she found nobody at home; the Moravecs were out. She did not know what to do, so she came back. Mirek was still there, but at first we did not know he had been out in the meantime. "What did Auntie Moravcova say?" he asked.

"She was not at home, so I have brought your letter back to you."

You could see Mirek was disappointed, but there was nothing to be done about it. That same evening the radio broadcast detailed news about the attack, with a description of the things found in the neighbourhood, including a bicycle, together with its manufacturer's number.

"Jesus Maria!" exclaimed Mirek (later we learnt that his real name was Valcik). "When Auntie hears that she will be furious."

"Why, Mirek?"

"The boys left the factory number on, so they will know it's her bike. You think you have thought of everything and then you forget some little detail that may turn out to be disastrous."

He had dinner and then went out for a few minutes. After that he went to bed. The next morning—it was Thursday—Madame Moravcova came. She was quite overwhelmed and she told us of all the harm the young men's carelessness might do. She was very angry—understandably, too. "I'm going to take Mirek away," she said.

"There's no need."

"He's been living with you a long time now and it might attract attention. And soon he and his friends will have a safe place to hide."

We did not ask where she was taking him. After we had said good-bye and just as they were leaving, I said to him, "Wait a minute, Mirek; I'll lend you a book. You can read it in the streetcar, so that no one will see your face."

I took H. W. Steed's *Thirty Years as a Journalist* from the shelf. That book could tell you many a story. It is back again in the shelf now, and if you open it you will see my surname and our Kosice address. I bought it when we were living in Slovakia. My name was there, but I had quite forgotten it when I lent the book to Valcik. He thanked us and left with Auntie Moravcova. When Mirek had gone, my wife went to tidy his room; and as she was making the bed she saw that the sheet was all covered with blood. The pillowcase was stained, too. We were astonished, because Mirek had never said a word; but then we remembered his exhausted look, and how pale he was—he must have been wounded.

We did not know where the young men were hidden. For us the weeks that followed were a nightmare. Every day in the newspapers and on the red posters we saw the lists of those who had been executed. Every day we thought the Gestapo would come for us. As we knew they worked at four in the morning we used to get up and wait.

Once Madame Moravcova came to ask whether we could send the young men coffee, food, and a kerosene stove. We had one that worked on paraffin, but it made too much noise, and I tried to find another when I was travelling about. My wife made up food parcels: she used to telephone Madame Moravcova from the public box and ask whether she had time to go to the dress-maker with her. When Auntie said yes, my wife took her the parcel. It would have coffee and kerosene in it.

Our last parcel was ready when the Gestapo came. They were combing through the district, searching all the houses, "*Was ist das?*" asked one, pointing to the case perched on top of the wardrobe.

"Things we don't use any more," said my wife. She was terrified.

The Gestapo man thought for a moment, then went on

looking through the flat. If he had known it was a parcel for the parachutists...

The next day my wife telephoned Madame Moravcova as usual. A man's voice answered. "Is my aunt at home?" asked my wife.

"Yes," said the man in Czech. Then after a moment he added, "Well, not exactly."

My wife hung up at once: she did not take the parcel to Zizkov. We understood—things had gone wrong. A few hours later the Gestapo surrounded our district; perhaps they had been tapping the Moravecs' phone and knew the call had come from Hanspaulka; but they found nothing.

So all through the summer of 1942 we waited for death. But Auntie Moravcova gave nothing away. Apart from her and the railwayman who had brought Valcik we knew nobody concerned with the organization of the attack.

In 1945, after the liberation, we handed in the things that Valcik had left with us when he left to hide in the crypt: it was then that the ministry gave us back Steed's book which I had lent him in 1942.

34

The caretaker's recollections: 3

(Frantisek Spinka)

AH YES, I haven't told you about the book Valcik brought here.

The day of the attack, 27 May, everything was very quiet at home. It so happened that my wife chanced to go and see M. Janacek who owned the next-door garage where the boys used to leave their bikes. In the street she heard that something had happened to Heydrich. The whole of Prague was talking about it; nobody knew anything exact but there were rumours of every kind; and to tell you the truth, we were delighted.

That afternoon Madame Moravcova came to ask if we knew; she was wild with joy. But when she heard that the boys had not removed the bicycle's number she went pale and she complained bitterly of their carelessness. She was to see them that evening somewhere in Hloubetin, but no one turned up.

About eleven the next morning she came to our place with Valcik—we called him Zdenda. "Can he stay with you two or three days?" she asked.

"Do you think you have to ask?" I said. I gave him the keys to the cellar and we agreed that if there were a search he should escape through the bathroom skylight. From there he could go down through a little door to the cellar, where I made him a good hiding place in the middle of the sacks of coal. He laughed, saying he would not need it—he wouldn't be staying long. But the very first night a policeman came, looking for a man who worked for them and who lived in the house, and Valcik had to use the refuge.

I remember that the day Zdenda came the Gestapo were in the neighbourhood. They were searching an inn that has now become a bakery. At that stage the Gestapo were everywhere—checking, arresting, frightening people, torturing them, putting them to death. That was their system.

That evening we played cards and listened to the BBC. Zdenda was waiting for a poem to be read on the Czech-language programme, but we did not hear it. My wife won several times; Zdenda laughed and promised he would have his revenge. The next day my wife made some cakes for him and he said they were as good as his mother's.

He stayed—let me see now: the attack was on the Wednesday, so he stayed with us from Thursday to Saturday 30 May. We wanted him to stay longer; he could have lived in the little attic on the fifth floor, where no one would ever have found him; but he'd been given orders to go, he said, and he was a soldier and had to carry them out. His comrades went too. He put on an overcoat and green spectacles, we said good-bye, and Madame Moravcova came to fetch him.

Madame Moravcova must have known where he was going, because she told us he would need warm underclothes; it would be cold in their hide-out. She had given him a pair of pyjamas and a dressing gown and asked me if I could help her pack up some mattresses.

"Where are the mattresses?"

"In our flat."

I went up to her place and made a neat parcel of them; but it was heavy.

So Zdenda went away. But he forgot a book: he left it behind. He'd brought it from the family he'd been living with before. It was about journalism—I don't remember the title now. But on the last page there was the name of the man it belonged to. It was a stroke of luck that Valcik didn't take it to the church with him. If the Gestapo had found it, the name would have given them a clue. All through the war we kept the book, and in May 1945 we handed it in to the ministry.

When Valcik had gone, Madame Moravcova said she felt

poorly and in need of rest; she was going to leave Prague for a while. She sent her son Ata to southern Bohemia, near Pisek, and her husband, if I remember rightly, to Suchdol, while she herself went to Brno or Holoubkov, I don't recall which. Before she went she gave my wife the suit Valcik had worn the day of the attack: blue-grey, I think it was. It was an ordinary suit; the pockets were empty; but still there was one thing that worried us—a bloodstain on the trousers, at thigh level. Madame Moravcova did not mention it to us; perhaps she had not noticed it. We sent this suit to my sister in the country, and after the war we handed it over to the ministry. Zdenda had given us his photo, but we buried it and it disappeared.

So Valcik left. Madame Moravcova too, leaving us the keys to the flat. Their place was empty and all the young men had disappeared; but still we were terribly uneasy—on hot bricks. We had entered into this business and now we were in it up to the neck; but in spite of everything, if it had to be done again, we'd do it.

But the calm did not last long. A few days went by and then Madame Moravcova appeared.

"Back already?" I said.

"I can't keep still anywhere. I go from place to place, and in the end I thought the best thing to do was to come back. So here I am. I am up to my eyes in work."

She took the keys of the flat and the next day it all began again. She washed clothes, ironed, went shopping. In a word, she couldn't rest or hide. My wife helped her. When Madame Moravcova was away, she carried a food parcel to the Olsany graveyard where M. Zelenka was waiting for her with a slim, grey-haired woman.

So that Madame Moravcova should not be noticed always carrying parcels, one day my wife took them to Charles Square and gave them to her there; another day she packed up the food in paper bags, took the same streetcar as Madame Moravcova, but got out after two or three stops, leaving the parcels on her seat. Twice we made cakes for the young men, and I found cigarettes and kerosene for them. Ata had come back, and he and I adopted the password Vratislav: before coming to the house he used to phone me. If the Gestapo or the police were there, I was to tell him he had the wrong number, so as to let him know he should escape. He was arrested and the Gestapo must have tortured him hideously.

We never saw Gabcik or Kubis again. Sometimes Madame Moravcova told us how they were doing, that they liked drinking coffee, that they had made a strainer out of a vest, and that they were cheerful, though they found the cold hard to bear. Ota (Kubis) and Zdenda (Valcik) were not very well; Kubis had been wounded in the eye during the attack and Valcik, whose trousers were marked with blood, must have been hurt too.

We had to get rid of Valcik's dog Moula. The day of the attack we gave him to a plumber named Jarov who had a big garden, where Moula could run about wherever he liked. But he did not live long: he missed his master so much that he died of grief.

In those days we did not know that the boys were hiding in a church crypt. Once Madame Moravcova said a man from Pardubice had decided that the parachutists should leave Prague for a farm or a monastery.

It was already the beginning of June, and the Nazis were growing more and more furious. They had shot hundreds of people, but they had not found the parachutists. We often thought of them, my wife and I, and we said they must be suffering terribly when they heard how many unfortunate people were paying for the attack with their lives.

On Saturday 13 June, an unknown man came and said he had been to the Moravecs, where he was to pick up a briefcase, but there was nobody at home. We said we knew nothing about it. That evening I told Madame Moravcova and she asked whether this man came from Kolin.

"I don't know, Madame; he didn't say anything." I described him, but I could see she had no idea who he might be.

"It's odd," she said. "What's more, not long ago I had the feeling someone was following me. I was taking the boys a parcel, and I thought it better to go right through the town—I didn't go to the place where they are hidden until I was sure this man was not following me any more."

It was said that the parachutist who betrayed all his comrades was living with a relative at Kolin.

On Monday 15 June, Madame Moravcova set off again with a parcel. She never suspected that it would be the last. When she returned she came to see us to say that soon it would be Adolf's birthday: later we found that Adolf was Captain Opalka's Christian name. "I'll have to make the boys a good lunch," she added.

"What will you make?" asked my wife.

"I'll try to find veal scallops; and I'd like to make them soup with liver balls in it."

From what she told us from time to time we gathered that the young men could not do any cooking where they were, except perhaps for breakfast; that was why Madame Moravcova wanted kerosene.

"They need hot meals; Zdenda has a temperature."

"That's because he was wounded," I thought; but I did not say anything.

Late on 16 June both M. and Madame Moravec came to see us. They were pale and looked worn out. He said, "We must hold out until the eighteenth."

35

People and happenings hitherto unmentioned

(*The author*)

A QUESTION arises: is it possible to reconcile the variations in the evidence and reports concerning the attempt on Heydrich's life—variations that persist even now?

The accounts given by those witnesses who by chance or good fortune escaped death, are very subjective. Their recollections leave some names out; each particular survivor knows only one side of the matter. Kubis and Gabcik lived with the Vojtechowskys for a brief period, but they are not mentioned, nor Bauc, Svatos or Hosek, nor Madame Bozena Kropackova nor Madame Slavomira Cechova, etc. The same applies to the events at Slany, where Karel Svoboda's people lived—Karel Svoboda, who, as we saw in the historian's first intervention, was to work with Gabcik but who was hurt in the course of training.

The facts were more complex than one might suppose. We cannot make the plain statement that on reaching Prague Kubis and Gabcik lived with the Khodls, then in Podoli, then in Zizkov, then with the Fafeks, where Dr. Johanovska had taken them, and lastly with the Dejvice schoolmaster. There were probably several other men and women who took them in, but now it is impossible to check this, since the Germans massacred the families, including the women and children, of all those who fell into their hands and whom they suspected of having sheltered parachutists.

Are the recollections of Jindra, the chemistry teacher, correct, for example? Sometimes yes and sometimes no. In the matter of some dates he is certainly mistaken. In his third account he says that he met Bartos in Captain Prochazka's flat towards the middle of February 1942. But we know this to be impossible. The records contain the dispatch, dated only 5 March 1942, in which Bartos informed London that by means of contacts in Plzn he had succeeded in getting into touch with the Anthropoid team, that is to say with Gabcik and Kubis. And he could not be acquainted with the people who were looking after the parachutists before he had found the parachutists themselves.

Let us move on to the question of what happened to the message drawn up by Jindra, which asked for the cancellation of the order for the attack. In this message he called Kubis and Gabcik by the Christian names Ota and Zdenda, and he states that his text ended with the words "If for international political reasons the action is nevertheless essential, pick another person to be killed." Did London receive Jindra's dispatch?

We discussed this with the officer who, in the Second World War, was in charge of the department of the Czechoslovak ministry of national defence in London which saw to the coding of dispatches sent to the Protectorate and to the decoding of those that came in. We asked whether he remembered Jindra's message.

The officer had no recollection of it. Yet we do possess an "official" confirmation of its existence, since K. H. Frank refers to it in his report to Berlin of 22 June 1942. He tells Berlin that the text of this dispatch was found among Bartos' documents seized at Pardubice and that it had been sent by the clandestine transmitter in that town, probably on 4 May 1942.

At that period Karl Hermann Frank already knew the true identity of the parachutists; he was therefore able to state that Ota was the cover-name of Kubis and Zdenek that of Gabcik. But his report contains certain errors: according to him Silver was the cover-name for Captain Sustr, the officer commanding the Czech parachutists in London. Silver was in fact the name of Bartos' team, and Sustr was not in command of the parachutists dropped over the Protectorate.

K. H. Frank understood who was meant by the Quisling E.M.; he tells Berlin that it refers to Emmanuel Moravec, the Protectorate government minister. He then quotes the entirety of Jindra's message calling for the abandonment of the attempt; and he adds that no reply to this *Funkspruch* was received.

We asked the officer who was the head of the section in London during the war the following question: "Do you remember the message confirming the order to carry out the attack? You passed every dispatch before it was coded."

"That is so. But I do not recall any such message. It may have taken the form of a cryptogram, that is to say of some ordinary phrase agreed beforehand. Or possibly Colonel Frantisek Moravec, the chief of intelligence in the London ministry of national defence, may have sent it himself without showing it to me. But that never did happen. I read everything. The incoming dispatches were shown to me uncoded, in clear, that is to say rewritten word by word. For my part I changed the uncoded text somewhat and varied the order of the words."

"Why?"

"If the enemy counterespionage were to have picked up the uncoded word-by-word text they might have used it to break our code. Every text had to be varied or amplified before it was passed to the other sections. But I knew nothing of any abandonment of the attack."

Yet according to the chemistry teacher, Bartos did receive a reply to the message, but one that he was unable to decode, since it was in a system known only to Kubis and Gabcik. Hana Krupkova, the wife of the survivor of Pardubice, has this to say: "I remember a dispatch that Freda Bartos could not decode. I went to Prague to deliver it to Valcik. Later Bartos thought it was the order to carry out the killing."

On 15 May 1942 Dr. Benes, the President of the Republic, speaking from London, broadcast a message to the partisans in occupied Czechoslovakia. He analysed the political situation, saying in particular, "In this situation, a proof of strength even in our own country—rebellion, open action, acts of sabotage and demonstrations—may become desirable or necessary. On the international plane action of this kind would contribute to the preservation of the nation itself, even if it had to be paid for by a great many sacrifices."

A reading of this message gives rise to another question: was the President informed of the preparations for the killing? Was the date set for it known in London?

In the war diary of the Czechoslovak ministry of national defence in London we find disturbing coincidences: on 3 October 1941 the interview between the Czechoslovak officers and the parachutists Gabcik and Svoboda took place, the interview at which the parachutists were told that a killing was to be carried out in the Protectorate. In the war diary for 2 October, that is the day before this interview, there is the statement: "At 1430 hours the minister of national defence left for an audience with the President of the Republic."

On 12 May 1942 London received the message asking for the abandonment of the attack. In the war diary for 13 May we read, "At 1300 hours the minister of national defence attended a private luncheon given by the President of the Republic."

Let us return to the question of the two messages. We now know the exact text of the UVOD (central direction of the home resistance) message received in London on 12 May 1942.

CHES.UVOD has probably guessed the task of Strnad and Vyskocil and asks for the following dispatch to be sent: From the preparations made by S and V we infer, despite their steady silence on the matter, that they are getting ready for the attempt on H's life. This attack, which could be of no advantage to the Allies, would have unforeseeable consequences for our nation. It would threaten not only those who are held as hostages and our political prisoners but also the lives of thousands of other citizens; it would cause the whole nation to suffer hideous oppression; at the same time it would result in the wiping-out of the last resistance networks we possess, and it would no longer be possible to provide the Allies with useful services from this country. That is why we beg you to give orders through Silver for the attack not to take place. Give the order at once. If action is needed for reasons of international politics, pick a Quisling: E.M. for example. PAR.

This is an exact quotation of the text received in London: it is to be seen in the Czechoslovak archives.

Certain differences between the texts of these messages may have arisen from the translations: the version found by the Gestapo in Bartos' papers was written in Czech; it had to be translated into German for K. H. Frank; and from the German report it was retranslated into Czech for this book.

There are other aspects of the matter that are still unexplained and open to question. The attack itself, for example. It was carried out on 27 May 1942: but what do we know about that day?

We do know the exact time of the ambush and we know where it took place. And we know who carried it out. We know that Gabcik, whose gun jammed, stood at the corner, together with Kubis, who threw the bomb. Who helped them?

Here opinions differ. Each of the passengers in the streetcar that had just reached the corner and whose doors were shattered by the explosion has a different tale to tell. Some assert that in the chaos—nobody knew what was happening—they saw the men who had carried out the attack on the left, others say they saw them on the right. It is difficult to rely on their evidence, except perhaps in the cases where several recollections coincide. Then again Valcik's wound is a fact that makes it still harder to interpret the happenings of that day. According to the evidence of the Zizkov woman, who lived in the same house as the schoolmaster Zelenka, Kubis said that Valcik gave the signal with his pocket mirror. But if one goes to the spot it is clear that in order to see Heydrich's car coming, Valcik must have stood farther up and at some distance from the corner. Yet he was wounded.

Several witnesses mention this wound. The people with whom he spent the night after the attack speak of it: his hostess said that after he left she found bloodstains on the sheet and the pillow. Furthermore the Zizkov caretaker to whose flat Valcik moved the next day states that when Madame Moravcova gave him Valcik's suit he saw a bloodstain on the trousers.

Hana Krupkova, the wife of the survivor of Pardubice, says, "The next day, 28 May, I left Prague with information on the attack for Bartos and the transmitter Libuse. It was Valcik who gave it to me that afternoon, at the Moravecs' flat. He was sitting on a sofa in the kitchen and he could not get up; he did not want me to tell Bartos about his wound; he said he had slipped and hurt his leg. As I was going to the station I saw newly stuck up posters with his photograph; so I telephoned from the station and told them to come and see something interesting."

Since Valcik's photograph was posted up for the first time on 28 May we know the exact date Madame Krupkova, the liaison agent, left Prague. Her account provides the third piece of evidence (after the railwayman's and the caretaker's) that Valcik was wounded on the day of the attack. Yet no article, book or document has ever mentioned it.

How could it have happened? Let us consider: Valcik, posted above the turning, gave the signal with his pocket mirror, and then perhaps he ran towards the place of the attack. Perhaps he was there just at the moment of the explosion. At that juncture Kubis and Gabcik were in the act of escaping. Kubis, his forehead bloody from a splinter, ran to his bicycle, left not far away, leapt on to it and rode towards Liben by the Kirchmayer Boulevard. Probably Gabcik was unable to get at his; perhaps the people who came out of the streetcar got in his way. So he ran up the turning down which Heydrich had come and took the first street on the left. Gabcik, with Klein, Heydrich's chauffeur, after him, ran towards Valcik. From time to time Gabcik turned and fired at Klein. Valcik, seeing this, helped Gabcik by firing too. And he was wounded by Klein.

This is a hypothesis that cannot perhaps be verified now. Then again, what if Valcik inflicted the wound upon himself? He had a pistol in his pocket, and in running round the corner he might have pressed the trigger by accident. If this is so, the first hypothesis is invalid.

It should be pointed out that the German report mentions only one man as being pursued by Klein. Is it not possible that the driver in his overexcited state should not have noticed that he was also being fired at by another man who came running down the hill?

But the Nazis must have known that at least three men were present at the attack. During the inquiry they tried to draw up a plan of the ambush at the corner as it was carried out; their map showed three men—the man with the bomb, the man with the gun, and the man with the mirror. The fact that the parachutists' names are not yet shown on the plan proves that it was drawn at the beginning of the inquiry. As we shall see later, the treachery of the parachutist Curda was necessary before the Gestapo could know these names. What we know about the mirror signal is not the result of research carried out after the war: the Gestapo were already aware of it in 1942.

A very important piece of evidence as to what really happened in the turning at the moment of the ambush is provided by the woman who got out of the streetcar and who was wounded by a splinter from the bomb Kubis had thrown. It was she who was nearest Heydrich's car and she was an eyewitness of the attack. She categorically states that there were three men on the pavement. Not two, as some have said, but three. One of them ran across the road at the last moment, perhaps to force Heydrich's driver to brake. Who was it? Opalka? Or Kubis? Hitherto it has been said that Gabcik and Kubis were both on the inner side of the turning; but is this really so?

According to the Dejvice schoolmaster who sheltered the two parachutists at that time, Kubis told him after the attack, "I was in reserve, on the other side of the road, about ten paces from Zdenek." It was Gabcik whom he called Zdenek.

Obviously no one can make an exact reconstruction of the various stages of the attack. The account given in the chapter entitled "The Journey" is based solely on the suppositions that seemed most probable to the author. Kubis and Gabcik left no record of their stay in the Protectorate; and the memories of the witnesses are often in conflict with one another.

What did the parachutists do after the attack? Let us, among so many differing recollections, choose the apparently conclusive evidence of M. Kriklan, the Dejvice schoolmaster's neighbour who knew that he was sheltering Kubis and Gabcik at his flat. M. Kriklan is dead, but his private notes of the day-by-day

events of the time have been found. They show that the parachutists went to Panenske Brezany again on the morning of
27 May. "When I questioned him," says Kriklan, "Kubis said
the attack had been carried out by him and Gabcik without any
assistance and that the same applied to the preparations." Having
described the attempt on Heydrich's life, Kriklan goes on:

> After the attack Zdenek [Gabcik] went to the Fafeks, where he
> had a hot bath. He had hurt his leg, jumping over a wall. He
> rinsed his hair with camomile to change its colour a little. With
> Libena Fafek he went to buy a green Tyrolean hat. At the corner
> of Charles Square an SS officer came up to them to ask for a light.
> He must have taken Gabcik for a German because of the hat.
> Zdenek provided it with a great show of politeness. That night
> Zdenek slept at the Fafeks' flat. For his part, Kubis spent the
> night after the attack going from one family he knew to another.
> In the afternoon of 28 May, Jarka [Kubis], wearing a railwayman's
> uniform, came to M. Ogoun, the Dejvice schoolmaster. Madame
> Ogoun treated his wounds all through that afternoon and the
> following night. When he arrived he was all swollen, bomb
> splinters having struck his face, particularly his eye, and his
> chest. At about five in the morning of the next day Madame
> Ogounova came to tell us that Jarka wanted to speak to me. I
> found him in bed, covered with bandages; but the treatment had
> reduced the swelling a great deal. There were green patches on his
> skin where the splinters had struck; they had all had to be taken
> out, even the smallest—the bomb had been poisoned. He was as
> composed as ever. No one could have believed that the day
> before this same hand had calmly . . . He urged Mama (Madame
> Ogounova) to go and rest. Then he told me about it.

Here M. Krilik repeats the known facts about the ambush and
Kubis' flight, and he adds, "He [Kubis] left his bicycle outside
the Bata shop and went to a workman's house—the wife was at
home—to wash and rest; the address had been given him beforehand; he had never been there before. He stayed some considerable time and then walked about the Prague suburbs, visiting
families he knew, one after another. He walked all night and the
next day he came back to the Ogouns for peace and quiet and to
have his shirt washed, because his wounds were still bleeding."

Perhaps we should return to the choice of what seemed the safest refuge for the parachutists. It was not the church of St. Cyril and St. Methodius in Resslova that was selected first. M. Fafek looked elsewhere, particularly, it seems, in a village near Sedlcany, and in the sanatorium belonging to the Masaryk League against Tuberculosis in the Budy forest, and in the Bethlehem chapel in Prague-Zizkov. Having thought it over, M. Zelenka–Hajsky picked the church of St. Cyril and St. Methodius.

And what do we really know about Gabcik's actions and movements? Some witnesses say that he came to Zizkov, bringing Madame Zelenka a bunch of violets, and that there he borrowed a raincoat. Another states that he borrowed it half an hour after the attack from the Svatos family, who lived near Wenceslas Square and who owned one of the briefcases, and that then he went to the Fafeks.

M. Kriklan confirms this. Gabcik must have been engaged to Libena, the Fafeks' daughter: M. Ogoun speaks of their engagement. What is more, we have the recollections of the priest of the Zizkov Evangelical Church—he says that Gabcik and Libena came "when the tulips were in flower" to ask him whether they might be married "a fortnight after the end of the war."

In the afternoon he went to buy a green Tyrolean hat with a white cord round it "so as to look like a German"—a purchase confirmed by M. Kriklan.

But on Thursday 3 September 1942 the trial of several persons accused of having given active assistance to the parachutists Gabcik and Kubis opened in Prague. In the dock sat Anna Malinova. She told the court that Gabcik came to her home the day before the attack, that is to say on Tuesday, 26 May 1942. He returned on Thursday, in a state of great tension. She asked him what had upset him so and he replied, "There was an attempt on Heydrich's life yesterday; do you know anything about it?" It was only later that he told Malinova he had taken part in the attack.

According to Anna Malinova's evidence, Gabcik stayed with her until 1 June. He did not leave the house. When he went away on the Monday he promised to come back, but he did not say where he was going. She had never seen him again since that day.

From the statement of Anna Malinova, who was sentenced to death and executed by the Germans, we may deduce that Gabcik remained hidden in her flat from Thursday 28 May until Monday 1 June, and that it was from her house that he went to the church. This version corresponds with the evidence of Dr. Petrek, the priest, who was also executed. He told the court that the seventh man, the one named Vyskocil on his identity card, came to the church on Monday 1 June. Now we know that Vyskocil was Gabcik.

According to Dr. Petrek, Kubis came to the church on Saturday 30 May. His identity card was in the name of Navratil and "he was wounded in the eye and in need of medical attention."

He was also in need of someone to whom he could confide his troubled conscience: had he done right in throwing the bomb? A man had killed another; and above all hundreds more had been put to death. This was no small spiritual matter for a man like Kubis. In a private letter which he wrote before the attack, on 12 May 1942, and which he signed Otta Jarotu, he said, "... but we are not like that. We have feelings too; we are not heartless."

And what of the others? What did they do?

The young Ata Moravec was sent to Pisek by his mother, and she herself, as we know from the caretaker's statement, left for Brno. After she had gone, she went to Pardubice to see Bartos, and she asked him for a capsule of poison. Bartos was in bed with articular rheumatism and he was unable to walk. He had no poison left; he had asked for some to be sent from London, but it had not yet arrived. It was Hana Krupkova who gave her capsule to Auntie Moravcova; and she affixed it behind the big brown cameo she always wore.

As everyone knows, the attempt on Heydrich's life was certainly carried out. Yet there are some details that remain obscure or in conflict with one another and that will always remain so.

A question may arise: if we are unable to clarify the whole

matter, if we cannot bring the whole truth to light, then what meaning does our account possess?

In spite of the variations between the statements and the contradictions in the evidence, and in spite of the possible mistakes in both, all accounts have this in common: they reflect the public opinion of the Czechoslovaks confronted with the Nazi occupier, whatever their social level, their calling, their political or religious beliefs.

THE HISTORIAN STEPS IN : IV

(*The author*)

Once they had recovered from their shock, the Nazis began to act. *The shock had been severe; eight months after Heydrich had entered Prague Castle, on 27 September 1941, proclaiming a state of emergency and shedding rivers of patriotic blood, two unknown men, in this Protectorate of Bohemia and Moravia that he had "pacified" by his exertions, had dared to throw a bomb at the Reichsprotektor's car, wounding him seriously.*

At 1215 hours Karl Hermann Frank telephoned Hitler and informed him of the attack. Hitler flew into a rage on hearing that Heydrich had been travelling without an escort. He told Frank to take over the functions of the Protector on a provisional basis, forbade him to move without guards, and promised him an armoured vehicle. He gave orders for the detection of the "criminals" and for the proclamation of a reward of a million marks to anyone who should bring about their arrest. He decided that any person who helped the culprits or supported their action, or who, knowing them, did not denounce them, should be shot together with his whole family. Lastly, he told Frank to arrest and execute ten thousand Czechs suspected of anti-German activities, by way of example: this was to be carried out immediately.

That afternoon, basing himself on Hitler's orders, K. H. Frank issued the following ordinance:

1. *On 27 May 1942 an attempt on the life of the acting-Reichsprotektor, SS Obergruppenführer Heydrich, was perpetrated in Prague. A reward of ten million crowns will be given for the arrest of the guilty men. Whoever shelters these criminals, provides them with help, or,*

206

knowing them, does not denounce them, will be shot with his whole family.

2. *In the region of the Prague Oberlandrat, the state of siege is proclaimed by the reading of this ordinance on the radio. The following measures are laid down:*

   a *The civilian population, without exception, is forbidden to go into the streets from 2100 hours on 27 May until 0600 hours on 28 May.*

   b *All inns and restaurants, cinemas, theatres and places of amusement are to be strictly shut and all traffic on public highways is forbidden during the same period.*

   c *Any person who appears in the streets in spite of this prohibition shall be shot if he does not stop at the first summons.*

   d *Other measures are foreseen, and if necessary they will be announced on the radio. Prague, 27 May 1942.*

The SS Obergruppenführer attached to the
Reichsprotektor in Bohemia and Moravia
(signed) K. H. Frank

Thus began one of the most bloodstained periods of modern Czech history. The German radio announced the state of siege at 1630 hours. The Czech radio did the same at 1704 hours. Every half an hour the ordinance was read again in its entirety. From 1940 hours Prague radio broadcast it every ten minutes, and from 2020 to 2100 hours it did so every five minutes.

K. H. Frank informed Himmler by teleprinter of the measures taken, particularly of the state of siege. Himmler acknowledged receipt of the message at 2005 hours, gave his consent, and insisted that that very night the "hundred most important" enemies of the Reich, chosen from the ten thousand hostages held, should be shot.

That evening, at 2132 hours, the radio broadcast a fresh ordinance announcing that the state of siege was extended to the whole Protectorate. It was again signed by K. H. Frank, who hoped to seize his chance of becoming the new Protector.

The next day, 28 May, he took a special plane to inform the Führer personally of the steps he had taken, and during the flight he made notes for the interview, touching particularly upon:

1. A display of German strength—powerful action [*underlined by K. H. Frank*]—*tanks to move through Prague.*

2. *The immediate execution of all persons suspected of opposition and of accomplices together with their entire families; but the exclusion of all mass arrests or executions.*

3. *Important rewards for those who helped in the search for the culprits.*

4. *An obvious threat—the abolition of the Protectorate's autonomy.*

   a *A pause: three weeks for the elimination of all resistance elements.*

   b *Positively: a call for the setting up of a "Front for the Reich" or some similar organization.*

   c *Measures to compel the Protectorate government led by Hacha to act: by means of proclamations to the people; furious attacks upon London—Benes—and upon Moscow and the Czech state of mind; the reward of ten million crowns; speeches addressed to the whole of the Protectorate; the broadcasting of these speeches with the participation of all the ministers and important personalities in order to influence the people—the government is ready for anything now!*

   d *The placing of Czech organizations under German command.*

   e *If, contrary to all expectation, the resistance spreads and the culprits are not found, the revocation of the Protectorate's status and the setting up of a Reich department run by the police—the execution of a large number of Czech prisoners in the concentration camps (7,000) and of several intellectuals still to be arrested.*

If we compare these notes jotted down by K. H. Frank—and they are authentic—with the orders Hitler gave him by telephone at 1215 hours on 27 May, we notice that whereas Hitler insisted upon the arrest and execution of ten thousand Czechs to make an example, the next day Frank submitted a counterproject—the immediate execution of all suspects and accomplices together with their families—but he was against mass arrests and executions.

In Frank's opinion, mass executions were, at least for the moment, ill-advised, "since they would play into the hands of our enemies, who wish to prove that killings and sabotage arise from the will of the entire Czech nation and that the nation as a whole supports them. World opinion must totally lose the impression that any national uprising is concerned: we must say that it is merely a question of individual actions."

This was subtler: Hitler agreed. But if the former Karlovy Vary (Karlsbad) bookseller had hoped to stay permanently at the head of the Protectorate, his hopes were disappointed. It was Daluege whom Hitler entrusted with the Reichsprotektor's functions and who moved into Prague Castle. Fresh ordinances were issued; lists of the first scores of executions appeared on the walls; the Nazi machine set itself to the detection of the "criminals." But it was merely groping; it had no real clue, no notion of who might have carried out the attack. Then the Gestapo remembered the man from Pardubice whose photograph had been found in Captain Moravek's briefcase after his death. They knew that this man had worked as a waiter in a Pardubice hotel and that he was probably a parachutist: he might therefore have been concerned in the outrage. Without realizing that their guess was right, on 28 May the Gestapo stuck up posters, for what they might be worth. The posters showed Josef Gabcik's photograph, and the text ran:

100,000 Crowns Reward!

Who knows this man? Who knows where he is living? His name is Miroslav Valcik, born 20 January 1920 at Hodonin. Description: medium height, about 5 foot 5 inches; fair hair brushed back and falling slightly to the right with the appearance of a parting; oval face; fresh complexion; no acne; clean-shaven. Eyes blue; nose normal; small ears.

A reward of 100,000 crowns for information leading to the arrest of the wanted man will be paid: the secret state police [the Gestapo] asks the population to apply to the Prague head office, 20 Bredovska, Prague II, telephone 200 41, extension 156, or to any other German or Protectorate police station. The reward will be paid with the utmost discretion. Prague, 28 May 1942.

The Head of the Main State Police Office in Prague
(signed) Dr. Geschke
SS Standartenführer

Since at this stage the Gestapo themselves looked upon the assumption that Gabcik was the author of the attempt on Heydrich's life as a remote hypothesis, their poster did not state why he was wanted. Then again, the Gestapo was in the dark as to Valcik's identity: they were mistaken in the particulars of his date and place of birth and in his Christian name.

The search for those who had carried out the attack began. All the people in the streetcar that stopped at the corner at the moment of the attack were summoned to the Gestapo; police brought in the inhabitants of the neighbouring houses, those who had been passing by, and everyone *who might have seen the "criminals." And the objects that Kubis and Gabcik had left behind them were minutely examined.*

The day K. H. Frank left for Berlin, a large poster printed in black on a red background appeared on the walls. This is a particularly important document because it shows what the Nazis had succeeded in finding out about the attack.

ATTEMPT UPON THE ACTING-REICHSPROTEKTOR'S LIFE

Ten million crowns reward for all information leading to the arrest of the guilty men. At about 1030 hours on 27 May 1942 an attempt on the life of the acting-Reichsprotektor, SS Obergruppenführer Heydrich, was committed. The acting-Reichsprotektor was travelling from Panenske Brezany by the Kirchmayer Boulevard and his car was turning to the right in V. Holesovickach Street, Prague-Liben, in order to reach the centre of the town. At this point a man stood in the roadway and endeavoured to open fire on the occupants of the car with a submachine gun. At the same time another man threw a bomb that exploded on touching the car. After the attack, one of the men ran away along the Kirchmayer Boulevard, Na Kolinske and Na Zapalci; there he entered Frantisek Brauner's butcher's shop at number 22. He fired several shots from the shop and then continued his flight along Na Zapalci and V. Holesovickach, probably towards the centre of the town. The other man made off on a bicycle towards Stara Liben.

The second man, of average height, slim, and dressed in a dark brown or black suit, wore a black hat.

The first, the man who fled by way of the Kirchmayer Boulevard and Na Kolinske, answers to the following description: height 5 foot 3 inches to 5 foot 4 inches, broad shoulders, strongly built, round suntanned face, thick lips, dark brushed-back hair, age 30–35. This man was wearing a brown or dark-brown suit with light stripes and brown shoes. He was bareheaded.

One of the criminals left behind him a pale beige waterproof-silk coat with light buttons. Each man had a dark-brown briefcase. These were found at the place of the outrage. One of the briefcases contained a dirty beige velour beret with the label of the Bila Labut [White Swan] stores. The criminal who fled on foot left a woman's bicycle near the spot: it has the mark Moto-Velo J. Krcmar, Teplice, and the manufacturer's number 40,363. The wheels have black rims with $\frac{3}{8}''$ red stripes; the frame and the forks are ivory and red; the handlebars red; the handgrips black; the saddle (in good condition) red-brown; the tool bag brown;

the chainguard black. The bicycle has nickelplated pump with a foot rest; the tube is 10" long. One of the briefcases found at the place of the crime was hung on the handlebars of this bicycle.

The criminals must certainly have been waiting for the Reichsprotektor at the place of the outrage a considerable time, perhaps for several hours.

With reference to the promised reward of ten million crowns for information leading to the arrest of the guilty men, which will be paid in full, it may be pointed out that the following questions arise:

1. Who can give information on the criminals?
2. Who noticed their presence at the place of the crime?
3. Who are the owners of the objects described, and above all, who has lost the woman's bicycle, the coat, the beret, and the briefcase described above?

These objects may be seen from 0900 hours today onward in the window of the Bata shoeshop at 6, Wenceslas Square, Prague II.

Whoever is capable of providing the information called for and who does not come forward voluntarily to the police will be shot together with his family, according to the terms of the ordinance of 27 May 1942 on the proclamation of the state of siege.

All may be assured that their information will be treated as strictly confidential.

Furthermore, from 28 May 1942 onward it is the duty of all owners of houses, flats, hotels, etc., to declare to the police the names of all persons in the whole Protectorate whose stay has not yet been registered at the police station. Disobedience to this regulation will be punished by death.

Information is received by the secret state police at the chief office in Prague (Staatspolizeileitstelle Prag) at 20 Bredovska, Prague II, telephone 200 41, or at any German or Protectorate police station; and this information may be given by word of mouth or by telephone.

Prague, 28 May 1942.

> The SS Obergruppenführer and Chief of
> Police attached to the Reichsprotektor
> in Bohemia and Moravia
> (signed) K. H. Frank

This edict gives a tolerably exact account of the events. It does not mention Valcik. The descriptions of Kubis and Gabcik are quite close to the facts: there are references to the beige coat Gabcik borrowed either from Ema Khodlova or from the Dejvice schoolmaster's son.

Madame Moravcova's bicycle is minutely described. Fortunately neither the police nor the Gestapo were able to trace the last owner by the serial number. The briefcases belonged to the Svatos family, who lived near Wenceslas Square and whom the parachutists often visited.

Later, on 31 May, the Nazis perfected their description. The new version of Kubis was "height 5 foot 6 inches–5 foot 8; age 30–35; slim figure. Face round, clean-shaven, full, high cheekbones, dark hair." The criminal "was bleeding and had a wound on the left cheek and the left ear or temple."

The description of Gabcik was equally detailed, but it appears that the Nazis had confused the outstanding features of the two parachutists. Gabcik was said to have "a straight nose, thick lips, high cheekbones, dark brushed-back hair." But we know that it was Kubis who had high cheekbones.

The Nazis had also taken exact measurements of the briefcases. One, they said, was made of good quality leather, and it measured $16\frac{1}{8} \times 8\frac{1}{4}$; the other, "brown, worn, made of crocodile skin," was $12\frac{3}{4} \times 8\frac{1}{2}$. "The side seams have been clumsily repaired with black thread: at the bottom right-hand corner a broad, short tear has been sewn together with four even stitches."

This, then, was the position towards the end of May 1942: Heydrich was living his last days in the Bulkova hospital and all the Gestapo possessed were clues that led nowhere. It is hard to believe that they supposed they could find the culprits by measuring a commonplace leather briefcase sewn up with black thread, or by looking for the owner of a beret with the label of the Bila Labut stores. The Nazis fully realized the trifling value of such clues as these, but they did not lose hope. They relied upon betrayal.

The Gestapo report states that the search began on the night of 27–28 May 1942: "On the orders of the secret state police head office in Prague a great sweep was organized in the city during the night of 27–28 May 1942. Four thousand five hundred men of the security police, SS and NSKK units, ordinary police and Protectorate police, together with three Wehrmacht battalions were required to seal off the town and to place sentries in the streets for the searching of the houses."

The sweep during the night of 27–28 May was primarily of a political nature, being a show of strength. But, as might be supposed from the use of units untrained in police methods, it did not carry the investigations a single step forward. A limited number of German and Czech members of the criminal police, reinforced by some members of the state police from Brno and a few country stations, was not enough, of course, to ensure a thorough check of every house. As the search had to stop at 0600 hours, since the population could go out at the end of the curfew thus rendering the police check inoperative, there was not enough time to search all the houses in certain districts.

In the course of the sweep 541 persons were arrested in the streets during the curfew because they had been unable to reach their homes in time or because they were not carrying identity cards. The stations in which members of the SD had been posted were able to release 430 persons at once, after checking their identity.

One hundred and eleven persons were transferred to the head office of the state police in Prague but eighty-eight were released after a very close check. In addition to this, three or four tramps, one prostitute and one juvenile delinquent were taken to the Prague police headquarters.

Among those detained in custody are: one leader of the resistance movement on our wanted list who has been living clandestinely since October 1941; four Jews and three Czech women suspected of having slandered the Aryan race; four persons in possession of excessive quantities of food; one woman in possession of ammunition without a permit; one Jew who had left his domicile; another Jew found in possession of books hostile to the Reich; and two Czech workers detailed for obligatory labour in Germany who had escaped.

This report implicitly admits the total failure of the sweep. The only success was the arrest of Jan Zika, a member of the clandestine central committee of the Communist party. But Zika, that "leader of the resistance movement," had not the least contact with Kubis and Gabcik. The searches did not provide any clue whatsoever as to the place or places where the authors of the attack might be found. The Gestapo were up a blind alley. Yet there was one little detail that passed unnoticed during the police sweep that might have led the Nazis to their goal.

36

The flat in Velvarska Street

(Tereza Kasperova)

"What's in here?" shouted one of the policemen in German, kicking the door with his boot.

"Our living room: a table, a chair, a sofa..."

There were cushions scattered over the sofa. The SS fell silent; his eyes darted here and there. Only one thing was in my mind: oh that he doesn't see that crack, oh that he doesn't see that crack. My daughter Alenka was sobbing. The crack opened on to a little box room where Opalka was hiding.

"Where do you sleep?" yelled the policeman. I showed them. "And where does the child sleep?" I pointed to the other bedroom: I could hardly hold myself upright. One of the policemen looked at Alenka. I had taught her what she was to say, taught her thoroughly; but a child, you know. He hesitated for a moment and then went into the side bedroom.

That was an appalling night. It was not my first contact with the Nazis. They had executed my husband in 1941 and I was left alone with my daughter. I hated them; they had destroyed our life; they had smashed our home and wiped out our family, and that was why I scarcely hesitated when some friends asked me whether I could shelter someone the Germans were after.

I was not interested in life any more. I had my daughter, of course; but if I vanished, relations would certainly look after her. So I waited impatiently for the day he should come.

I did not know his name; I did not know what he was doing here, or whether he came from the East or the West: all that mattered to me was that he needed a safe refuge and that he had important work to do.

We lived in Prague-Dejvice, in Velvarska Street near the modern high school. When you got out of the streetcar you had to turn left and take a path through the birches in a little park. The windows of our flat looked onto the path.

One day there came a ring on the bell at last and there he was. My friend Bozena, at whose home he had been living for about twenty days and who brought him to me, said good-bye and when she had gone he stayed there in the kitchen. Rather tall, slim, intelligent-looking. "Call me Adolf," he said with a pleasant smile.

I showed him where he was to sleep and where he could keep his things—he had very few—and we settled about everything he would need. We had three rooms, and in one of them a low door opened onto a kind of a little box room or cupboard, so small that a man could hardly stand up in it. I kept things in it that I did not often need, and now this little space turned out to be very useful. The door was hidden by a sofa; the upper line or crack of the door was four or five inches above the back of the sofa, but I put a blue and yellow cushion on it, concealing the door entirely. It was in this room with the cupboard that I put Adolf, showing him the hiding place he could use in case of danger.

I said nothing to the caretaker of our house. We arranged that Adolf should tell me the exact time he would come back every day so that I could open the front door for him. Sometimes he stayed in his room all day, reading; and after lunch he would help me with the washing-up. Sometimes he went away: he did not talk much, but you could see from his eyes that he had a fine character. He told me nothing about his mission, and I never questioned him at all. He was working against the Nazis: that was enough.

On 27 May he left very early in the morning. He carefully checked the clothes he was wearing, including the pockets; he took the revolver he kept under his pillow at night and said good-bye as usual; but he added, "We have a great deal of work to do today. If I am not on the path in the park at eight this evening, I shall not be coming back, so don't worry." He went down the stairs: I saw him again, passing through the trees, and he turned and waved.

At that time I worked for a dentist, keeping his appointment book up to date. That day at about eleven o'clock I heard there had been an attempt on Heydrich's life. I was staggered, and straightaway I thought of Adolf. Was he concerned in this affair? I could do nothing all day long; I dropped everything, and all I thought of was this attack and Adolf and Alenka—she was only seven then. That evening Alenka wanted to play with me, but I had no heart for it. I kept looking out of the window. Would he come? At last I saw him there on the path; he was walking slowly, with his head bowed. I opened the door for him. I made him dinner, but he ate little. "Forgive me, Madame Tereza," he said, "I've no appetite." He said these words sadly, and then he fell silent. I did not want to be a nuisance, so I went into my daughter's room. I felt he was uneasy and anxious; he did not mention the attack and I asked him no questions.

I shall never forget that night—the night of 27–28 May. Right through the whole city of Prague the Gestapo and the SS searched flats and houses, shouting and roaring, looking everywhere for the men who were responsible for the attack. They came to us too, as I have already told you. I was asleep and then suddenly I heard the bell. One ring, two rings: the ringing never stopped. I looked out of the window and there at the door I saw men in uniform, Germans. I was frightened but straightaway I began to move like an oiled machine. I ran to the bedroom, took Adolf by the shoulder and shook him; he woke up, stared at me in amazement, not understanding. "Get up quick," I said. "There are Germans downstairs—SS."

He leapt out of bed, snatched up his clothes, and together we pulled out the sofa. I opened the little door. He had to crawl—there were boxes and skis and baskets.

He got in and I pushed the sofa back to its usual place. I was hurrying out of the room when my foot caught in something soft—his tie. I took it, ran to the bed where he had been sleeping, tidied the pillows and felt something cold under my fingers. The revolver. He had forgotten it. I ran to the sofa again, pulled it out, knocked on the door: he opened it a crack; I passed him the tie and his revolver; and only then I went to open the door. The SS were outside the flat, ringing like lunatics. They bellowed, "What the hell are they up to in there, making us hang about like this?"

"I was asleep," I said quietly; but my heart was thumping.

They came in cautiously at first, but after a few moments they lost all restraint. They opened the wardrobes, they searched everywhere, throwing the quilts on the floor. Alenka was crying. Before this I had told her not to utter a word about Uncle Adolf. They looked at the sofa that stood in front of the little door, but fortunately they did not move the cushions—it was by the merest chance that they found neither the crack of the low door nor Adolf. When they had gone I had to sit down, my knees were trembling so.

What more can I tell you? Once Adolf asked me to go for a letter: I was given it by a young man with a little black moustache. He was waiting for me, looking at a poster on a wall that said that Valcik was wanted, and he laughed at it.

I did not know the other parachutists. Later I learnt that Adolf was Captain Opalka, but he never spoke to me of his men. Once he did say a few words about just one of them; he was very displeased, and I suppose he was referring to Curda. Opalka stayed with us about a week, from 24–30 May: then Bozena came for him. While he was staying with us a man from the German state police came and asked me what I did, what I was living on, etc. There was no time for Adolf to hide in the cupboard and he stayed in the kitchen with his revolver in his hand; but this German did not search the house.

When he left Opalka told me he had to join his men. "Why?" I asked. "It's more dangerous, all together in one hiding place."

"Their morale is going. I have to be there, Madame Tereza."

I did not try to keep him: he knew his duty. For his last journey I gave him a raincoat, my husband's raincoat that they had sent me from Pankrac prison after he had been executed. And some warm underclothes.

So Adolf left and I stayed there alone with Alenka. Later I often used to think of those young men. Perhaps they ought to have given themselves up to the Gestapo—Kubis and Gabcik, I mean: perhaps by doing so they might have put a stop to the massacre—but perhaps not. It is hard to say.

After the fight in the church I saw a photograph of Opalka, dead. He was no longer the same man who had lived with us. Death had changed him. At that moment I remembered my husband's raincoat: perhaps I had been wrong giving it to him. What if the Germans were to find some number or mark showing that the coat had been sent back from the Pankrac prison after the execution of a Czech officer, my husband? Every moment I expected the Gestapo to come.

They did not come. And we went on living, my daughter and I. We had escaped from death. Curda did not know our address and Adolf did not speak. The Germans murdered his family— the aunt who had taken his mother's place and his father; but they knew nothing about his fiancée in Moravia. But for my part I know how he thought of her all the time, and how he loved her.

37

A Communist from the neighbourhood of the Kobylisy firing range

(*Antonin Novy*)

I WOKE WITH a start, not knowing why. Then I heard a noise like the humming of a swarm of bees, first far away and then coming nearer. I recognized the sound of motors, of cars moving along; I got up quietly so as not to wake my wife and I went to look out of the window.

In those days of the blackout every window had to be covered with a dark-blue curtain: I raised it and put my head out. In the darkness I could see shafts of bluish light on the road, and I realized that they were the headlights of German army trucks, coming from Prague. Where are they going at this time, I wondered. It was a warm night, full of stars, and the air smelled pleasant; but before I could wonder what flowers they were that smelled so sweet I heard a song. A muffled song, lost every now and then in the noise of engines and tires. Why, I know that tune, I said to myself, it's ... At our meetings before the war we always used to sing that song. And the trucks were moving towards the firing range nearby, in Kobylisy.

My God, I thought. I was standing there barefoot in pyjamas, and my hands began to tremble: I raised the curtain with one hand and I leant on the other so as to be able to stretch out as far as I could. No, there was no possible doubt: the trucks were taking the road to the firing range.

They passed in front of our house and I could make out the

tune and the words of the song. It was the men in the second truck who were singing; in the first and the third they were silent. A shiver ran down my back. Trying to comfort myself I said: perhaps they are taking them there for some work or other: they will give them picks and shovels and then in a few hours they will come back towards the prison. But who could work now, in the darkness of the night? I tried to stop myself thinking of the worst: but how could that be done?

Impossible to go back to bed: you'll never get off to sleep again, I said to myself. But I knew very well what it was that weighed upon me so. I waited, I *waited* for them to come back again: I ended up by persuading myself they had come back. But nothing of the kind.

Who were these people in the trucks and who could tell where they had come from? For the moment that did not matter in the least. Was I going to hear a burst of fire or not? I felt for the matches, groping on the bedside table, and at that second I heard it. The burst of fire.

A hideous burst of fire. My wife sat up in bed. "Jesus, what's happening?" she cried. I tried to answer, but I could not. I dropped the matchbox and ran to the window: I saw nothing. And then again another burst.

"It's from the firing range," said my wife. "What are the Huns doing there? They can't leave us in peace, even at night."

I tried to persuade her she was mistaken—that no one had fired. But I could only think what a fool I had been, trying to believe a working party had been taken there to work at night. I let slip the words, "It's executions. They passed in front of the house in their trucks."

"Oh no! How could you possibly tell?"

"They were singing—"

At that moment, another burst, the third. I stopped counting them: my wife began sobbing into her pillow. I let the blue curtain fall back, lit the lamp and put on my trousers.

"Where are you going?" asked my wife, raising her head.

"To see Pepik." Pepik was the secretary of our Communist party cell at the factory; both before the war, and now when we were working for the underground network. My wife said nothing: she wept. "Well," I said, "I'm off," and I went out. It was dark everywhere. The trucks were not coming back; not a soul in the street. The firing squads must have woken people; but perhaps they thought it more prudent not to put on the light.

I took the first street on the right; Pepik lived close at hand. We had worked in the same factory for a great while. The house was shut up and I had to throw a little pebble at the window. But he was not asleep; he immediately appeared at the window to see who was below. He opened the door and we went upstairs.

"You heard?"

"Of course."

"They went by in front of our house. They woke me; they were singing."

Pepik was silent. We heard the sound of engines again; the trucks were coming back, empty. "We must do something," he said at last. "I'll find out what's going on."

The next day we met at Franta's. Pepik brought a tract and we copied it. It said the Czech nation would not allow itself to be terrorized even by firing squads. We handed out this tract and prepared and distributed others. We collected money and passed it on to the families of those who had been executed.

After that night I could never sleep. It began again: it was always the same noise. First the distant rumble, then the trucks coming nearer. They passed in front of our house and I was at the window; I wanted to cry out. If only I had been able to do something.

Then the bursts of fire. The hideous bursts of fire. That was in the summer of 1942—after the killing.

We had to move away from Kobylisy. For years and years my wife woke up at the sound of car engines in the road, even after the end of the war. I was the same: I could not bear the rumble of traffic moving in the night.

And as soon as anyone plays or hums the song the condemned men sang as the trucks were taking them to the firing squad, the song that we too sang at our meetings before the war, I remember that summer of 1942.

The Germans shot the best men we had.

38

The chemistry teacher's account: 4

(*Ladislav Vanek*)

THERE WAS NO telling now what would have happened if the attack had been countermanded. It had been carried out—it was done. For us this meant we must find a safe shelter for the young men and try to defend or preserve the underground network. The Nazis, out of their minds with fury, were shooting innocent people, hundreds of people "guilty of approving the outrage." It was an appalling time.

Zelenka–Hajsky, the schoolmaster, was given the task of looking for a safe hiding place for the parachutists. Through Petr Fafek, a brave, straightforward, reliable man, he got into touch with Jan Sonnevend, the Dean of the Orthodox Church in Prague, who promised his help. More specifically, he suggested the crypt of his church of St. Cyril and St. Methodius in Resslova Street.

Looking back now, one might think that gathering all the parachutists we knew into the same church was not the best solution, and that it would have been better to scatter them in different houses or to get them out of Prague. But it must not be forgotten that the town was surrounded; the Nazis were checking every road into it, searching houses and flats; and they were not going to content themselves with the great sweep they had organized during the night of 27–28 May. To us it seemed safer to hide the young men in the church—religious buildings and especially crypts were not searched—and to get them out into the country at some favourable moment.

The crypt was very cold; one froze down there. I went twice without difficulties of any kind. When I was going back a third time I saw the church surrounded by SS units and the Gestapo. That was on the morning of 18 June.

During my first visit I was able to have a talk with Opalka. On reaching the church I at once told Dr. Petrek, the Orthodox priest, why I had come. He asked me to turn my face to the wall so that I should not be able to see where Opalka came from, and then he went away. A few moments later he returned and said, "Come: Adolf is waiting for you."

Opalka was sitting in a chair. Although the June sun was shining outside, he wore a thick sweater. "How are you?" I asked. He did not reply. "Where are the boys? I should like to speak to them."

"They are wretched." That I could well understand. Every day, the execution of innocent people; every day new posters with lists of names, lists of the dead. Gabcik almost out of his mind because his gun had jammed, and the others near despair because of the horrors that were going on outside. Opalka added, "They worry me. They think everything might change if ... "

"If?"

"They want to go and see Moravec, the minister."

"What for?"

"Every day they read the execution lists in the papers. Gabcik and Kubis came to me and suggested that they should go to Emmanuel Moravec and tell him they had committed the attack—it was they the Gestapo were looking for. Their idea was they should kill him before killing themselves."

"But that's madness. I hope you forbade it."

"Of course."

"And what about them? How did they react?"

"They said nothing. They are finding it hard to keep a hold on themselves."

A wild, desperate notion. The Nazis wanted blood, the blood of thousands of victims to pay for Heydrich's death; and even if those two went there alone and gave themselves up, their sacrifice would not stop the massacre.

I looked at Opalka: he was still the same conscientious leader, fully alive to his duty. I had come to tell him that we were finding them other hiding places outside the town.

"Where do you mean to take us?"

"You will stay in Prague: we shall be needing you—you have abilities. The others will go into the country. But first we have to get you out of here." Our plan was that four parachutists should go to Kladno in a police car. A Kladno policeman had helped us to find a temporary refuge for them in a shopkeeper's warehouse.

"What about Kubis and Gabcik?"

"They will go to Oubenice, a village near Benesov; everything is ready for them there, and they will stay with a carpenter. For greater safety we shall hide them in some of the coffins that are being taken out of Prague."

Opalka agreed and I left. A few days later, on 16 June, I came back to tell him what we had arranged. The parachutists were to leave the church on Friday 19 June, because the sacristan's wife was to come back from a stay in the country at the end of that week, and we did not want her to suspect that men were hidden in the crypt. It was agreed that Opalka and I should make a trip to Kladno on Sunday 21 June, to see the young men and their new hideout.

Kubis and Gabcik were to stay in Oubenice a few days. I was to join them there and leave with them for London in a plane sent to fetch us. Opalka had a homing device that would enable him to guide a small plane in to land. While I was away, Opalka was to look after the underground network; and then I was to be flown back from London.

The four parachutists hidden in Kladno were not to remain there long either. We meant to take them to Drahanska vysocina, the mountain where groups of partisans were hiding. In the forest there lived a reliable Czech, a gamekeeper; and his house had become a kind of headquarters for all the operations carried out by the partisans.

The Silver A team, Bartos and the radiotelegraphist Potucek (Valcik was now in the church), were no longer able to work in the neighbourhood of Pardubice. It was too dangerous for them there, too. For Silver A we had found a hiding place in a quarry near the village of Rousinov, a quarry belonging to the mayor. The mayor was in agreement, and with him keeping watch Bartos and Potucek would be able to carry on with their work; the transmitter Libuse would continue to send out intelligence for London—if all went well.

39

The child from Lidice

(*Vaclav Zelenka*)

THAT EVENING we had potato soup. Papa said "Be good and eat it up," and he asked Mama whether there was any news. He went to work every day at Kladno; he was a metalworker.

After supper I went to bed. To begin with I did not dream at all: then later I had a fine dream. We were playing hide-and-seek in the village square, and some of the older children were in school, singing. We made too much noise, so the rural police-man came and there in front of the church he beat his drum and told us to be quiet. Yet it was not really the beating of a drum; it was Mama waking me up, crying. I was not in the village square but in my bed at home, and running about our house there were men in foreign uniforms. After many years I learnt that these were SS and it was they who had drummed on our windows to wake us up and ordered us to dress and leave our houses.

They told Mama to take all her valuable possessions. I did not know what the words meant, but she answered, "I have none; I've only got one ring." And to provide ourselves with food for three days. Papa was very pale. He was standing in front of the wardrobe: they had ordered him not to move. Then we all went outside and they took us to the square; a lot of people were there already—Ema, Dagmar, Eva and Venda and many others. The men in foreign uniforms were coming and going, carrying sew-ing machines, radios, bicycles. Our dogs ran round us, barking, but the SS shot at them; and they wounded our Vorech. But he crawled as far as our house. One of the Germans kicked him, and I began to cry again.

"It's nothing, nothing; don't be afraid," said my mother, stroking my hair to soothe me: but she was sobbing too. In front of the church, the square was strewn with books and pictures and other fine things the soldiers were throwing out of the windows.

Papa smiled, took me in his arms and kissed me; he had hardly had time to say a few words to Mama before the men came to take him to where they were assembling the fathers, the grand-fathers, and the biggest boys. He turned and waved to us once more. As for us, they took us to the school; our mothers came too, carrying the very little ones and the babies. It was wretched in the school; sobs everywhere; the little ones cried, the mothers cried, and we cried too.

Very early in the morning trucks came and they piled us into them. We left without seeing Papa: the men all remained at Horak's farm. They took us to Kladno high school.

I had never been to Kladno and this was the first time I had ever seen a town. Houses as high as the church at Lidice; and the school they took us to was very big, too. They housed us in the gymnasium. After that some men came to see us—the mothers said they were the Gestapo. The questioned us and looked at our hair, our eyes, and our heads, wrote down our names and left. We were given coffee and dry bread. For lunch they brought us soup and a few potatoes. For supper, the same thing.

That day—it was a Wednesday—no one knew that our fathers and grandfathers had been shot at dawn in Lidice. We were sure, and so were our mothers, that we should see them again soon.

When night came all you could hear was weeping every-where; and we did not sleep much. Mama sat by me and I went off; but I did not dream of anything, neither of the drum nor of the men in foreign uniforms. Nothing happened on the Thursday. Black coffee in the morning, potatoes at midday; and from time to time a man came and asked something. Our mothers were tired, and we were tired too. We couldn't play, but then we didn't want to, either. I asked Mama why we were in this gymnasium and she said she didn't know—that the Germans were looking for foreigners, but there were none in our village. We, the boys of the village, knew every cowshed, every bush by the stream and round the mill, but we had never seen anybody. Mama also said these German gentlemen had made up the whole thing: but I thought to myself, why do they make up things that are not true? It is wrong to tell lies.

Towards evening on the Friday a group of men came into the gymnasium. They lined us up on one side and our mothers on the other, saying they were to go somewhere by train and we were to join them by bus. But our mothers would not believe it and each one took her children and clung to them and the men had to pull hard to separate us. They managed it because there were a great many of them.

I was not to see Mama again for a long time after that. I called out to her not to be afraid and I would take care in the bus, holding on properly so as not to fall; but then these men began firing their revolvers at the ceiling to silence us.

In another room they put strings with numbers round our necks, and we, the boys of the village, pretended to be brave, saying to one another we were not to cry, so as to show the girls how to behave. But presently we were crying too.

They picked two other children and me and took us away by car without saying where we were going. An hour later we came to a big town with a great many towers and houses and a broad river, and when we had gone over a bridge we stopped. "Prag," said one of the men with us. So this was Prague.

We got out at the square—I think now it must have been Charles Square—and the men took us to a hospital. We did not know we had been selected as "suitable for Germanization." They did not speak Czech: they spoke German, but we did not know they were speaking German—all we knew was that we did not understand them at all.

I do not remember now how long we stayed in that hospital. After that they drove us in a car all day and all night. We came to a town—perhaps it was Lodz—and there we found the other children from Lidice in a camp. They put us in an old cowshed; we had no warm clothes and we were very cold. We could not wash; everything was filthy and presently we had lice. We were hungry—now and then they brought us black coffee and bread. Our clothes were all torn; we slept on the bare ground; and we knew nothing about our mothers. They did not come and yet these men in uniform had promised they would join us.

I did not stay there long. They came to see me several times: they looked at my fair hair, and in the end they sent me to Puskov—it was a house where children like me were assembled. Or an orphanage. After I got there I fell ill and they sent me to hospital. I never saw the children of our village again. At Puskov I did meet just one: that was Vasek—he had fair hair too. When I came back from hospital he told me we were going to be given to families. They took us both to Oberweis; I remember there were ruins there and a camp and a firing range; and Vasek stayed at Oberweis. I went farther on.

A man and woman from Dresden adopted me. They wanted me to call them Mutterchen and Väterchen, but I couldn't. And I wouldn't: I could still see my own father and mother. But they spoke no other language than German and I went to a German school—and I began to forget. They called me Rolf; that astonished me at first, but they told me that was my name now, and I was to forget the old one. At school they called me by my new father's surname. He was a truck driver. Later he went to the war; he was wounded, and then he came back. My German mother used to tell me German fairy tales and I forgot Czech. And so the time went by, and perhaps I should really have forgotten where I came from. The war came to an end and I was still there. I no longer remembered Lidice by name.

The Czechoslovak authorities did not find me until 1947, and I went home nearly two years after the end of the war. Home, to my own country.

It was only then that they told me the Nazis had killed eighty of the children of Lidice. No more than a few survived. My fair hair and blue eyes saved my life. And I had to begin learning to speak Czech again.

Here I heard that my father had been shot that first morning with all the men of Lidice. All that was left of our village was a flat place with thick grass growing over it. How sad it was looking at that plain. At one end there had been the school, then a little farther on the village square. And then the church and our houses. Everything had vanished.

The only person I found again was Mama. She recognized me by the three scars I had had on my chest from my earliest days. And although I had forgotten how to speak Czech, I remembered the colour of our cow exactly, and that she was called Stracena.

40

The girl and the bicycle

(*Ruzena Cizkova*)

SOMETIMES I wonder where all that hatred comes from—the hatred in a man that can make him capable of killing even a child.

In our house there lived the Novaks; they had three daughters and one son. It was an ordinary house of our working-class district with the washbasins in the corridors, and we all knew one another—you saw everybody and you knew what your neighbour was having for lunch. The walls were thin, and you heard whatever was said next door. A plain working-man's tenement like so many others in Prague.

The Novaks came here after Munich. Before that they lived at Podmokly, but they had to flee when the Nazis occupied the country in autumn 1938—that is to say, the Sudetenland.

M. Novak worked as a joiner in the railway workshops at Prague-Vrsovice. He used to get up very early and go to the streetcar stop, and at night he came back late. Since he did not make much money, his wife often used to cook very humble meals. The children worked too; but a growing girl needs a great many things, you know—now she'll be wanting a frock, and then a hat and so on. And the parents just go on working and working. But I must say the young Novaks were very good, kind children.

They had been living here quite a long while. Madame Novak used to come in now and then to borrow something from us, and we would talk, gossiping about all sorts of things. And once she said to me, "Our eldest girl Marie, you know ... " Then she stopped, embarrassed.

And at that I said, "So you have another daughter, Madame Novakova?"

At first she didn't like to answer. I had to promise never to tell anyone—and I never did—and then she told me her eldest daughter Marie had fallen in love with a German before the war, when they were still living at Podmokly. And when M. Novak heard about it he said, "Either your German, my girl, or us." In those times when Henlein's men, the future Nazis I mean, were carrying out raids against the Czechs, it was no kind of a joke to say that.

Well, in spite of everything, the girl married her German. After the occupation of the Sudetenland the Novaks fled to Prague and the daughter stayed in Podmokly. Sometimes Madame Novakova wept and wrote to her daughter, but Novak was to know nothing about it. A mother's heart, you know.

So that was how it happened nobody knew the Novaks had another daughter; and it was that which saved her life—the daughter's life. They had a son called Vasek who worked as a locksmith at a station, and three daughters, Anicka, Slavka, and Jindriska. Anicka worked in a blanket factory. She was very pretty. She kept company with a young man and they wanted to get married as soon as possible. Slavka worked at a dressmaker's here in Liben. Jindriska, the youngest, was just finishing school, and Madame Novakova told me this dressmaker had agreed to take Jindriska too after the holidays, as an apprentice. But at the time when all this happened Jindriska was still at school.

Sometimes Slavka did sewing at home for the neighbours, but it was forbidden, and once the stuff was still spread out on the table when someone knocked. Her mother took fright and threw a tablecloth over the stuff; a needle went right into her hand, all the way. It hurt, and I went to the doctor's with her; he took it out and bandaged her. We were leaving the surgery when Novakova said to me, "We need dark-blue curtains for the windows"—you had to have them during the war, you know—"come and look for some with me." Not far from the house there was a workshop that made these curtains; we went there, liked what we saw, and bought some. That was in the morning; and as we carried the curtains home we talked about what we should cook for lunch. Madame Novakova said, "I must buy some yeast."

"So must I," I said. We went to the grocer, we bought our things, and then all at once a railwayman ran in, crying, "A killing! They've shot a German up there in Liben!"

"Oh nonsense," I said, and I meant to ask Novakova if she was going to buy a cabbage too when I saw she had gone all white: her hands were trembling, and drawing a deep breath she stammered out, "So they've done it."

I'll never forget those words—never. But it was only later I understood them—at that moment I never suspected anything at all. We left the shop; Novakova was walking very slowly. "What's the matter?" I said. "Is your hand hurting you?"

"Yes."

"Go home and lie down," I said.

"No. There's something else I've got to buy." She turned round and hurried off. I watched her turn her back; I didn't understand. Then I shrugged—oh, let her do as she likes—and went home.

In the lower part of our house there was a bar, then a winding staircase. I went up slowly, ladened down with my heavy shopping basket and the curtains, and then all of a sudden I saw a man in front of me, all out of breath. He was standing further up the stairs; he was out of breath and his face was half-hidden by his hand. You would have said he had had too much to drink. I took care not to go near him, but still I did say, "Are you looking for somebody?"

"Madame Novakova," he replied.

"I've just this minute left her; she has gone to buy something and she will be back at once."

"Thank you, Madame," he said, and he ran up the stairs. He must have known the house because he did not look at the names; he went straight to the Novaks' flat and opened the door. It was not locked.

Yes, I should tell you that for three days past Madame Nova-kova had been leaving the door open. I had asked her why she did not lock it and she answered, "Why? No one will come."

No doubt the parachutist was to change his clothes in her flat, but she did not know when and that was the reason why she had not locked the kitchen door for some while. And at that time I supposed that she had forgotten.

The man went in and closed the door. I followed him up the stairs, carrying my basket—we lived in the next-door flat—and wondering who he might be. The thought came to me that per-haps he was a thief. Once I was inside, I leant my ear against the wall, but there was not a sound at the Novaks'; then I went into the bedroom and put my head out of the window to see if she was coming.

There she was at last, looking round as though she were afraid. She came slowly towards the house. I called out, "Madame Novakova, you have a visitor!"

When she heard me she was frightened; she did not reply but began to walk faster. She came into the building and hurried up the stairs. The door of their flat opened and I heard a low-voiced conversation without being able to make out the words. A few moments later the man came out again and through the partly-open door I saw he went to the sink. Blood was running from his forehead. He turned on the tap, leant over and washed. The house was quiet: no one anywhere.

Then Madame Novakova came to me and said her visitor was one of their friends from Podmokly who had hurt himself on a bicycle, braking in front of a coal truck. That was why he had come to them, to dress his wound. And she asked if I could lend her a little mirror and whether I had any iodine. I gave her the mirror and the iodine and she returned a few minutes later to give them back. She said her friend's shirt was stained with blood and her husband's were too small for him.

"Here's one of my husband's," I said, and I brought out a white shirt with blue stripes.

She thanked me, took it, and left. The man went away about midday: he had put on a railwayman's uniform. I did not see him again. Later I heard it was Kubis, the one who threw the bomb at Heydrich's car.

Ah, but before he went there was that business about the bicycle, too. Madame Novakova said to me, "Just think, Madame—he has left his bicycle there."

"Where?" I asked.

"There, where he had this accident, near the level-crossing gates."

At that moment we heard Jindriska. She was quite a big girl, but she was a little devil, and she shouted as only children can shout, "I'm back, Mama. I'm hungry." She had no notion of walking or coming up the stairs slowly; she ran and jumped and everything shook all round her.

"You've come just at the right moment," said her mother. "You must go somewhere first, and then I'll give you something to eat."

"Where?"

"A gentleman I know has left his bicycle outside Bata's. Go and bring it back and put it in the courtyard. If anyone asks whose it is, don't answer: there's been an accident and it might get him into trouble." Jindriska ran off, and Madame Novakova called out to say, "And don't try to ride it; you don't know how to. And take care of the traffic."

But Jindriska was already gone. She came back a quarter of an hour later and leant the bicycle up against the wall down below in the courtyard.

"Did anyone see you?" asked her mother.

"A lady asked me questions, but I didn't answer," said Jindriska.

That evening there were police checks through the whole district. The SS searched the houses, looking for the men who had carried out the attack. Later the Gestapo came in cars and called in all the Liben girls. I began to suspect what had happened. Madame Novakova took Jindriska to the hairdresser's and had her long hair cut short and given a permanent wave. She said she would pay when Novak had his wages. And Jindriska did not go to school; they said she was ill.

But she had to go to the Gestapo. Four girls from our building went. That day, when Novak went off to work, he brought his wife to us. She looked terrible; her hair was all over the place and I did not recognize her. Her eyes were staring, and all she did was to murmur over and over again, "Jindriska, my Jindriska."

M. Novak made her sit on a chair by the window and said, "You stay there and look out of the window. She'll come back for sure." Then he asked me to keep an eye on his wife, who was not well. "And above all, please don't let her go out, not for any reason at all."

I promised. But an hour later Madame Novakova began weeping and tearing her hair; I had to make her lie down and I put cold compresses on her forehead.

Three of the girls from our building came back that afternoon. But not Jindriska. Why, it was almost dark before we saw her in the gateway.

"What have you been doing? Where have you been all this while?"

"They lined us all up in a big room, then they brought a bicycle, the one that had been left there at the corner, and each of us had to take it by the handlebars and walk across the room; and there were several women watching us and they were supposed to recognize which girl from Liben it was who had taken the bicycle from outside Bata's."

"And what then?"

"It was hot and I felt ill and it was not my turn until almost the end. But those women did not recognize me." She began to laugh, hopping on one leg. But Madame Novakova was at the end of her tether and when Novak came back from work he and their son Vasek had to carry her back to their flat: she looked dreadful.

After that we waited for something to happen. In the end we thought everything was going to go off all right for the Novaks. That was what we thought until that evening.

I was in the bedroom and I heard M. Novak talking loud; as far as I could make out his wife had been to see someone. She had been carrying food—for the parachutists, probably—and she arrived at the very moment the Gestapo were there. Madame Novakova had told them she had just come to fetch something;

the Gestapo had said nothing, but they had confiscated her identity card.

The next day it was fine; the sun was shining and the school holidays had begun. I went out with my little girl to go for a walk by the river. Jindriska saw me and said she would come with us and push the baby carriage. She had put her school attendance papers in a drawer, and she was afraid that when her father came back in the evening he would say she had been foolish.

We came back about five that afternoon; I took the baby in my arms and told Jindriska to leave the baby carriage in the courtyard. I went slowly upstairs and then all at once there in front of me I saw Vasek Novak in shorts, without a shirt, and behind him Madame Novakova and her daughter Slavka, surrounded by unknown men. Vasek's hands were chained.

The Gestapo! I knew it at once, and all I felt was a dreadful, helpless horror. They went by me; I said something to Madame Novakova and stood there petrified. I could not take another step. They led them down, left the building, and at that moment Jindriska darted into the courtyard. She had not seen them—she knew nothing.

"What's the matter with you?" she asked me. I did not answer. What could I say? "Aren't you well? It must be the sun." She tried to help me; she held me up. I did not know what I ought to do, and at that moment a neighbour appeared on her balcony and called out, "Jindriska, run—get away. The Gestapo are here. They've come for you!"

Jindriska's eyes opened wide; she did not stir for a moment and then she flew up the stairs—only Jindriska could go so fast. She opened the door and cried, "Mama!"

And I ran up after her, two steps at a time. I opened the kitchen door and looked. Everything was upside down, thrown open, you can't imagine the mess.

At this moment a Gestapo man came out of the bedroom and shouted something in German. We had made a dreadful mistake.

Three and a half hours I had to sit there in the Novaks' kitchen, holding my baby on my lap with Jindriska sitting opposite me. He had slapped her in the face.

And when you think that when we were coming back from the river Jindriska had kept saying she was hungry. "Now you can have something to eat," I said to her as we were sitting there staring at nothing and this Gestapo man behind, keeping watch on us.

"But I'm not hungry any more," she said, so sadly.

A few minutes later she got up and went to the stove. Madame Novakova had made noodles that day. And the Gestapo man jumped up and began hitting her. Because she had not asked his permission.

It was already dark outside. Downstairs boys came to the pub with jugs for beer, but no one was allowed out of the building— they could only come in. So when someone's son was late coming home and his mother happened to go out to find him, they would arrest her in the courtyard; and when the father came to see what was the matter, he was made to stay in the corridor. In this way a whole crowd of people were gathered together; and the Gestapo waited for M. Novak to come home from work. And so that no one could warn him, they stopped everyone going into their flats.

The last of the family the Gestapo arrested was Anicka. She came back from seeing her fiancé, smiling, wearing a big new white straw hat with a ribbon, looking so very happy.

They shut up the flat and left. We never saw the Novaks again. About a week later I went to the Pecek Palace—that was the Gestapo's headquarters—to ask how the Novaks were and whether they needed anything. But the man at the desk shouted that they were quite all right and what was I worrying about them for? Did I want to stay there too? I looked at him and I said, "It's nothing to do with that, but they had cooked noodles in their kitchen and the noodles must have gone bad—the whole house smells." He did not know what to say to that and he turned me out.

The Novaks all died in a gas chamber. Little Jindriska too. Madame Novakova went mad in prison before the execution.

The only one who escaped was their eldest daughter, the one who had married a German. But what kind of a life can hers be? I would not be in her shoes for anything on earth.

41

A letter of denunciation

(*Josef Stula*)

IN THOSE DAYS I worked at the Benesov Czech police station. After the attempt on Heydrich's life all stations were sent photographs of the coat, the briefcase and perhaps of the bicycle, though I don't remember that, found on the spot after the attack, together with orders to show them to all the adult population. These people were to sign a declaration to the effect that they had seen the photographs, that they did not recognize the objects, and that they did not know their owners. This clever idea was supposed to lead to the arrest of the guilty men.

The Nazi authorities also ordered us to send them any information received, even anonymous information, that might help in the search; and it was to be forwarded immediately. The Benesov station was to communicate with the Gestapo at Tabor, the nearest town in the region.

Occasionally we received anonymous denunciations of some-one or other suspected of anti-Nazi activities: it was unusual, but it did happen. At our station we systematically destroyed all letters of this kind. All the policemen in our section did so—we thought it a useful thing to do—except for one sergeant who was given to talking, particularly when he had drunk a little too much. When he was in that state he did not realize the danger, and therefore we avoided speaking of our anti-Nazi opinions when he was around.

On the crucial day the officer in command of our section was ill and I had to take his place. And this sergeant was on duty.

His first job in the morning was to fetch the mail for the three sections of police, which were all in the same building. I very clearly remember the moment this talkative sergeant came back from the post office and put the mail addressed to our section on my desk, particularly pointing out what he thought a suspicious letter taken from a white envelope. The letter had been posted in the town of Trebon and it was addressed to the Benesov police station. It attracted my attention, but I thought it better to wait until the sergeant had gone before I read it. The letter was anonymous; the handwriting strong and firm. If I remember rightly, it began like this: "Stop the search for the men who committed the attempt on Heydrich's life, stop the murder of innocent people, because I can tell you that the attack was carried out by Gabcik and … " I forget the second name, so let us say it was X. The anonymous denunciation went on, "Gabcik comes from Slovakia and X has a brother in Moravia who is a butcher."

The later passages were unimportant, I think; I do not remember them now. The denunciation was not signed and so in my view it had not the least significance; I showed it to my colleagues and they too were all of the opinion that it was a commonplace piece of nonsense. I said that we should burn it, as we usually did with anonymous letters. But one of my colleagues pointed out that the sergeant knew of it; that he had already mentioned the letter in the next-door office, and that we ought to take care not to get into unnecessary trouble.

We did not know the names mentioned in the letter; they were not usual in our district; so we thought it was some kind of a practical joke.

No, the letter was not registered: it was a perfectly ordinary letter.

Before we could make up our minds how to get rid of it, a lieutenant from the next section came in and asked what we were talking about. I showed him the denunciation.

"What do you mean to do with it?"

"It would be best to destroy it," I said.

"Wouldn't you like to give it to me?"

"What would be the point?"

"Listen," he said, "I have a little house at Jindrichuv Hradec—it's quite close to Trebon—and I need to do some repairs there. If you give me this letter, I'll have a reason for going there on duty—going to find the person who wrote it—and I'll be able to use a service car."

I glanced round the room. No one said anything. I should tell you, by the way, that according to the instructions in force in those days there had to be serious reasons for undertaking a service journey in a car, and in this case it was quite a long trip, outside our district. I gave him the letter.

The next day the lieutenant asked the commanding officer for permission to go on duty to the district of Trebon, where the letter had been posted, telling him at the same time of his private reasons for this "investigation on the spot." The commanding officer agreed on condition that the journey should be put off until the next day so that he could go too—it was beautiful weather at that time. But the next day he had an important piece of business to deal with, and the journey did not take place until three days later.

The two officers and their driver left at about ten o'clock in the morning. We had no notion that they would soon be back. But at one in the afternoon I met them in the corridor, looking pale and anxious.

"What are you doing here?" I asked, astonished.

"Things have turned nasty."

"How?"

"Well, you see… that letter was genuine!"

In the commanding officer's room they told us about it. "The trip began well; the weather was fine, the sun shone, and we delighted to have such a fine day for our so-called investigation. We stopped at Tabor to tell the Gestapo we were beginning our search for the writer of the anonymous letter. As soon as we got there and before we could say a word, the Gestapo man shouted 'Where is that letter?' It was like a thunderbolt. Straightaway he started bawling and barking, so I brought the letter out of my pocket; he read it quickly and cried, 'Why have you brought it so late?' We did not know what to say and he roared 'Get out!' We came back at once."

Thinking it over, we saw that we were all in danger. But that particular afternoon we were convinced that the Gestapo had fabricated the denunciation to check our "loyalty"—we knew other cases of the same kind.

That evening, listening to the radio, we heard that Gabcik and the other whose name I forget were the men who had committed the attempt on Heydrich's life. "God above," said my colleague, "but those ... those are the names in that anonymous letter."

We waited for the coming of the Gestapo—for arrests. At that point our lives were not worth two cents.

42

What an archivist knows: 2

(*The author*)

KAREL CURDA received his millions of crowns and marks. He was not to escape his just deserts, however: in 1947 he was judged by a Czech court, sentenced to death and hanged.

In our records there is an important document dealing with his treachery. It was written by the SS Standartenführer Dr. Hans Geschke, Commander-in-Chief of the Prague Gestapo, and addressed to the Reichsprotektor Daluege and to K. H. Frank. It is dated 25 June 1942 and it runs as follows:

In order to investigate the attempt on SS Obergruppenführer Reinhard Heydrich's life, committed 27 May 1942, the central office of the state police in Prague set up a special commission. At the beginning of its work, all this commission had at its disposal were a certain number of statements, which included a good description of the criminals and of the objects they left on the spot. For three weeks all possible and imaginable means were resorted to, but in vain: not the smallest useful clue was discovered. A comparatively large number of the Czech inhabitants, as we found later, could have given information about the objects; but they remained silent.

It is not the intention of this report to give details of the immense amount of detective work carried out by the state police; it is confined to an account of the following up of those clues that were later to result in the discovery and liquidation of the criminals.

On 16 June 1942 Karel Curda, a native of the Protectorate, born 10 October 1911 at Stara Hlina, working-man, Catholic, unmarried, formerly domiciled with his parents at Trebon no. 12, came to the special commission of the head office of the state police and stated that he recognized one of the briefcases left behind at the place of the outrage. During the interrogation, whose results agreed with those of the technical criminal investigation, it at once became apparent that we were dealing with a clue of the first importance and that Curda's statements were true. Later he admitted that he was a parachutist and that he had landed in Protectorate territory during the night of 28–29 March 1942 together with five other agents. He recognized the briefcase immediately, saying that he had seen it in the possession of another parachutist at the flat occupied by the Svatos family; and he confirmed that this briefcase contained an English light machine gun with which he was familiar.

As his description of this parachutist agreed with the description of one of the criminals, Josef Gabcik (cover-name Zdenda), formerly domiciled at Poluvsie near Zilina, was set down as a suspect. Curda did not know Gabcik's present dwelling place. The head office of the state police worked upon this clue with the utmost energy; and employing all possible means it discovered a direct lead after no more than thirty-six hours of the most concentrated activity; this clue pointed to the criminals, and in the subsequent five hours it led to their discovery and liquidation.

Curda mentioned his suspicion that the second criminal might be Jan Kubis (cover-name Navratil), Gabcik's best friend; but he was unable to confirm this. The two parachutists named by Curda were unknown to us as enemy agents: their names too were unknown. The weapons of English manufacture found at the place of the attack showed that parachutists had certainly taken part in the outrage. When at last Curda, in the course of subsequent interrogations, betrayed part of the clandestine shelter network used by enemy agents and known to him, these shelters were discreetly watched according to our tactical methods, all at the same time and as rapidly as possible. This investigation finally resulted in the identification of the Svatos family, the owners of the second briefcase found at the place of the outrage, and of Madame Moravcova, the owner of the woman's bicycle.

The bicycle had in fact been lent to Zdenda, alias Gabcik, and the Svatos family's briefcases to Ota, alias Kubis; from the criminal point of view this entirely proved these persons' complicity in the attempt on the life of SS Obergruppenführer Heinrich Reinhard Heydrich.

The church of St. Charles Borromeo is a Greek Orthodox church, although in view of its origin the term Czech Orthodox would be preferable. At 0415 hours on 18 June 1942 the operation against this church began.

These are extracts from the Gestapo's report to Kurt Daluege and K. H. Frank. They tell us the name of the traitor—Karel Curda. But at the same time we see that without Curda's betrayal the investigation would not have taken a "favourable turn." The report states this plainly: "for three weeks all possible and imaginable means were resorted to, but in vain: not the smallest useful clue was discovered."

It was at this juncture that Curda appeared: it was he who betrayed Gabcik and Kubis, but he did not know their hiding place. That is important. The report also confirms that the Nazis did not even know their names.

Nowhere does the report state how the parachutists' hiding place was discovered—the church of St. Cyril and St. Methodius, which the Nazis called St. Charles Borromeo. It speaks only of the shelter network that Curda betrayed. It says that these people were arrested immediately; one may have been tortured. There were many who knew of the hiding place; they took food there, kerosene for the stove, and other things.

There is another document that throws light upon this question. It is the "final report," the Abschlussbericht, that was sent to Berlin on 5 August 1942 and that states: "The operation against the church was carried out for the following reasons: first, the criminals might have been warned by the liquidation of the resistance cells; and secondly, it was not known whether subterranean passages might possibly enable the criminals to escape from the crypt. During two interrogations on the day of 17 June and the night of 18 June we at last obtained two clues concerning the church of St. Charles Borromeo, in which the authors of the outrage were hidden. Plans of the church were immediately sent for. ...."

The liquidation of the resistance cells referred to in the report means that of the betrayed shelter network—the Moravec family, the family of the schoolmaster Zelenka–Hajsky, the flats in

Pardubice and elsewhere. But it was not until 17 June and the night of 18 June that the Nazis had two clues leading to the church.

Who knew the place where the parachutists were hidden? The Abschlussbericht sent to Berlin says: "In the course of the interrogations, fourteen persons admitted that they were aware of the preparations for the outrage. Thirty-five persons knew the place where the parachutists hid after the attack."

Thirty-five persons, then, according to the Nazis. They are not named. It is said that one who successfully resisted torture was the young Ata Moravec. There are certain clues that point to the church—but here it is not a question of the priests of St. Cyril and St. Methodius.

For a better understanding of the situation let us quote the statement of Karel Curda, a statement made to the Czech authorities at the time of his arrest in June 1945.

On 16 June 1942 I travelled to Prague and went to the Gestapo at the Pedek Palace in Bredovska Street. They began questioning me. To start with they showed me photographs of a few parachutists and asked whether I knew them. I recognized them all: the photographs were of Lieutenant Pechal, and of Kolarik, Miks and Gerik. But I said I did not know them. They beat me, saying they had already captured Gerik and they knew more about it than I thought. Then I admitted I knew the men whose photographs they had shown me. Then they showed me an album with photographs of our Czech soldiers in Poland. I recognized four or five of them, and since I was forced to, I told them so.

I also admitted that I was a parachutist, dropped on 27 March 1942 in the neighbourhood of Telc in Moravia with two other men of my team, and that we had hidden a bundle in a field: they did not even ask me which of us had hidden it. I also admitted that Gerik was in the plane with me, but that he had not jumped at the same time as I did. I told them my whole history since my landing, and during my account I betrayed the people who had sheltered and helped me, that is to say my brother-in-law Antonin Maca at Kolin, the owner of the printing works at Lazne Belohrad, M. Krupka and Alois Moravec, the Svatoses in Michalska Street in Prague, Sergeants Valcik and Kubis, Madame Baucova, and my mother and sister at Nova Hlina.

I know nothing about these people's fate: all I know is that my mother and sister were arrested and then released. Superintendent Jantura and the Gestapo officer Horny questioned me through interpreters. I did not betray the postman Drobil of Jindrichuv Hradec nor Mrvik of Kolin, who gave me clothes. I spoke of the man who had housed us with the Svatoses, but I did not give his name because I did not know it.

They asked me whether I knew someone called Motycka. I did not. They said that was impossible, because Gerik knew him. They also asked me if I was a radio technician and if I knew how to work receivers and transmitters and other instruments. When I said no they were surprised that I should not understand Gerik's trade. They questioned me about a man called Navratil, whom I had known in the Czechoslovak battalion in England. I told them he had killed himself cleaning a weapon.

The next day the interrogation went on. This time I betrayed the names of Captain Sustr and Major Blavic, and their duties and where they worked, and the airfields at Velesbourne and near Narvick. I did not admit anything else. As I was forced to it, I gave away the names of Captain Opalka and Kolarik and the parachutists of two other teams. Since I had seen in the paper that Kolarik's family had been executed I told where he lived. As for Captain Opalka, I said I did not know where he lived; I told them I had seen him for the last time at the Svatoses'. I also told them how he treated me. And I admitted that a lady who was a liaison agent had come to see me in Madame Baucova's flat. I betrayed the names of Lieutenant Pechal and Sergeant Miks, saying that they had come in the plane with me but that I did not know where they had been dropped.

After the interrogation they took me into the cellar. There I saw Ata Moravec.

The fact that someone should have spoken of the church under torture is not the most serious aspect of this case. It was from Curda that the bloody trail originated. Curda went to the Gestapo of his own free will. No one forced him to do it; he was in no kind of need; he had a safe refuge, he had clothes, he had papers, he was fed.

Later he changed his name and called himself Jerhot; he received his millions, became a trusted associate of the Gestapo, married a Nazi woman and began a new life. Life, money, peace, under the shadow of hundreds of deaths.

He did not escape punishment. In 1947 he was hanged. But what punishment could make him pay for his treachery and its consequences?

And did not responsibility lie with those who sent him to Czechoslovakia, although they had been warned of his dubious character? The soldiers of the Czechoslovak military unit in England sent a letter to the former minister of national defence in London, General Ingr, in which they said that Curda was not trustworthy, that he drank too much, that in two English families he had attempted fraudulent marriage proceedings, that he admired Hitler, and that he said he had behaved foolishly in leaving the Protectorate, where he might have had a better life.

What did General Ingr do with this letter? He passed it on to Colonel Frantisek Moravec, the chief of intelligence in the ministry of national defence.

And what did Colonel Moravec do? It seems that he made a note on the letter to the effect that Curda was a good athlete and that he had undoubted physical qualities.

43

The interpreter's account: 1

(Josef Chalupsky)

HERE IN 1930 I opted for Czech nationality, although I lived in the frontier region where the situation was often difficult. Before that, that is to say after the First World War, I was employed in the regional administration. In 1925 I was transferred to Sokolov, then to Prisecnice, and lastly to Vejprty, in the district administration. In 1937 a section of the state police was set up at Vejprty and I was appointed head of it. Then came Munich; the Germans occupied the region, and I fled to Prague, where I worked in the central police station. And it was there, on 18 August 1939, that the officer in command told me I was placed at the disposal of the German state police as an interpreter in the counterespionage section.

That frightened me. A colleague said, "Go on: you will be in a position to help decent people."

It was easy enough to say, but actually doing it ... You risked your life. When I spoke to the chief of the counterespionage section, Fleischer, he said to me plainly, "Your parents were German: why did you opt for Czech nationality?"

"Because I am a Czech, sir."

"Well, think it over. What is it you want? To go to a concentration camp?"

I thought it over and accepted, comforting myself with the thought that perhaps I might really be able to help my own countrymen. Maybe another man, acting the hero's part, would have chosen the concentration camp: but I was not brave enough for that.

The first affair in which I had to translate concerned a military espionage group; the second was to do with a man called Bondy, who had organized a clandestine group in Budapest. Among the people arrested were several very well-known Czech hockey players, such as Pacalt and Tozicka, members of the Prague team that played in Hungary.

During those days I looked around me, and I got to know my chief. Fleischer was a cruel, illiterate brute; he had only one way of interrogating suspects—torture; and he flogged and flogged and flogged.

I also came to know a Nazi officer called Thümmel; but he used the cover-name of Holm. It was said that he had been a baker in Saxony, yet he had an important position in Prague. He was on good terms with Fleischer, who gave him various papers and the results of interrogations, to keep him informed. He was a strange man, and later he was arrested by the Gestapo: it was said he was an English spy. But at that time Fleischer trusted him completely and let him read the documents—he could even take them home.

At that period the Gestapo were carrying on an investigation into the case of an unknown traitor who was telling the Allies about the Nazis' most secret plans. They arrested an important Nazi official in the town of Liberec and brought him handcuffed to Prague; but after questioning him they were obliged to let him go. Fleischer was censured for this. How could he have told the unknown traitor was Holm?

One day Fleischer received a postcard from abroad, written in Czech, and he brought it to me to translate. I looked at the card: it had been posted in Belgrade and it said that the Three Musketeers sent Fleischer their best wishes. It was from Captain Moravec and two other officers, Masin and Balaban, whom the Gestapo had been vainly trying to find for a long while. Fleischer frothed with rage. I found him a very amusing sight, though I did not let him know it; but I had no idea that the man behind this joke was Holm—he had sent the card during one of his journeys on duty. "How come they are in Belgrade?" said Fleischer over and over again.

Holm and his wife lived near the Dusty Bridge: they had no children. In the end the Gestapo arrested him. It was said that a captured Czech officer, under torture, gave the description of a Nazi officer to whom he had passed money for secret information. Holm was on the list of suspects, and when he was tortured he confessed that he was the traitor they had been looking for.

Moravek and Holm worked together for a long time. For example, Holm gave Fleischer the address of the flat where Captain Moravec was hiding; but he also warned Moravec, and when Fleischer's men got there, all they found was an empty room and two full wastepaper baskets. On one was written *For Goebbels*, and on the other *For Göring*.

Two months after I had been posted to the Gestapo I heard a conversation between Fleischer and Herschelmann, one of his subordinates. Fleischer said he had not yet received information from Gustav. I did not forget that name, and later I found that it referred to a Gestapo agent, a certain Preucil. Fleischer had had him taken to the Polish frontier, and a few shots were fired after him to make the Poles believe that Preucil was escaping from the Protectorate illegally: then the Gestapo waited for the intelligence he would send. His mission was to go to England and join the Czechoslovak forces. He succeeded: he was drafted into the air force and from time to time he sent cards and letters with information. I had to translate them; but I took copies, and in May 1945, after the liberation, I handed them to the Czech authorities. Preucil was condemned to death, and he had thoroughly deserved it. He did not stay long in England: perhaps they had begun to suspect him. He escaped in a plane and landed in Belgium. Fleischer went to fetch him and brought him back to Prague. Here Preucil went on working for the Gestapo; he denounced members of the resistance, and helped Superintendent Pannwitz, who was hunting the parachutists and who, together with Fleischer, was in charge of the investigations into the attempt on Heydrich's life.

After the attack I translated a few letters of denunciation sent to the Gestapo. There were not many of them: they were often

anonymous and had nothing to do with the matter—two neighbours would quarrel and then one out of revenge would denounce the other, saying he had hidden parachutists or something
of that kind.

But there was one I cannot forget: it was the anonymous letter
which said that parachutists were living at the home of a schoolmaster called Zelenka in Prague-Vrsovice. I do not remember
where it was sent from. I could not destroy correspondence of
that kind: these letters were numbered and recorded. I did think
I should go and find the schoolmaster that evening to warn him;
but all at once the investigation took an unexpected turn. Curda
came to the Gestapo and gave them almost unbelievable
information.

A round-faced man with thick lips and uneasy eyes. For a few
interrogations I was his interpreter. Once we were alone together
for a few moments and I said to him, "Why do this?"

"I could not bear the killing of innocent people," he said.

"And are you satisfied now? Do you think they are going to
stop all this, all these killings and reprisals?"

He looked at me with astonishment and said nothing. Later I
was sorry I had spoken to him: he was a coward, and he had
talked for the money, not to save innocent people. There was a
strange look on his face when I came in again to translate his interrogation. I was afraid he would tell Fleischer of our conversation. Fleischer did not trust me: I know he had me watched.

But let us go back to Curda. He denounced everybody who had
helped him. Even the woman who had sheltered and hidden
him during the police-raids. And the Moravec family of Prague-
Zizkov. He did not know the place where the parachutists were
hidden, that church in Resslova Street. But the name of Madame
Moravcova was enough for Superintendent Pannwitz. He had
the building surrounded.

"You will come with us," he said, turning to me.

"But I have work to do, Superintendent."

"No arguing. Come on."

I do not remember the exact time, but it was about dawn, perhaps on Wednesday 17 June. The cars set out: we drove through

the middle of the city and went to Zizkov. The superintendent was like a hound on a scent. He trembled with eagerness and kept telling the driver to go faster. I was ordered to stay with him. We crossed the Bulhar circle, turned to the left and went up the hill. This was Zizkov: old, commonplace houses, little shops. Prague was not awake yet. Tomorrow there would be fresh red posters all over the walls.

I closed my eyes: I should have liked to be a great way off, to know nothing about it. If only these people could be warned— if only one could wake them up and cry "Run, Madame Moravcova: you have only five minutes. Hide your son, above all hide your son: it is important. We still have one block to go—hurry, hurry." Then here was the street and here was the house. The cars pulled up. "What is Curda doing just at this moment?" I wondered.

Fleischer ran to the front door and began ringing. He skipped with impatience there at the door, but still he kept looking round him, his hand on his revolver. The door remained shut. Fleischer rang again, swearing. At last we heard footsteps and a woman appeared, perhaps the caretaker. She opened her mouth to say something, but the superintendent thrust her back and walked in. He stopped in front of the elevator. "Where do the Moravecs live?" he asked. I had to translate.

The caretaker gave a start. She was frightened. She muttered something and then all at once she answered very loud, "Would you like to take the stairs or the elevator?"

It seemed to me that she was shouting on purpose, to warn the people in the house. But Fleischer did not notice anything: I translated the question; he made a gesture and began running up the stairs. She asked whether she might close the front door and he shouted "Get the hell out of here, and quick about it!"

When he reached the landing he looked at the names on the doors, found the Moravecs' and pressed the bell. We waited: the house was quiet, peaceful. A movement could be heard inside the flat and then the door opened. Without a word the superintendent stepped quickly into the hall, followed by his men. He ordered me to stay outside the door.

I do not know what happened inside. A few minutes later they called me. When I went in I saw three people standing with their faces to the wall, an elderly man, a woman, and a youth. It was the Moravec family.

"Where are the parachutists?" shouted Fleischer and I translated.

The superintendent was mad with fury; he had been convinced that he would find the men who killed Heydrich in the Moravecs' flat; but there was no one there. His men had turned the whole place over without finding the least trace. All M. Moravec said was, "I don't know anyone."

"You'll remember," shouted Fleischer, and he rushed into the next room.

"I must go the toilet," said Madame Moravcova gently. The Gestapo man watching them only answered with an oath. "Please, please: I have to."

"Another bloody lie," cried the Gestapo man, hitting her. A few moments later Fleischer called him and I was left alone with them.

Madame Moravcova, leaning against the wall, turned towards me and asked me the same thing that had just been refused a few moments before. "Go on, Madame," I said, although I had no right to do so. She thanked me and left. Coming back into the room, the superintendent cried, "Where's the woman?"

"In the toilet."

Furiously he bellowed "Idiot, fool." He rushed at the door, broke it down; Madame Moravcova was still standing; a strange smile lit up her face; then she collapsed.

"*Wasser*," shouted Fleischer. His men came running with water; they did everything possible to bring her back to life. They did not succeed: she had poisoned herself. "I shan't forget what you have done," said Fleischer to me.

They carried Madame Moravcova's body into her sister-in-law's flat next door, and I translated a little more while the search in the Moravecs' went on. From the first moment one thing was obvious: the parachutists were not living there. Madame Moravcova could no longer speak: there remained her husband and

Ata. The boy's eyes were filled with horror. The superintendent went up to him, looked at him and smiled. He knew a great deal about men. They were taken to the Gestapo, in their pyjamas, just as they had been woken; and I did not see them again.

Then we left. Before we went I began to vomit. Fleischer ordered me not to leave my office. I was not called upon to translate Ata's interrogation.

A hideous morning. And I had no suspicion of what was still in store for me.

44

The sister next door

(Bozena Moravcova)

I'M SEVENTY now, so what can I possibly remember? Nothing. And what did I know in those days? Nothing. We lived next door to one another, and every day I used to go to my brother's flat for my meals. I had only had breakfast at home. But they never told me anything. I had not the least idea my sister-in-law was looking after parachutists and sheltering them.

I had two lodgers—two young ladies—so my sister-in-law couldn't house anyone in my flat. I saw Valcik in her flat just once; but it was only later that I knew his name.

My nephew Ata was a fine boy. We used to call him the Fighter for God—it was a name we took from one of the Hussite army hymns. He had a boisterous nature, and in 1939, after the Germans came to Prague, he had a fight with a Nazi and put one of his fingers out of joint. His brother Mirek, the one who fled abroad and then became an airman in our army, was quieter.

That dawn, 17 June, my bell rang. I opened the door and there was a Gestapo man. He came in and shouted "Where are the parachutists?"

I had no notion of what he wanted; I went behind the curtain and I said to the two young ladies, "Get up, get up, if you please. Hitler's gentlemen are in the house."

He began telling me something, but he spoke German and he spoke fast, so I said to him, "Excuse me, but I don't know what you want."

He called the interpreter. I gathered that they had come to the

Moravecs. They searched my flat, looking at everything, even the toothbrushes. They even squeezed out the tubes of toothpaste: perhaps they were looking for poison. I had to open the wardrobes and the drawers and the baskets; one pushed his rifle under the bath and knocked against a chamber pot—it made a noise, and he jumped and cried out. The young ladies were trembling with fear, and so was I. We had to stand against the wall with our arms in the air and one of them pointed his revolver at us. Their officer came and said something to the interpreter, who asked whether they could bring a sick person from next door. With a kind smile the interpreter said to me, "Will you let her be brought here?" My throat closed up; I could not get out a sound.

I bent my head and they carried in my sister-in-law and put her on my bed. She was all wet. They had tried to bring her round with water—but she was dead. As I learnt afterwards, she had swallowed the poison the parachutists had given her.

I don't know what happened to me then; my legs wouldn't hold me and I started to weep. Such horrors.

A doctor came, and he said "There was no point in sending for me," and they said he was to write a death certificate. About seven o'clock in the morning they brought a coffin. I was still standing against the wall; I was not allowed to sit down. Meanwhile they had taken my brother and Ata away; then they put my sister-in-law into the coffin and took that away too. But as they carried it down they bumped it on the stairs and I heard the sound of a coffin on the stone steps. I kept hearing that noise for a great while.

They forbade me to leave the flat; the young ladies could not go either. The Gestapo stayed there in the Moravecs' flat next door. Their men were waiting for someone to come, probably a parachutist—someone who did not know the family had been arrested. Later they moved into the pharmacy opposite our house; they watched the door and the windows of the flat with a telescope, and they stayed there several weeks. They did not capture anybody at all.

Not one of the Moravec family ever came back. My brother and Ata were executed in the Mauthausen concentration camp, and Mirek died somewhere abroad during the war. I have their photographs and I often look at them and talk to them. Every Sunday I do the housework and put on my best dress and wait. But I am old and I am alone, so very much alone. If only I knew that at least they had not died in vain.

That is what makes me suffer; suffer all the time.

45

The interpreter's account: 2

(*Josef Chalupsky*)

I SAT THERE in my office waiting for someone to call me to translate, but nobody took any notice of me. They were all coming and going—something was up. Fleischer passed through the room, darting a furious glance at me: he must be remembering that I let Madame Moravcova go—that was it. They were probably questioning M. Moravec and Ata.

Towards midday I was thinking of asking leave to go and get something to eat when Superintendent Pannwitz appeared at the door and said, "Come on. We are going." I put on my coat and went out with them.

The cars were waiting outside the building. We left at once. We took the same road, the road we had taken at dawn, and the people passing by looked at us with hatred in their eyes and in their hearts. And once again we turned to the left and climbed to Zizkov. We stopped in the same street, but we went to another house.

This time the Gestapo chiefs went straight ahead. They asked no questions, they did not look around, but went directly up the stairs with their men after them. I, being the interpreter, came last. I do not remember which floor it was. Fleischer went to a door and rang. Silence. He rang again. We heard slow, cautious footsteps, and someone looked through the peep hole. Pannwitz noticed it, gave an order, and instantly his men began to smash the door in. It began to yield, and then a woman opened it. We caught sight of a man running into the bathroom. Herschelmann

259

of the Gestapo opened fire; so did the others. I leapt back and I saw the name on the door: Jan Zelenka, schoolmaster. So it was that teacher, that Zelenka.

Just then a voice called from the bathroom. No point in translating—it was in German. Zelenka spoke the language well. *"Nicht schliessen! Ich komme heraus!"*

The Gestapo men stopped firing: they must have been surprised. Fleischer motioned to them, with his revolver pointing at the door. The bathroom door opened. M. Zelenka came out. He took two or three steps; Superintendent Pannwitz advanced to arrest him and at that instant the schoolmaster stretched out his arms and drew himself up; his body twisted, and before the superintendent could touch him he fell. He had poisoned himself.

"Himmel Hergott," roared Fleischer. Once again he had come too late. They took a rug, rolled the body in it and probably took it to a doctor—the superintendent wanted the stomach emptied: but the schoolmaster was quite dead.

They were mad with fury when they returned to the Gestapo building. Again I was ordered not to stir from my office. The hours went slowly by. People left their work, and there I stayed. The sun set and evening came on; I ate a roll and a piece of sausage. I tried working so as to forget, and I took up a paper, meaning to translate it: but I could not. All these events passed through my head, one after the other. I remembered how they set fire to the village of Lidice a week before, and when they came back they celebrated what they had done. The day after one of the Gestapo men had said to me, "Nothing was found; nobody was hidden there. But it was wonderful."

Where were the parachutists now, I wondered. Did they know what had happened at Zizkov? Had they been warned?

The coming and going outside my door never stopped. Night had fallen. I left the room and asked the nearest Gestapo man what was happening now. With a little smile he said we should be going somewhere presently.

"Where?"

"To rout out the criminals who committed the outrage."

"Is it already known where they are?"

He shrugged. A little later he came and told me from Pannwitz that it was forbidden to leave the building. The alert was on and nobody was to move.

About one o'clock in the morning they began saying in the corridors that we should leave any minute now. They spoke of a church, but they did not know which. I remembered that a few days earlier K. H. Frank had launched an ultimatum to the Czech nation: if he did not know the killers of Heydrich by 18 June, if the Czech people did not give them up, then ...

And here we were at 18 June. Was it mere chance? Was not the Gestapo trying to cover up the shameful fact that they had been unable to capture the parachutists? The attack had been made three weeks ago; a fortnight ago Heydrich had died; a week ago Lidice had been wiped out: reprisals, searches, police sweeps, the state of siege, hundreds of executions, ten million marks and ten million crowns promised—and was all that to be in vain? Did they not mean to put on a show of "arresting the criminals"? Pannwitz was perfectly capable of planting a few men in a church and staging a "battle" to tell the whole world that the Gestapo had arrested Heydrich's killers. I had seen the Gestapo trying to preserve its reputation by tricks of that kind. For example, at Jeneralka—that is a farm near Prague—they set up a transmitter and sent out "intelligence from the resistance" for foreign consumption, fabricated by themselves. Might they not be preparing another of these swindles?

They sent for me at about four o'clock. From the psychological point of view this is a well-chosen time. Suppose you were waiting for the Gestapo to come and arrest you: all the evening you listen for a car stopping outside your house; you keep watch until midnight, until one o'clock in the morning—nothing happens, and a spark of hope begins to glow. Maybe you say to yourself, "Perhaps I have escaped the net." You are tired; you are happy. You go to bed to lie down for a few minutes, for a few hours, and at that moment there is a ring on the bell. The Gestapo.

The morning of 18 June was clear and cold. A Thursday, if I am not mistaken. The cars took the road along the river; they crossed Charles Square and stopped at the beginning of Resslova

Street. A little farther along this street was the church of St. Cyril and St. Methodius, which the Nazis called St. Charles Borromeo. The streets and the blocks of houses were already surrounded by SS units and the Gestapo.

"Here we are," murmured Pannwitz. He got out and began to walk. His men followed, and as usual the interpreter came last.

No one suspected anything yet: the streets were empty and quiet, the houses shut up; the air was cool, the air of a June morning. The sky was a light blue and the flowers in the Charles Square beds smelled delightful. I looked around: there were several battalions of men armed to the teeth. Altogether too many for putting on an act. Was it possible that the parachutists were really hidden in that church? Pannwitz might merely have posted a few confederates inside, but he had certainly not hesitated to lay on an impressive outward show. I did not care for the look on his face, however.

The church was immediately next to some houses. You could get into it by one of the doors of the presbytery, next to the church. A Gestapo man rang on the bell of this door. A long pause; then someone opened it. One of Pannwitz's men knocked him down and clapped on the handcuffs. I do not know whether it was the priest or the sacristan. The group went into the corridor: a closed door at the far end. "Who has the keys? Where does this door lead to?" A quick series of questions; Pannwitz was given the key and he walked into the church with his men.

I stopped at the threshold. Pannwitz's group was already in front of the altar when all at once shots rang out from above, from the gallery over the nave. This was unexpected—at least for me. I do not know where Pannwitz thought he would find the parachutists, but judging by the calm way he walked into the church, he had not reckoned on this attack. One of the Gestapo men cried out in pain—he was shot through the arm. Kahlo was his name, and he was distinguished by his zeal, everywhere.

The superintendent gave orders to fall back towards the corridor. But his men were caught in a plunging fire and they milled about in the middle of the church, unable to tell which way round they were. At last they all managed to escape.

Pannwitz caught sight of me in the doorway and shouted furiously, "What the hell are you doing here?"

"You told me to follow you."

"There's nothing for you to do here. Get out, do you hear me?"

"May I go back to the office?" I asked.

"No. Go into the building next door, the technical school, and wait there at the switchboard. If I need you I'll send someone."

In the street the situation was tense: the SS had heard the firing and they did not know what they ought to do. A machine gun had been set up in the window of a high school opposite the church. A few minutes later the SS opened fire with it on the gallery. They even set up a small piece of artillery. I went into the technical school, sat down, and closed my eyes. Now I knew that they were not putting on a show.

What happened then in the church? I can tell you what I heard from eyewitness accounts. Pannwitz gave orders for the men in the church to be liquidated. At first he would very much have liked to take them alive, but he soon realized that that was impossible. The battle began. The men in the gallery were excellent shots. They were in no hurry; they aimed carefully, and their bullets reached every corner. Several wounded SS rushed to the first-aid post, happy to be able to get out of the church. But again and again there came the order—attack, attack! In small groups the SS made their way into the church, fired a burst and retreated to the shelter of the corridor. Up in the gallery three men held out like heroes.

In the end the commander of the SS gave orders to use grenades. The firing and the explosions could be heard in the street and even in the school where I was.

Then suddenly there was silence up there, an agonizing silence throughout the church. The SS waited a moment and then they went up: they found three parachutists covered with blood.

They came out of the church carrying one body and two dying men. They laid the dead man on a church carpet outside, on the pavement. They took the two others to hospital, but they died without having recovered consciousness.

This was at about seven o'clock in the morning. The Gestapo brought the traitor Curda and Ata Moravec. They showed them the dead man and asked his name. Pannwitz did not know who was hidden in the church: perhaps he was thinking only of Kubis and Gabcik.

Curda was silent, confused, ashamed; at last he muttered, "Opalka."

Meanwhile they were searching the inside of the church for the way into the crypt. The nave was almost destroyed, the windows were broken and the altar overturned. Through loudspeakers set up in the street the Germans called upon the besieged men to surrender, promising that they would be treated as prisoners of war. The men hidden in the crypt said nothing. I do not know how the Gestapo learnt they were there. Possibly from clues inside the church. No sound had come from the crypt during the battle.

But now they began to fight: and they knew how to fight. It is said the Germans brought Curda to the only window to tell his former friends to stop firing. It seems that Ata Moravec refused to do so. The parachutists replied with a burst of fire. From that moment on they knew who had betrayed them.

The loudspeakers and the machine guns were no use. Either someone suggested it to him or Pannwitz himself had the idea of calling for the fire brigade. A Nazi officer came to the switchboard where I was waiting and telephoned for the pumps to be sent to Resslova Street. What time was that? Probably about eight.

As he left, the officer said to me, "We shall need you in a few minutes. As soon as the firemen get here."

46

I was a driver in the fire brigade

(*Jan Vobecky*)

I WAS A MEMBER of the Prague fire brigade, and I was on twenty-four-hour-shift duty that very day. It had been a still night and nothing had happened.

I sat there, thinking of nothing in particular; the sun rose, the sky was clear, and I was pleased with the idea that I should be going home soon. And then the alarm! All the alarm bells going at once. I stared about. The alert? All out, all out! We're off.

Nobody knew what it was about—not the least suspicion. They had phoned our chief; I was at the wheel of the motor pump and he said to me, "Charles Square, Resslova Street."

Off we went at full speed; I crossed the circle, reached the square: no smoke anywhere. But SS all over the place. That seemed queer to us: we stopped, and we looked at these Huns who had sealed off the quarter. A Nazi major appeared and began telling us the bandits who had attacked Heydrich were hidden in that church in Resslova Street and we were to flood them out.

"Don't you reckon on us for that," said one of the firemen.

Our chief started foaming with rage. "Who said that?" We none of us uttered a word. "Just you look around you—there's the Gestapo and there's the SS. Anyone who doesn't like the job will pay heavy." He was a swine, our chief; and after the liberation in 1945 he was sentenced for collaborating with the Nazis. "Jump to it," he went on.

There was a corpse stretched out on the pavement. A little later I heard there had been a battle with three parachutists inside the church. Two were dying: one of them had his legs broken by a grenade and the other was very badly wounded too; the Germans had hurried them off to hospital, but they died on the way. And the third was the one lying there on the pavement.

The SS kept coming and going, firing at the church, but they could not manage to hit the little barred window into the crypt. A Nazi officer came and asked us if we knew the lower part of the church. We shrugged and made no answer.

Our chief rushed up again and ordered one of us to take a hammer and knock in the bars over that single window. The fireman obeyed. I don't know whether he wanted to do it and I don't know what I should have done in his place. That was chance again: he was an inquisitive type and to see better he'd shoved himself into the front. So now there he was with a hammer in his hand. If he didn't go, he would be arrested: we'd see his name on the red placard the next day—shot for sympathizing with the perpetrators of the outrage. He preferred going to the window and so he made his name stink forever.

He gave the bars two or three blows and they fell. K. H. Frank cheered him; and I felt sick. No, I said to myself at that moment, I wouldn't have gone: it would be better for them to read my name on the red placard than be able to say I'd helped those bastards.

The Nazis meant to throw little tear-gas bombs into the crypt and block the window with a mattress; but the men inside had a ladder—they tossed the bombs back into the street and used the ladder to push the mattress away. And they never stopped firing and the SS didn't dare go and fetch the mattress.

Then the Germans thought up something else. They made us set up a floodlight in the street to blind the parachutists and stop them aiming as they fired. But before the floodlight had even begun to work the boys in the crypt had smashed it—it was completely out of action.

Our chief put himself forward again. "We'll smoke them out," he said. And he gave orders for a pipe to be brought to the window; but the men in the crypt pushed it away with their ladder. Then someone suggested flooding them. That was a hideous idea.

We had to get the pumps going and push the hoses in at the window. The water began to flow and we all wondered what was going to happen. But the boys in the crypt did not let that get them down. They took their ladder and shoved the hoses out. An SS man ordered them to be put back and the firemen obeyed, but a few moments later there they were back in the street again.

At last K. H. Frank arrived back on the scene. He was white with rage, shouting, swearing, and in spite of the tragic situation just looking at him was a treat for us. So the water did not succeed. Not for the moment, anyhow. As for me, I was watching from a distance, staying by my pump carrier; I thought it was better not to be too close to the church or they might find a job for me too; and then—chance again—a bullet fired by an SS struck a stone and a splinter hit me in the eye. I was able to go off for a few minutes to have it dressed.

Meanwhile several fireman had been picked and taken into the church. The Gestapo had found a stone and they thought by raising it they could get into the crypt. The firemen were to smash the stone with hammers. They hit the stone, but with no result. They didn't put much heart into it, of course, but they made a show of doing their best for the benefit of the SS who were standing behind them with revolvers. Lord, I was glad I had been hit by that splinter.

Hours went by. K. H. Frank appeared in the church again, shouting something in German. I didn't understand, but no doubt he thought the fighting had gone on too long. The Germans were afraid the parachutists might be able to escape by a tunnel: people said that in the old days there had been one that went down to the river. What a swipe in the eye for the Gestapo if they got where they wanted at last and then found nobody, after having besieged the church for hours with every possible weapon, and the whole of Prague talking about it.

An officer started telling K. H. Frank about how brave the SS had been—a friend of mine who spoke German told me—but Frank hardly took any notice. You only had to look at them to see they were scared stiff of that little window. Several things found on the parachutists killed in the church were brought to Frank, but he shoved them away and started bellowing again, pointing at the window. What he wanted was to take them alive and right away: and now for hours and hours he had been coming and going without getting one step nearer.

The Nazis tried to break through the wall of the church near the window, but the stonework was too strong. And, Lord, how that pleased us!

47

The interpreter's account: 3

(*Josef Chalupsky*)

THE FIRING could be heard in the street. I did not want to think about it, but I knew the parachutists in the crypt were fighting a hopeless battle. Unless they could escape by a tunnel. But I knew the Germans had lined the banks of the Vltava and that they were watching the exits of the drains. Even if the parachutists succeeded in finding a way out, death was waiting for them at its mouth.

The SS came for me. "Come to the church." Once again I went in by the priest's corridor. To one side there was the sacristan's flat: through a small window in the kitchen one could see the inside of the church. An earthquake could not have caused more damage. The door through which Pannwitz and his men had passed, and through which they had fled from the fire of the parachutists hidden in the gallery, was no more than a blackened hole. This door led to the altar, which was separated from the nave, as it is in all Orthodox churches, by a high wooden screen. Now the screen and the altar were overturned and riddled with bullet holes. The ground was strewn with paintings and books and other religious objects.

It was a baroque church, and it measured roughly a hundred feet by fifty: the main door opened opposite the altar. Close to this entrance a group of SS were leaning over a hole, quite a narrow hole; one of the Gestapo said that the men used it for getting in and out, probably with the help of a ladder.

"You're too late," said an SS to me. I saw what he meant: by

the dark hole there stood a man; he was translating what Pannwitz said into Czech. Leaning forward a little, but not too much,
so as to avoid the bullets, he called down the hole, "Surrender!
You will not be harmed."

Silence below: then the parachutists began firing again. The
answer was clear. Pannwitz beckoned to a man with a black
beard, wearing handcuffs: Dr. Petrek, the priest of the church.
The superintendent ordered him to tell the men in the crypt to
surrender. The priest hesitated. His eyes had a feverish light, and
his pain-racked face showed they had tortured him. "Hurry up.
We haven't much time to spare," cried Pannwitz ironically.

Dr. Petrek looked at us all, took a step towards the hole, and
said, "I am ordered to tell you that you must surrender. Therefore I do so. And that nothing unpleasant will happen to you—
that you will be treated as prisoners of war."

Now for the first time voices were heard from below. "We
are Czechs! We shall never surrender: never, do you hear?
Never! Never!"

Once more a voice from the crypt cried "Never!" and there
was a burst of fire.

Petrek stepped back; the SS too. Pannwitz, all ablaze with
zeal and fury, was talking to the commander of the SS. I had
time to look around. There were pools of blood on the stairs:
that was where they had carried down the bodies of the parachutists. Later I went up into the gallery: the floor and the walls were
spotted with blood; there were empty cartridge cases everywhere. The gallery was quite large, and it overhung the whole
of the nave. At the bottom a bricked-up door led to the adjoining house, but the parachutists had not had time to break through
it. Indeed, perhaps they had not wished to do so; their companions were in the crypt, and they had to gain time for them. They
fought to the last bullet.

The men in the crypt were still holding out. Once again the
loudspeakers in the street called upon them to surrender: an ultimatum was delivered—if they did not surrender, the whole
church would be destroyed and they would die in the ruins. But
the parachutists' only reply was a burst of fire.

The SS officers called for volunteers. The group formed with no great haste. At first no one at all came forward; then after a fresh appeal a few men made up their minds and then the commanding officer picked the rest. They were taken into the church. Superintendent Pannwitz addressed them with a few well-chosen words. He spoke of the call of honour and showed them the black hole. A rope was brought; one end was put round a "volunteer's" chest, and he was lowered into the hole. A howl of pain. He had been hit by the parachutists and had to be hauled out with a wounded leg. The hole was so narrow that it did not allow of the smallest movement.

The superintendent and the SS commander were completely at a loss: they saw they could lower one volunteer after another without achieving anything. And outside, in the street, K. H. Frank was stamping up and down.

So now in their baffled fury they gave orders for the carpets to be rolled back and the whole floor of the nave examined. In a few minutes the ground was bare; one SS watched the hole and the others searched feverishly. Pannwitz hurried to and fro: there must certainly be a way into the crypt—in former times the coffins of the monks had been laid there. How were the coffins taken down? There must be stairs, but where were they? Somewhere at the place where a stone sounded hollow. At last to their delight they found it, a heavy slab concealed beneath the altar.

The superintendent sent for the firemen and ordered them to break it. Behind them stood the SS, their rifles in their hands. But the slab held firm, and after twenty minutes a fireman tried to explain in pidgin German that it was impossible to deal with it with the tools they had there. The firemen were sent away and the SS ordered in with dynamite. They did something round the slab, then we were told to leave the church. They blasted the slab, and the heavy stone broke in two. An eager, inquisitive Gestapo man pulled away part of the wreckage and peered in to see what was inside—bullets whipped past his head. Pannwitz grinned with satisfaction: there were wooden steps leading into the crypt; this was the way down.

Once again the SS were called upon. They were to go down the steps, and this time they were sent group by group, in waves of attack.

How I admired those men in the crypt: for hours now they must have known that their struggle was hopeless, that sooner or later they would be killed; but they did not give in. They fought like lions.

The first SS attack failed. When they had gone a few steps down a burst of fire stopped them dead and some of them fell; they could not see clearly, and the stairs being so narrow and steep the wounded men threw the others into disorder. They had to retreat.

Meanwhile, in the street, a fireman was ordered to get hold of the ladder the besieged men used for pushing away the hoses. Frank wanted to flood them out—the fireman obeyed. He went along the wall of the church and just as a parachutist was thrusting at the hose he grasped the end of the ladder and pulled it out. K. H. Frank praised him, of course—it was a step nearer victory. They say that later the Nazis rewarded this fireman; and after the war a Czech court condemned him.

Now the parachutists' position was becoming critical. Water was flowing into the crypt and they no longer had anything to push the hose away with, for the little barred window was too high. At the same time the SS launched another attack, throwing grenades—and steadily the water flooded into the crypt.

Yet the parachutists went on firing. They hit back without a pause, resisting ferociously. How long could they hold out? Five minutes? Half an hour?

And then suddenly, at about noon, four isolated shots rang out below. After that, a great silence.

Pannwitz stiffened. He looked at the way into the crypt and beckoned to an SS officer. The SS hesitated, then sent two soldiers, who went cautiously down: one step, two steps, three. Still silence. They looked back at the officer, who waved them on. They moved down further still, everyone in the church watching them, hardly breathing. They vanished into the crypt and then called up: the officer hesitated no longer; with his revolver in his hand he rushed down. A moment later he reappeared, wet above the knees, and cried, *"Fertig!"*

It was over. It was all over.

What more can I tell you? It was no longer dramatic: it was deeply sad. The firemen took their hoses and went away; the Nazis laid the bodies on the pavement—K. H. Frank wanted to see them. Before they were taken out of the church I looked at their faces. You must certainly have seen the photographs. I did not know their names; they were soaking and covered with blood. Each had kept his last bullet, had killed himself with it and had fallen in the water. There they lay beside one another, in civilian clothes; their eyes open. The vanquished or the victors?

Later the Gestapo took them away to the Pathological Institute and brought witnesses to identify them there. Even Curda was sent for.

I went down into the crypt, dimly lit by the little window, the one the water had come through. The place was bigger than I had expected. I had to stay on the steps—the floor was quite hidden under the water: a couple of feet deep or rather more. I was too overwhelmed to attend to details of that kind. There were spaces cut out in the walls; the monks' coffins had been placed in them in former days. Some of these niches had mattresses in them, and there the parachutists had slept. They made me think of the cells in a honeycomb. And I saw some stoves and a book.

I lit a match. There were scraps of paper floating in the water—money and identity papers torn to shreds: they had thought of everything. Bloody marks on the walls; bloody marks on the steps. And water everywhere. But the ceiling of the crypt was high, and they could have held out for a long time, probably for a whole day, before it was completely flooded. No, it was not the water that beat the parachutists.

What was it, then? There is only one likely explanation—lack of ammunition. Later the crypt was cleaned out: underclothes were found, stoves, tins of food; but not a single round of ammunition. It is true that the Gestapo report speaks of the flooding, but there is not the least foundation for it. No: the parachutists fought to the death. It was only lack of ammunition that put an end to their struggle.

A heap of bricks was found near the little window. They had vainly tried to pierce the wall of the church: there was no way out. From that moment on, they had known they were condemned.

I left the church. A German band was marching down Resslova Street, playing a strident Nazi victory march. It was attempting to conceal the Germans' immense disappointment that the parachutists should have chosen their own death. Not one of them would ever speak now.

THE HISTORIAN STEPS IN : V

(*The author*)

We are nearing the end of our account of the killing of Heydrich. In the death register, volume 1/1942, number 348, a painstaking clerk wrote:

Reinhard Tristan Heydrich
Todesursache: Schussverletzung/Mordanschlag/Wundinfektion.

On 29 September 1942 a no less painstaking registrar recorded the sentence of the German court martial in Prague: 252 Czech patriots condemned to death for sheltering or giving support to parachutists.

From this it would seem that 252 Czech citizens paid for one German. But the facts are quite different. To these 252 must be added all those who were put to death during the state of siege, which lasted from 27 May to 18 June; the men, women and children of the villages of Lidice, Lezaky, Bernartice, Pardubice, and other places; all the parachutists who killed themselves or who were shot; and the systematic murder of Czech political prisoners in the concentration camps of Terezin, Mauthausen, and Dachau after the attack.

On 3 September 1942 the Prague court martial passed sentence of death on the representatives of the Orthodox Church, Dr. Petrek, Bishop Gorazd, Cikl and Sonnevend.

So many, many executions: it was revenge run mad.

The last day of Karl Heinz Frank's ultimatum to the Czech people was, as it turned out, the last day of the parachutists' lives. According to the chemistry teacher's account, they were to have been taken out into the country on 19 June, the next day, and this might have saved them; although it seems to us that the plan for their going to England could not have been carried into execution at that period. In the first place, there was no suitable landing-ground in the neighbourhood of Oubenice, the village where Kubis and Gabcik were to have been sheltered; and secondly, in 1942 there was no Allied plane that could fly so great a distance without landing at a properly equipped airfield. There were indeed smaller planes that could land even in a field; but their supply of gasoline would not have allowed them to make the journey there and back again.

But it is probable that the members of the resistance were unaware of these purely technical reasons; they could hope for the escape of Kubis and Gabcik by plane, and given the atmosphere of terror then reigning in the country, this hope was psychologically of the first importance.

We do possess evidence that Ludvik Vanek, a joiner from Oubenice, looked for a clearing in the nearby forests that might serve as a landing-place: but he and his family and other people of the village were executed. The fact remains that from the technical point of view an operation of this kind was impossible in 1942.

Let us return to the battle in the church. We have German records showing that nineteen officers and 740 other ranks took part in it: and perhaps the Gestapo should be added to this number. Are these figures true? It should not be forgotten that Nazi accounts are often tendencious, particularly when they originate with the Gestapo or the SS.

The first orders for the operation against the church were given at two in the morning. According to instructions received at about three, the SS units were to be in Norimberska Street at 0345 hours: there they were told to surround a given zone. Two sets of barriers were set up, the outer set surrounding the neighbourhood of the church, the banks of the Vltava by Trohanova and Myslikova Streets, and Charles Square; the inner shut off the block of houses adjoining the church. The SS trucks were to reach the outer line at 0410 hours. The Gestapo men intended for searching the block were given a strong guard of twenty-five SS.

At 0415 hours the zone was sealed off. A little later, towards 0420 or 0430 hours, Superintendent Pannwitz with his team and the interpreter made their way into the priest's corridor. The battle began.

The report of Dr. Geschke, SS Standartenführer and chief of the

*state police central office in Prague, dated 25 June 1942 and addressed to
the Protector Kurt Daluege and Karl Heinz Frank, continues:*

At 0415 hours on 18 June 1942 the state police central office launched the
operation against the church with the intention of searching the catacombs
… A few minutes after making their way into the interior of the church
the central office commando was caught under the fire of men in the church
gallery. For several hours fruitless attempts to take the enemy alive were
made: three of them were firmly ensconced behind massive columns in the
gallery and four others had shut themselves into the crypt. These attempts
had to be abandoned; they could have succeeded only at the cost of heavy
losses, since the enemy resistance even included bombs. An SS shock-
force was thrown in, overcoming resistance by means of grenades and
machine guns.

Five enemy agents were found already dead; two others died without
recovering consciousness. Among the latter was one of the perpetrators
of the outrage, the man who threw the bomb.

In order to confirm the results of the investigation carried out by the
state police, all the witnesses at our disposal who had known the criminals
were at once brought into the presence of the bodies. Eighteen persons,
including two parachutists who had known the criminals when they were
living together before the outrage, recognized them immediately.

Eleven weapons were found in the church, two of them being Colt
pistols numbers 539,370 and 540,416: the technical criminal tests confirm
that these weapons were used by the criminals at the place of the outrage
and during their flight. The Svatos family recognized the body of one
of the men guilty of the outrage, he being the person to whom they had
lent a briefcase. They also recognized the remains of the other criminal,
the one who had placed an automatic weapon in the briefcase and who
borrowed an overcoat from them half an hour before the outrage.

Madame Moravcova's son recognized one of the criminals as the man
to whom his mother had lent the woman's bicycle abandoned where the
attack was committed, and the other as the one who some weeks before
had shown him a bomb, also found on the spot. Thus the identity of the
guilty men was established beyond all possible question.

The ammunition, the mattresses, the blankets, books, clothes and other
objects accumulated in the church show that the criminals had the support
of a large number of accomplices. The dean, the priest, the sacristan, the
president of the laymen's committee, and the church clerk were fully aware
of everything that was going on. The dean himself was of the opinion that

the perpetrators of the outrage were among the enemy agents, since one of them (the man who had thrown the bomb) had to have his eye treated, while the other criminals talked about the preparation for the attack and its execution. The clergy's unbounded indulgence towards the criminals is shown by the fact that although Bishop Gorazd was told of the matter some days before the state police stepped in, and although he was anxious for the church's good name, he did not denounce these proceedings, in spite of knowing that this rendered him liable to the death penalty.

Dr. Petrek compelled Ornest, the sacristan, to remain silent by making him take an oath on the altar by the light of candles; in administering this oath he wore his chasuble. His support for the perpetrators of the outrage went so far as the emptying with his own hands of the bucket containing lime and chlorine that was put in the crypt as a toilet.

This Nazi report simplifies the matter; but there is another, dated 23 June 1942, that describes it in quite another way. In the first place, the Germans did not know how many parachutists were hidden there; nor did they know just where they were to be found. "*Several criminals are in the neighbourhood of the buildings shown in the enclosed drawing no. 1a: it appears that the murderers of the SS Obergruppenführer are among them. Attention must be paid to the church, situated in the southwest corner of the sketch.*" Later there was a misunderstanding between the SD, the Gestapo, and the SS.

Immediately after the suspected area had been sealed off by the inner barrier, SD agents, together with some SS soldiers, were fired upon inside the church. A clash took place, in the course of which grenades were thrown on the German side. At the same time the SD opened machine-gun fire on the large windows of the church from the buildings opposite. This step endangered our own men inside the church. The officer commanding the SS then realized that the operation in the church called for tactical manoeuvres and that unregulated fire would jeopardize his troops; he therefore gave the following orders:

(a) immediate cessation of the fire from the buildings opposite the church

(b) immediate departure of the SD and the protecting SS from the church

(c) the advance of E/SS shock-squad D under the command of an officer with war experience.

The shock-troops were to attack and arrest the criminals, who were defending themselves obstinately. Their numbers and positions were not yet exactly known. The step mentioned under (b) was wholly necessary, since the SD were in civilian clothes without any distinctive markings, and mistakes were possible ...

The report goes on to describe the battle in the church. "The shock-squad mentioned under (c) were ordered to take the criminals alive. These orders were difficult to carry out, since the only way to reach the gallery from the nave was by a winding staircase that was defended from above by one of the criminals. The commander of the shock-team made intelligent use of detachments armed with grenades and machine guns, and under cover of their fire he succeeded in reaching the gallery. At the top of the stairs it was only possible to advance in single file; each of the pillar recesses had to be taken one by one in hand-to-hand combat. After two hours of fighting, at about 0700 hours, the three criminals holding the upper part of the church, were seized and arrested."

This part of the Nazi report confirms that the Germans' huge military superiority did not prevent the parachutists from fighting to the end. The battle in the church, that is to say in the gallery, went on, therefore, until seven o'clock. Three men, of whom only Captain Opalka, "the criminal who defended the stairs," was a regular officer, fought an SS shock-squad and detachments with machine guns and grenades for three hours.

K. H. Frank wanted the parachutists alive, and the report ends with the untrue statement "they were seized and arrested" without pointing out that it applied to one dead man and two others in a dying state who never recovered consciousness nor uttered a word.

At this point a question arises. Before they went into action the Nazis did not know how many parachutists were hidden in the church, and they might have been satisfied with the three killed in the gallery. Did the priest or an arrested suspect tell them under torture that other parachutists were concealed in the church? No, they did not: the Gestapo were guided there by chance alone.

"In the church there were found not only these three parachutists: a fourth garment was discovered. It was therefore evident that at least one more criminal was hiding somewhere."

That was the reason they began searching for a fourth parachutist— the man whose clothes had been found in the church. Who can imagine the feelings of the parachutists in the crypt as they heard their comrades fighting, but without being able to intervene? For close on three hours they could still hope that the Nazis would find no sign of their being there. For close on three hours they held their weapons ready in silence, never suspecting that an unaccounted-for piece of clothing would attract the Germans' attention.

The report goes on to give an account of the reduction of the crypt, and it speaks of the priest who "hid and sheltered the criminals for a fortnight in the sacred edifice and who was ordered on several occasions to speak down the hole into the crypt, calling upon the criminals to surrender. But they replied 'Never!' "

The report also deals with the means the Germans had to employ to get into the crypt: tear gas, water, grenades. These statements corroborate the interpreter's account.

Without intending to do so, the report implicitly acknowledges the parachutists' heroic defence: "firemen who tried to point their hoses into the hole in the outer wall of the church were driven away from the window with a ladder. The SS were then ordered to throw bombs or tear gas through this opening, but the criminals tossed them back into the street … " Water did not answer, either. "After a certain period of time it was realized that the level of the water in the cellar was rising only very slowly. It was feared that it was draining away by some opening and that the criminals might be able to escape through a tunnel."

How did the flooding of the crypt proceed? In the plans drawn by the Nazis after the battle, the water level in the crypt is shown as two feet four inches. The crypt was nearly seventeen feet high. So flooding was not the greatest danger the parachutists had to face. Besides, a little later the Nazis began to drain the water away; in the fifty-foot-long crypt it might have hindered their attack—and after the furious battle in the church they expected hand-to-hand fighting. No: the greatest danger for the men in the crypt was lack of ammunition. And they kept their last rounds for themselves. "… four dead criminals were found in the crypt. Apart from serious injuries, they had wounds in the temple showing that they had killed themselves with their own revolvers."

What more does this report tell us? It gives a list of "the heroes" of the SS units; of those who "particularly distinguished themselves," of those who "displayed extraordinary courage," "fighting qualities" or "outstanding activity ..."; then follow the names of those suggested for decorations.

They left behind them the ravaged church. They rolled up the carpets on which the dead parachutists lay and carried them off. They swept the pavement.

But the tragedy was not over. Potucek, the radiotelegraphist, sat at his transmitter that evening sending out intelligence for London. In the neighbourhood of Pardubice Libuse carried on with its broadcasts.

Major Bartos, suffering from articular rheumatism, still had to stay in bed. His health was only slowly improving. The situation was desperate. The Krupkas, in whose flat he was living, left for a short rest in the country; they had been living in dread for a long time and their nervous tension had almost reached breaking point. As soon as Bartos could walk a little he left too. Perhaps he was concealed in the neighbourhood of Cerveny Kostelec, where he wanted to find a hideout for the transmitter Libuse and its operator. They were then near the village of Lezaky.

But during his interrogations Curda betrayed Bartos' team and the place where he was staying, together with the names of those who were sheltering him and giving him assistance. The Gestapo came to Pardubice, found out the Krupkas' new address, arrested them and occupied their flat. What is more, a note sent by Bartos told them that he would be coming there on 21 June. The Gestapo took Madame Krupkova back to the flat; they meant to compel her to open the door for Bartos and ask him to come in, where they would be waiting for him.

What the Gestapo did not know was that long before this the Krupkas and Bartos had agreed on a signal: a curtain drawn in one room meant Danger: take care. That day the sun streamed into the room: the arrested woman, having waited for some time, watched by the Gestapo got up and drew the curtain, without attracting attention. She remained sitting in an armchair and two Gestapo men waited by the door, with revolvers in their hands. Outside, the sun set: Bartos did not come.

They took her back to prison, only one Gestapo man staying in the flat. Time passed. The sun no longer shone into the room: the German drew back the curtain. Now at last came a ring on the front door below.

The Gestapo man ran to the window; Bartos saw him and fled. The Gestapo agents rushed from the house and the chase through the streets began. They opened fire; Bartos fired back. In the end he was surrounded, and he shot himself with his own revolver. The Gestapo instantly took him to hospital to keep him alive until he could speak; but he never regained consciousness.

Since Bartos had killed himself, and since Curda did not know all his helpers, it might have been hoped that the arrests in the region of Pardubice would stop there. But alas, the Gestapo chanced to find the red notebook in which Bartos had written his notes, extracts from London dispatches, names—enough for the arrest and execution of scores of patriots.

So now the commanding officer of Silver A was dead too. The only man left was the radiotelegraphist Potucek. He succeeded in escaping from Lezaky to Bohdasin, near Cerveny Kostelec. From there he sent out his last message by Libuse on 26 June 1942. He said, "The village of Lezaky, near Skutec, where I was with my transmitter, has been destroyed. The people who helped us have been arrested. Thanks to them I was able to escape and to save the transmitter. Freda [Bartos] was not at Lezaky that day. I do not know where he is, and he does not know where I am now. But I hope we shall manage to find each other. Now I am alone. Tell me the name and address of the man who will take Freda's place if I do not see him again. Next transmission 2300 hours 28 June."

The tragedy was near its end. In Prague, all the partisans had been arrested or were dead; the villages of Lidice and Lezaky had been wiped out, their inhabitants murdered—only two little girls thought suitable for Germanization survived at Lezaky; all who had helped Bartos' team in the entire region were put to death at Pardubice.

The team's radiotelegraphist wandered about the country, looking for his commanding officer. He did not yet know that Bartos had killed himself some days before the sending of the last message.

What became of him, the last of them all? The Gestapo found him at Bohdasin and the village was surrounded. Once again Potucek managed to escape, shooting his way out. But he was hunted; he was starving; and on 2 July 1942 he was shot near Pardubice.

What more is there to add?

The parachutists were dead—and with them thousands of Czech citizens. Some did not even know why they were being executed. The Czech nation had to pay for the killing of Heydrich—the blood flowed.

If Curda had imagined that his betrayal would put an end to the murder of innocent people he was simple-minded indeed. Far from it: after his betrayal the Nazis began to strike with full force, arresting, torturing people savagely to make them denounce their associates. They no longer used any form of law; they no longer interrogated; they killed. A massacre. No one was sure of his life: they did not even spare children. Every morning, every noon, every evening the radio gave the lists of names: for having approved of the outrage; for having helped persons not registered with the police; for—no matter what.

If the Nazis imagined that by these hideous reprisals they would succeed in smothering the resistance movements in Bohemia and Moravia, they were wrong. For a while underground activity might diminish, but the Czech nation began to fight again and in spite of everything the resistance grew.

At first, the killing had, in the opinion of some politicians, been no more than a gesture. Others had seen it as a plot worked out against the will of several representatives of the home resistance movements; but it became a powerful and unanimous verdict against Fascism, a kind of judgment emanating from the people as a whole.

The world learnt that in spite of Munich and in spite of the occupation, the Czech nation was continuing to fight for its independence. From the international point of view, the attempt on Heydrich's life formed invaluable moral capital for Dr. Benes, the President of the Czechoslovak republic in exile, maintaining the prestige of the Czechoslovak government in London and allowing it to develop its policies.

The heroism and the sufferings of the Czechs at that time were known: wholly against the Nazis' will this became an example for the nations enslaved by Hitler, an encouragement for all who were fighting in the occupied countries. Speeches rang out from London, Moscow, and Washington expressing deep admiration for the Czech men and women who did not bow down before Hitler's Nazism.

For eight hours, as the interpreter has told us, seven men had held out to the very last against some eight hundred Germans.

Jan Kubis, Josef Gabcik, Adolf Opalka, Josef Valcik, Josef Bublik, Jan Hruby, and Jaroslav Svarc. They were joined in death, lying there on the pavement outside the church of St. Cyril and St. Methodius in Prague.

Death also united their helpers, and forever: Madame Moravcova, Zelenka–Hajsky, the Khodls, the Piskaceks, the Novaks, the Fafeks, the Svatoses, and scores of other families. Hundreds of hostages were taken in convoys from Terezin to the extermination camp of Mauthausen, as though to a slaughterhouse: their children under fourteen were sent to concentration camps. The children of Lezaky were shot with their parents; the children of Lidice died in a gas chamber.

They all had their loves, dreams, duties, life.

48

The last journey

(Antonin Novacek)

HELL COULD not have been worse. We were standing in the courtyard of the smaller fortress at Terezin, shivering with cold and hunger, bruised and knocked about, dressed in rags, covered with lice. The evening roll call was over, but we had been ordered to stay where we were.

We suspected the Germans were up to something: but what? A convoy? Executions? Some of the prisoners stood with bowed heads; others tried to work out the reason why we were forbidden to go back to our barrack rooms, the reason why we were left standing there in the yard.

At last two SS came out of the building carrying a table and two chairs. One sat on a chair, piled a heap of papers on the table and started to call over our names. Each prisoner called had to run to the table, state his identity in German and then run as fast as he could into the next courtyard and line up with the other prisoners. Presently several other SS came to join the fun, and they hit us as we passed by them.

They called my name too. You know those cold October nights with a furious wind tearing heavy clouds across the sky— showers of rain every now and then. Our teeth were chattering. After a few minutes we realized that most of our group was made up of what we called the parachutists. By that we did not mean real parachutists, but the patriots who had sheltered them, helped them, found them food. By chance or not, I was in this group, although I had been arrested for underground Communist activity; then again for this convoy the Germans had also picked about twenty Jews and thirty young Ukrainians who had been deported to the Reich for forced labour and had managed to escape; but they had been recaptured in the Protectorate.

In the "parachutists" group there were Valcik's and Kubis' families, all of them: their fathers, grandfathers, brothers, nephews—just boys. In the next yard, the women's yard, stood their mothers, sisters, aunts, nieces. During this roll call all you heard was Valcik, Kubis, Kubisova, Valcikova, Valcik, Kubis. The Kubises and the Valciks were large families and the Nazis had arrested all of them from various parts of the Protectorate. Now they were standing here, awaiting their fate.

Only Gabcik's family had escaped. Gabcik was a Slovak, and at that time Slovakia was an independent Fascist state where the Germans did not yet interfere a great deal. That is why his father and his family survived.

Together with the Kubis and Valcik families in those two yards there were Captain Opalka's father and his aunt, and all those who had helped the parachutists: Madame Zelenkova, the wife of the schoolmaster Zelenka–Hajsky who had killed himself; M. Moravec; Madame Moravcova's son Ata and their relations; the Fafeks and their two daughters; and the Khodls; all the Piskaceks; all the Novaks with their Jindriska, the youngest of us all, the child with the bicycle; all the Svatoses; Madame Sramkova and Madame Kaliberova of the Red Cross; and dozens of others.

Finally an SS said that the next day, 22 October 1942, we should not be going to work but should stay in our cells and barrack rooms: then we were taken back to them. But none of us slept. One said an enormous trial was being prepared; another thought it meant death without any form of law. I too stayed awake all that night. My roommates, those who were not in our group, tried to comfort me, saying perhaps we were going to be sent home. That was an enchanting, beautiful idea; but we knew the Nazis too well.

"They'll take us to a labour camp, I'm sure of it," said my neighbour the next morning. Another was convinced we should be brought before a court, and that at least the trial would be conducted in heated rooms.

So we waited. We knew that something was going to happen, and that we could do nothing to defend ourselves. We did not even know whether we should look forward to this "something" with dread or delight.

Our companions went off to their work. We remained shut up in our cells. We no longer had any desire to talk: we looked at one another in silence. At last there came an order—everyone to the barber's.

Hope? Would they have our hair cut off if we were going to be killed?

Hand in all your things. The blanket, cup, spoon. Hand in your rags.

Now it was joy that began to come to the top: they were giving us back our clothes, the clothes in which we had been arrested. "Why do they give you back your suit?" cried one of the Kubises, a mere boy. "To go home, that's why!" He began hugging the others. "What did I do wrong? I had nothing to do with it—I was working in the fields." But seeing the others' faces he fell silent at once.

"Go and wash!"

Did they really mean to release us? But they knocked us about savagely: why? A few slow steps on the way to the showers and they hit out.

"They are enjoying it while they can," said a young Valcik. "It's the last time. This Sunday there's a pilgrimage in our village."

At about four o'clock that afternoon the SS took us into two barrack rooms large enough for perhaps fifty people—these rooms were in the second courtyard of the fortress. The beds were only bare planks. They shoved us in like a flock of sheep and locked the door. There were too many of us to lie down or sit, so we remained standing, all squeezed together. Some were still hopeful; others swore. In one corner there were voices that joined in reciting a Pater aloud.

"Fools, idiots," cried a white-haired old man. "They are going to let us out."

It was dark: the October night comes early. We were hungry, cold, thirsty. Outside the rain fell in torrents.

At nightfall the door opened and an SS came in. Behind him, two cooks with a pot of "black coffee" so vile that your stomach heaved when you tasted it; but we had eaten nothing all day and it was hot. We drank it.

The night dragged on forever and ever. Standing there motionless, crammed together, there was no hope of rest. Outside it was raining again. The air was thick, hardly breathable; some men fainted, others looked wild and feverish.

At dawn the next day, 23 October 1942, the SS came. Outside: form up in ranks of five! Everything was dark and wet. They began counting us, lashing out and bellowing.

Jöckl, the commandant of Terezin, appeared. Straightaway he saw that some of us had put on all the clothes we possessed. He gave the order that no one was to wear more than one shirt, a pair of drawers, a coat, and shoes. Then the blows and the shouting again. The SS checked our clothes, hitting us, and the first to be hit fell to the ground. Beside us there rose a heap of the clothes and linen that the SS had snatched from the prisoners: an icy wind was blowing, and we froze; we gazed at the heap of shirts, sweaters.

At last we were marched to the front of the camp's administration building. Day broke; the prisoners were led off to work, and we stood there waiting. At about seven o'clock they brought the group of women, some eighty of them. They were crying.

Towards half past seven, a meal appeared. Half a pound of bread and a scrap of margarine. "Your ration for the whole day," said the cook, with a grimace.

We set off. There were about three hundred of us. We marched surrounded by our SS guards with their rifles pointing at us. They shouted, "Faster, faster!" But we could not go faster—the women were in front of us. We took the road leading to the station. Snow began to fall.

A train was waiting for us, the engine turned towards Prague. "We're going to Prague to be tried," said someone, and everybody looked up and stared, fascinated by that commonplace old engine. The SS gave their orders: no talking, no moving, no opening the windows and so on during the journey.

The train pulled out. Two or three SS in each carriage, keeping watch on us, talking among themselves. We looked at the floor or the ceiling: there were some who rejoiced even at the idea of seeing Prague once more. The rhythm of the wheels soothed us; but in our uncertainty we could not sleep.

My neighbour murmured that there were two possibilities: either a trial at Prague, or a concentration camp. If, after Prague, we travelled on in the direction of Kolin, that would mean Poland—Auschwitz: and if we went towards Benesov, that would mean Austria—Mauthausen. Which would be best, Prague, Kolin, or Benesov?

Outside the windows the stations went by; sometimes we saw people—men on their way to work, women going shopping. Then a group of children coming back from school. It was strange to see people walking about freely in streets with no barbed wire or SS guards.

And we reached Prague. The central station. The loudspeaker made an announcement, first in German, then in Czech. People going to and fro and we could hear them talking in Czech, but not a movement nor a gesture could we make. One minute, two minutes, ten: it was obvious that we were not going to get out here. So no trial, then: all that remained to us was Kolin or Benesov.

I remembered a game of my childhood, a game of counting to see how things would turn out. Kolin or Benesov, Kolin, Benesov. We moved off southwards. Towards eight at night we passed through Ceske Budejovice and ran on in the direction of Linz. So it was to be Mauthausen. The extermination camp. The most optimistic among us no longer said a word. Outside the windows, darkness and rain.

"Let's sing something," suggested a man. The guard uttered a roar. Night came, and with it fatigue: our bodies were exhausted, our spirits too. We no longer knew the time of day: time did not exist for us—it had its being only outside our train.

"We are in Austria," muttered the man next to me; but nobody replied.

All at once the train stopped. "*Alles heraus, los, los, zu fünften—* Get out, get out, jump to it, form up in fives."

We could not see one another; we were staggering. The rain

poured down, and in a few moments we were soaked. A dark, dark night. Other guards appeared; guards from the camp. They had machine guns. We were lined up at last. And then we marched. Kicks, blows: *los, los, schneller*, step out, faster, faster: shouts and roaring. The streets of the little town were narrow; we left the houses, but we could see nothing of the landscape—could only guess at it. The road began to rise: at the top an avenue lined with leafless trees. It began to snow, and the wind blew stronger.

They forced us to go faster and faster. Two and a half miles to the upper camp, said someone; but I knew nothing about it: I marched; I counted my steps, I counted the trees; now and then I closed my eyes; and I marched on and on. Endless road; that must be a camp up there. From the darkness there loomed granite walls. Endless walls; all you could see was long, long walls. At last we stopped in front of a great door. Floodlights inside lit up a courtyard—it made you think of a stage, set for a tragedy.

It was 24 October 1942. At this point all the Kubises, Valciks, Moravecs, Fafeks, Khodls, Novaks and the others were still with us. But a moment later they began to sort us into two groups, the "parachutists" and us.

Snowflakes fell on our shaved heads; it was terribly cold. We stood there, waiting. Orders; the roll call; the checking of names. We went down stone steps into the cellars: here there were the baths. SS were waiting: they hit and beat us. Some of my comrades fell dead. We had to take our clothes off and then we were taken back to the courtyard: it was already covered with snow.

At that moment the "parachutists" group was taken away: some two hundred and fifty men, women, boys, and girls. Their heads shaved: their bodies bruised all over. They were thrust forward; we could still see them; then they vanished. Forever.

That afternoon thick smoke rose from the tall chimney of the neighbouring building. Sometimes flames showed at the top: it was the crematorium. And the snow fell and the smoke swirled in the furious gusts of wind and rose towards the sky. It was a low sky, dark and sad.*

*Antonin Novacek, to whom we owe this account, was one of the few survivors of that convoy of prisoners deported to Mauthausen.

EPILOGUE

(*The author*)

I stand here in the courtyard of the Mauthausen camp. Twenty years after the killing. A few buildings have already been pulled down; others are falling to pieces; grass grows over the ruins.

The wall is cold: the stone of Mauthausen will remain cold until the day of doom. But here the world has already known its end.

The camp blocks, one beside the other; beyond them, a meadow. At one time there were huts there, too. A bare mountain rises against the sky and down below the Danube flows in a curve—on its bank stands the little town that gave its name to the atrocities. In the evening the neon signs shine out, cars come to the parking place, and people sit at little tables outside the restaurants to eat steaks or bowls of whipped cream.

Everybody ought to come up this winding road on foot, bareheaded. But the world has not a very feeling heart and sometimes cars travel along it. Sometimes a coach will go by.

Over my head, the sky; all round me, a dank, humid wall; and in the distance beyond that wall, hills, little woods, villages with pointed steeples. A contrast saddening enough in itself.

At the edge of the crematorium, an abrupt slope; below, a little plain. That was where they once threw the ashes. Now grass and wild flowers grow there, green and blue: the dark blue of the sage in flower.

When I was a little boy I used to go for walks with my father. He showed me that flower, telling me that when he was young he and the other boys called it "gypsy's trousers." "I can't remember why now," he added, laughing.

The sage beneath the crematorium grows on ashes. It was here that so many died whose death was neither glorious nor heroic; but it was quite as full of pain, distress, and sorrow. Ordinary people. Czechs whose names are neither outstanding nor famous. And my father was among them.